CURIOUS CUSTOMS
&
BIZARRE BELIEFS

AROUND the WORLD

By Wesley M. Wilson, B.S., M.B.A., J.D.

ISBN # 0-89716-865-8
LOC 99-63055
11.0049
Cover design: David Marty
Production: Elizabeth Lake

First printing April 1999
10 9 8 7 6 5 4 3 2 1

Peanut Butter Publishing
Pier 55, Suite 301 1101 Alaskan Way • Seattle, WA 98101-2982
(206) 748-0345 • FAX (206) 748-0343
Portland, OR (503) 222-5527 • Denver, CO (303) 322-0065
Vancouver, B.C. (604) 688-0320 • Scottsdale, AZ (602) 947-3575
St. Paul, MN (612) 922-3355 • Milwaukee, WI (414) 228-0800
e mail: pnutpub@aol.com
WWW home page: http://www.pbpublishing.com

Printed in Canada

Table of Contents

INTRODUCTION

Ideally, we should pick out the best parts, the best ideas, of other cultures to adopt. We should abandon those parts and ideas that do not lead to our goals. But we must know what are the alternatives before we can make an educated choice. That is one of the purposes of this book—to wake us up, to present alternatives, other ways of doing things, new ideas. *Erweitern Sie Ihren Horizont.* **Learn how people in the rest of the world live.** To understand people today we must also look at their past—their history. I have analyzed curious customs and beliefs that I learned about during travels in more than 140 countries, including four extensive round-the-world trips, and travels in all 50 states in the U.S. I reexamined my daily journal notes made during more than 340 city tours, visits to some 290 history and ethnographic museums, 75 art museums, 35 science museums, 90 outdoor village museums, and 90 important archeological sites around the world.

Man, around the globe and over the centuries, has faced somewhat similar problems, fears, and joys. Man has met those problems and fears with a great variety of practices or customs. We look at a situation or an event based upon our experiences and our culture. We are convinced that our interpretation is the truth. We tend to get into a narrow-minded rut, considering only some of many alternatives. Sometimes other peoples have beliefs that differ from ours but they are also convinced that their beliefs are true. There may be more than one "truth." We still have a great diversity of customs, cultures, beliefs, religions, and peoples on our crowded little planet. Observant travelers with an open mind are fascinated by the variety. *Vive la différence!* Those who seek to impose their customs, beliefs, and religion on unwilling people are today's imperialists. They are as harmful as the religious leaders and mercantile imperialists who used military power to impose their authority over others in the past.

Many of us have as a goal the happiness, security, and feeling of well-being of ourselves, our friends and family. Others may find that goal to be too dull; they may prefer to lead an exciting adventurous life, even one that is dangerous. We value progress and want an ever- increasing standard of living, improvements in technology, and other changes. Other cultures are not interested in changes, they want to preserve traditions. Our culture in the U.S. is a mixture inherited from immigrants coming from much of the world. We have taken the best, and a little of the worst, from their backgrounds. We are not limited to any one background. We have not inherited a long-standing hatred of any other people or nation. After World War II, the U.S. did something amazing—it financed the recovery of defeated enemies, Germany, Italy, and Japan, as well as other countries that were devastated during World War II. We have a high standard of living, measured by comfort and material possessions. We have the best technology that man has invented, designed, or perfected over the centuries. However, many in the U.S. are still too poor or too poorly educated to share in our progress. In the past, someone with a particular body malfunction or non-function might be disabled or die early. If we are rich or have a good health-care plan it is now possible to replace or repair a weak or defective part of our body, so we function almost like new, and life span has been extended. But we can still learn a lot from traditional cultures, even from "primitive" cultures.

We have a "free press," with news gathered from around the globe. But even the best newspapers print only a tiny percentage of the news that is reported daily in the world. Newspapers, magazines, or TV or radio news broadcasts only present news highlights, and the reports are usually slanted to accommodate to the customs and traditions of the typical reader, listener, or advertiser. When I am at home, I listen to short-wave radio news broadcasts from other countries in any of the five languages that I understand. Their version of what is happening is often much different from, and more complete than what we read or hear in the U.S.

In presenting the customs and beliefs here, I reexamined several filing cabinets filled with articles, travel brochures, and maps, and several bookcases filled with travel books. I also reexamined my new set of books, *Countries & Cultures of the World, Then & Now*, published by Professional Press in 1997 in three volumes. Volume I covers ancient civilizations plus countries in Africa and Asia. Volume II gives the background of, and describes what a traveler would see in Europe, the former Soviet Union, and the Pacific. Volume III covers all countries in South, Central, and North America, including the 50 states of the U.S., plus the Caribbean. My varied background—farm boy, merchant seaman, soldier, pilot, electrical engineer, personnel director, labor relations attorney, and university lecturer—whets my appetite to learn the many aspects of other cultures. I retired in 1985 to travel, to study other cultures and languages. I have another advantage, in speaking five languages. My other recently-published book is *Five Languages Made Simpler—French, Italian, English, Spanish, and German, Grammar, Vocabulary, Phrases and Conversation*. I completed 14 "total immersion courses" abroad, usually while living with a local family. This helped me to expand my views beyond a narrow U.S.-North American way, and to have more of a world view.

Some people may not like my observations and conclusions. It may conflict with the facts they "know" and with their opinions. If I have made any error of fact I apologize. I have carefully scrutinized my sources but it is possible that a guide abroad may have been in error when he told me the "facts." I am also aware that "a man convinced against his will is of the same opinion still." However, intelligent people are willing to admit that there may be the basis of an opinion different from theirs. I do not agree with all of the beliefs I report here. I likewise do not support some of the customs that I found to exist. Some customs may appear to be immoral to residents of the U.S.

We must be alert to **seven developments that are weakening traditional cultures and governments** in the world:

1. International trade-agreement provisions recently agreed to or proposed will supersede and invalidate many laws of individual nations, including the U.S. and its 50 states.

2. There has been a trend for several decades for large groups of investors to buy newspapers, magazines, TV stations, radio stations, and book publishers—the molders of public opinion. This trend has developed not only in the U.S. but also in Europe, Asia, and much of the world. Large book retailer corporations are buying formerly independent book wholesalers. News reports on radio, TV, and newspapers must not alienate major advertisers, owners, or a government coveted as a trading partner. A newspaper, TV station, or publisher must temporize its reporting everywhere to avoid offending a major market served by a commonly-owned newspaper, station, or publisher. There are fewer truly independent courageous news sources. Most TV and radio networks are now owned by giant corporations. The networks now own most of the TV programs, giving them control over the content. In the past, TV programs were owned mostly by independent production companies. The U.S. and other nations are almost ignoring antitrust laws that were passed after many years of effort.

3. Governments in poor countries borrow huge sums from big banks and international funds to buy military equipment or to build dams, roads, huge mosques, palaces for rulers, etc. The lenders insist that more cash crops be grown or that minerals or timber be exported for money to pay the debt. Many countries struggle to pay interest on loans and do not make payments on the principal. The poor countries will forever be indebted to rich lenders. Land that is needed to grow food for starving local people is used to grow food for export.

4. Those in power in lesser-developed countries often steal the money and other assets of a country for their personal wealth, which is

transferred to a "safer" country abroad. Many wealthy countries have been made poor by corruption, mismanagement, military expenses, war, overpopulation, and poor distribution of wealth.

5. Some 50 huge banks and other corporations in the U.S., Europe, and Asia each controls more trade and money than all but a handful of nations in the world. They force nations to comply with their terms. Large international corporations move their operations to and do their banking in a country with the lowest labor costs and the lowest taxes. They are unpatriotic in any country, a poor citizen that only provides jobs while conditions are favorable to them. **Greedy grasping global giants gag governments.**

6. If the Euro currency is successful it will challenge the U.S. dollar, which has been the standard for trade and storage of assets since World War II. What will be the impact?

7. Movies and TV programs, translated into many languages, popular music, soft drinks, and fast foods from the U.S., are popular in much of the world, especially with the young. They are overwhelming and weakening traditional family cultures everywhere.

8. FAX machines, E Mail, the Internet, and TV satellite antennas are piercing government censorship and the attempts of many nations and some religions to control outside influences.

Wesley M. Wilson, Olympia, WA, February, 1999

PART I:

PEOPLE & HOW THEY LIVE

All men are brothers and all women are sisters.
We must avoid family quarrels on our crowded planet.

CHAPTER 1:
YOUTHS, GIRLS, MEETING & MARRYING

Who Is Eligible to be A Spouse?

It is taboo to marry anyone in the same clan in most cultures. Some villages in the Pacific and Southeast Asia have two or more clans, so marriage may be permitted with someone in the other clan. Ruling families, such as pharaohs in ancient Egypt, Incas in Peru and Ecuador, and Polynesian rulers in old Hawaii, have married within the family—a sister or cousin—to keep power in the family. But the ruler usually had other concubines or lovers. Cleopatra married her brother but she had Julius Caesar, then Mark Antony, as lovers. It is common in some Arab countries, including Yemen and Oman, to marry a relative, to keep the dowry and bride-price within the same extended family. A man often marries a daughter of his father's brother. In other societies, such as the Dogon in Mali, a man marries the daughter of his mother's brother. The Dogon consider it incest for a man to marry a girl from his father's side of the family, even though she is a distant relative. In contrast, one of my guides on Efate Island, Vanuatu, said he had known since he was very young that he will marry a particular daughter of his father's sister. He was 17, he must wait until he is 25 to marry the girl, a year younger. He must have his own house and garden, and at least three pigs to marry at age 25. Seven to 20 pigs are usually given, half of those are killed for the wedding celebrations. He must also pay a certain number of mats and taro and *kava* (a drink) to the bride's family. His two brothers will marry the sisters of his future wife. His three sisters will all marry sons of his father's sister. He said one of his sisters is pregnant, but he did not think that would affect the marriage. Among some African tribes, such as the Anlo (Ewe) of Togo and Ghana, marriage between cousins is preferred. This keeps the bride-price within the extended family.

Intermarriage is believed to cause the many albinos seen in parts of Melanesia where people usually have dark brown skin and hair. In villages on the east coast of New Caledonia people with white skin and curly blonde hair are often seen. They sunburn easily. On the Fijian islands, I saw several young white men or women with their darker spouse. The Fijian Whites are usually descendants of the Andrews, Pickerings, or Whipples, English sailors who passed through a few generations ago. Marco Polo, the great traveler from Venice, wrote about his travels through Asia in the Thirteenth Century. Polo was repulsed by the common practice of people in Kanchau, in the former province of Tangut (northwest China), for men to go to bed with their cousins and mother-in-law. The Mosuo, a branch of the Naxi minority group, in the Lugu Lake area of China's Yunnan province, practice *axia* or "walking marriage." Men live with their mother, children and women live with their mother. Women own and inherit the property, children always have the mother's surname. A youth borrows jewelry from a girl during the day, then returns it when he visits her in the evening. He also gives tea, sugar, and wine to a new girlfriend. Youths sleep with a girlfriend at night, leaving at dawn to return home. Children in the matrilineal society do not know who is their father, it seems to make no difference in their culture. The grandmother is the head of the family group, in charge of financial matters. Sex is usually with a cousin, but it is forbidden to have sex with anyone with the same surname. Nearly everyone is a "cousin." The prettier girls and the better-looking youths tend to have more partners. Local people are quite handsome, they say they inherited their good looks from many generations of ancestors.

On some islands, such as Fiji and Samoa it is common for a child to live for several months at a time with someone other than the parents, perhaps living at the far end of the village. Everyone in the village is considered to be a brother, sister, aunt, uncle, or grandparent. "It takes an entire village to raise a child." In New Caledonia, the mother's brother acts like a father and mentor to a boy, instructing him in things that a village boy should know. He is more important to the boy than his father. Among China's Mosuo the mother's older brother acts as a mentor and is in charge of traditional family ceremonies. If the mother has no brother she chooses a real husband for her most mature daughter. He is expected to be monogamous, and is called "uncle." There is no stigma in much of the Pacific against an illegitimate child, who usually lives with the mother's family, as in the U.S. If the father acknowledges the child as his, they may live together as a family. A young person in the Pacific islands usually must go to another village to find a spouse. Villages may share a feast, dance, school or church, or have sports competitions, so young people can meet a potential spouse.

In Fiji, Hindus and Fijians may go to the same secondary school but cannot marry, neither family would permit it. In the U.S. and most of Europe, parents and others discourage or prohibit Blacks and Whites from marrying. If a White girl marries a Black man she is treated by Whites as a Black. In South Africa under *Apartheid*, Blacks and Whites could not marry, although a White or Asian man sometimes had a

Black or "Coloured" mistress. In countries where Blacks were slaves a White Man often had a slave girl as a mistress. The White administrators of big castles along the coast of West Africa, where slaves captured from the interior were held awaiting a ship, often selected a Black mistress. Ghana's St. George of Almino Castle had peepholes where the administrator could look down upon the female slave quarters and select the one he wanted for the night. A female slave who was obviously pregnant sold for more money—for almost the price of two slaves. A baby with a light skin color was worth more. Hindus of India, Nepal, and Bali can only marry someone from the same caste, or perhaps a foreigner. Chinese girls living in Vietnam are not permitted to marry a Vietnamese man, but a Chinese man there may marry a Vietnamese girl. Chinese girls in Cambodia or Thailand may marry a local non-Chinese man if he is ambitious and likely to succeed. Most Buddhist girls in strongly Buddhist countries—Thailand, Cambodia, Laos, and Vietnam—will marry a Buddhist man only if he has served time as a monk, usually at least a few months. In Singapore, parents often forbid a daughter to marry a Caucasian. They consider Asians to be superior. In strongly Islamic countries such as Syria there are no civil marriages. Therefore, a Muslim imam or mullah will marry only a Muslim man and woman, or an Orthodox Christian priest will marry only a couple that he approves of, such as an Armenian Christian couple or a Gypsy Christian couple. In countries where the Catholic Church is strong, such as much of Latin America, a man or woman may only marry another Catholic.

In China, young women, aware that there are far more single men than women, are becoming more particular. Several educated Chinese and Japanese women told me that they had rather stay single than to marry any of the available men. Chinese women often say "I won't marry unless he has 48 legs of furniture, savings, a good job, and he accepts that women are equal." Chinese girls want a man at least 175 cm. tall (5 ft. 9 in.). China has 10 eligible men for every nine eligible women. In India the ratio is almost as lopsided. Boy babies have been favored, girl babies often die "accidentally" at birth. Now Chinese village girls are becoming more valuable. Teenage girls go to the booming coastal areas and work in factories, sending money home regularly. Parents in many countries without a pension system hope that a baby will be a boy, who will have a *duty* to support them in their old age. A girl is likely to marry, then she will owe her loyalty to her husband's family, not to her parents. Chinese say "a daughter is like water that is flushed away." When she marries she leaves her family and joins her husband's family. A son continues the long family line that began with ancestors. But in many Pacific islands and African countries where the bride-price is high a family hope that a baby will be a girl, they are worth more.

In Islamic countries and among many Hindus of India, a girl "must" be a virgin when she is married. In the rural U.S. and in much of Europe, a bride was also expected to be a virgin. It was common in the rural U.S. in the Nineteenth Century to give a *shivaree* for a newly-married couple. Groups of young men and women waited outside the bedroom window where the couple were. After an hour or so the bride was expected to display at the window a bloody pair of panties, indicating the breaking of her hymen. In other cultures, such as the two main tribes in Zimbabwe, and the Aini of southern China, a female is not considered to be eligible for marriage until she has had at least one child, to prove that she is fertile. It makes little difference who is the father.

The date of birth is important in Buddhist countries. Some boys or girls try to select a spouse who was born during the reign, the year and day, of a particular animal among the eight animals that are important in Buddhism. I was often asked in Southeast Asia on what day of the week I was born. I confessed that I didn't know—they were surprised. In France, it is considered to be important that a spouse be born during one of the 12 signs of the Zodiac that is compatible with your sign. My teachers in schools in Quebec and France often asked each student what was his or her sign. The teachers were surprised when the intelligent but practical students from "Anglophone" Canada, Switzerland or Germany answered that they didn't know. In China, astrologers are hired to explain in detail (year of their birth) the partners who would make a good or poor choice. In Japan, the Chinese zodiac is used, often by a matchmaker, to weed out a partner who is considered to be incompatible. A Japanese man or woman also asks a partner "what is your blood type?" A person with *A* type blood is considered to be incompatible with someone with *B* type blood. They may marry someone with the same type of blood, and a person with *O* type blood may marry either an *A* or a *B*. Japanese physicians say there is no relationship between blood type and personality, but most Japanese are still superstitious.

You may remember the old British folk saying:
Monday's child is fair of face;
Tuesday's child is full of grace;
Wednesday's child has sorrow and woe;
Thursday's child has far to go;
Friday's child is loving and giving;
Saturday's child works hard for a living;
And the child that is born on the Sabbath day,
Is blithe and happy, good, and gay.

In Russia and many other socialist or former socialist countries there is still a terrible housing shortage. Families are cramped together in tiny apartments. Young men and women cannot marry because they cannot find a place to live except in the crowded home of a parent. Sometimes neither the man nor the woman is working—they can't afford to marry. In Romania, I was told two years ago that marriages and births are rare. We traveled throughout Romania, Bulgaria, and Albania, but never saw a woman who was obviously pregnant. Palestinian girls in Gaza told me that during the *intifada* boys were no longer interested in girls or in school, they only wanted to try to get even with Israelis for some of the atrocities Israeli soldiers and settlers did. In Brazil's free-trade zone of Manaus girls outnumber young men 15 to one. The girls work in assembly plants, the men are in the jungle in dangerous activities, working in drug smuggling or mining for precious metals and stones.

Soon after the beginning of World War II, in 1940, many U.S. soldiers were stationed in northern England. The local girls were too friendly. They sometimes suggested that the couple have a mock wedding at the village blacksmith just across the border at Gretna Green, Scotland. The blacksmith performed a simple ceremony in his shop. Sometime later the soldier learned that the wedding was legal! When the U.S. military complained, the law was changed to require that the girl be at least 18 and to make it more difficult to marry.

In many African and Asian countries, a boy or girl must have reached puberty before being eligible to marry, typically age 14. In Mali one of our guides of the Dogon tribe was angry because the four parents had selected an eight-year old as his bride, but he must wait until she is 14. He said he knows the little girl and likes her. He finally became reconciled to the parents' binding decision and said that he would "play the field" for six years. Some African and Asian countries permit a girl age 11 to marry, and boys have married even younger. European and North American countries usually require that either partner be at least age 18, but in some places, with the consent of a parent, a child of 15 may legally marry. China, to help control births in the crowded country, usually requires that a woman be at least 23 and a man age 25. Until recently, a young Chinese man had to have a certain number of "points" to marry. Points were earned by working in agriculture, serving in the military, and by being over a certain age. Among the Ashanti in Ghana, a girl's mother announces a girl's first menstruation by beating a hoe with a rock, to let everyone in the village know that the girl is now marriageable. Village women sing *bara* songs to celebrate her coming of age. However, the birth of a new "woman" means that an old woman will die. When a Zulu girl of South Africa has her first period she stops eating sour milk. Her father slaughters an animal for a feast, to let everyone know that the girl is now of marriageable age. In Vanuatu, to determine if a girl is old enough to marry, a man hides and watches her cook. If she cooks efficiently without complaining she is old enough.

Parents select the spouse in many lesser-developed countries, especially those where boys and girls go to separate schools, are not permitted to go alone to dances or other social functions, and have few opportunities to meet the opposite sex. In some countries such as Papua New Guinea, either the boy or girl can veto marriage agreed to among the two fathers, or among all four parents. In countries where parents select the spouse they may agree to marriage between a son or daughter and a person with whom he or she has fallen in love, "Western style." In much of the world, love has no connection with the business of marriage. In cultures where a son or daughter cannot refuse a spouse chosen by the parents, many choose suicide rather than an unwanted marriage. In Korea, older boys and girls have few opportunities to meet each other. Half of all marriages are arranged by parents. In Sri Lanka, the pretty young waitress whom we had known only for a week asked my wife and me many questions about our two single young adult sons. After an hour she said "I'll take the older." I finally realized that she thought we would select the bride, as parents do in Sri Lanka. In many Arab countries boys and girls go to separate schools and have little chance of meeting each other. Girls age 10 or older may be required to wear a veil outside of the home. A happily married young man in Yemen described how his parents chose as his bride a relative in another village. He did not know her and did not want to accept her. Once, when she thought he was watching, she "accidentally" briefly removed her veil. He saw that she was quite pretty and wanted to marry her at once. The Islamic Koran is usually interpreted that a girl has the right to veto a proposed marriage. However, in some countries neither a boy or girl has the right to see the face of the proposed spouse.

In southern China, Yi (pronounced *Ge*, meaning tiger"—earlier they hunted tigers; they were also called *barbarian*) parents often agree with a neighbor that their boy baby will marry the neighbor's girl baby, and the girl and boy must later marry. However, they can now divorce, but if the girl leaves, her family must pay a lot of money to the boy's family. A recent survey in Wenzhou, a wealthy part of Zhijiang province in China, found that 86 percent of the children age 14 or younger were already engaged to marry. Little more than 100 years ago parents often selected the spouse or refused to accept a proposed spouse in Canada, the U.S., and Europe. My wife and I studied four summers at the University of Quebec. All classes were in French and we learned much about local customs. Until recently a young man in Quebec had to convince the parents of a girl that he would help *them*, that was more important than his being the favorite of their daughter.

The Bride-Price

In much of Asia, Africa, and the Pacific the groom must pay money or goods to the girl's parents to compensate them for the cost of raising the girl and to get her parents to relinquish all rights to her children. In the U.S., the bride's father often "gives her" to the groom. In Russia until the last 100 years, the groom paid the bride price to the oldest male in the bride's family. In some Pacific islands, payment is made to the bride's oldest brother, but the payment is distributed among many of her relatives. Those who receive part of the bride-price then have an obligation to help the bride, if she has trouble with her husband, or for any other need.

The bride-price varies a lot among cultures, depending partly upon how many boys and girls are available—the law of supply and demand. In some countries with Islamic or animistic religions where a man may legally have several wives, the rich older men buy a lions' share of the girls, driving up the bride-price. In Zimbabwe and much of Africa, wealthier men kept several men busy at a crude forge, making iron hoes or knives. Several hoes would buy a bride. A Zulu girl usually refuses to marry a man she loves unless he has paid her bride-price, the *lobola*. In African cattle-growing areas, such as among the Masai, a bride may cost 15 head of cattle. An average young *moran* may be around age 30 before he can accumulate enough cattle to pay the bride-price. However, the moran live in a hut separate from the family or at a far end of the hut. At night prepuberty girls age 11 or 12 visit the moran, sometimes changing partners. However, the moran are forbidden to sleep with girls during the moran's initiation period around age 14. I have watched the little girls primping, with their beads and necklaces while they sing love songs about the moran. When a girl is born she is often assigned a future husband, so girls learn to have fun before they enter the business of marriage. The hair of girls and women is shaved but the moran have elaborate hairdos, often colored with red ocher.

In Papua New Guinea, particularly in the Highlands, the bride-price is based upon pigs. The bride, but not the groom, is present during negotiations over the bride-price. A bride's relatives may also insist upon a few *cassowaries*—a big wild fowl, like Australia's emu. Big crescent-shape kino pearl shells from the coast are also used as money. The furry feathers are prized for decorations and to make *bilums*, a kind of bag. The bones make knife handles and clubs. A young pretty bride with an unusual secondary school education may cost 30 pigs. Girls have boyfriends but single girls don't have sex, their bride-price would then be much lower. The marriage is not consummated until the final payment of the bride-price is made. A woman can divorce but her family must then negotiate the paying back of a large part of the bride-price received earlier. These negotiations become highly disputed. One girl told me she decided to stay married, even though she did not like her husband. The members of the groom's extended family loan him enough pigs, but he must later repay them, with interest. If they do not believe the man is responsible, a good worker, and friendly, he will not get a loan. Some men in Africa, Japan, and elsewhere don't like a girl to be educated, for she will cost more and she may not accept orders from the man. A woman who has been married but divorced, or an older or ugly bride, or a poorly educated girl, may cost only five or 10 pigs in Papua New Guinea. Sometimes a bride is free, especially in the Lowlands, where most men have only one wife, so there are enough girls for everyone. Local people rarely drink milk and don't like cows; they call a cow "the White man's pig." On many Pacific islands if a woman who divorces remarries, the second husband must pay the bride-price to the first husband. Five pigs is often the standard bride-price. On some of the Solomon Islands a bride may cost only one spear, but on other islands she may cost several strings of *bakiha* shell money more than 20-feet long, or many curved pigs' tusks. A boy's family is in debt for many years; some churches in the Solomon Islands are trying to limit the bride price to about 2,000 U.S. dollars. Another common type of shell money used for the bride-price in the Pacific is circular, six inches or so in diameter, like a big washer. Long rolls of money made from the red feathers of birds are used to pay the bride-price on some Pacific islands. On New Caledonia the bone of a flying fox was sometimes wrapped in a cloth made from the hair of the flying fox. The combination is considered to be valuable, and in the past it was used for the bride-price. Some objects are associated with the spirits, and have an importance greater than merely the gathering of the raw material and the time needed to manufacture the "money." In Mali the bride-price is often only two goats, two shirts, and two pairs of trousers. Among the Ashanti of Ghana the bride-price paid by the husband also guarantees that she will be faithful to him. If she is not faithful the bride's family or *abusa* must return the bride-price, or most of it.

Men in some countries, such as the Black Thai in Laos, steal the bride and have sex with her, thus requiring that she marry him. This saves the bride-price but often results in a clan or tribal war. Reports are that with China's shortage of women some men pay a kidnapper to bring him a girl. A groom of the Yi minority group in Yunnan province sometimes stages the "kidnapping" of his bride before a wedding, even though the wedding has been agreed to. A major object in battles between some African and North American Indian tribes was to steal women and girls. Some tribes near the Amazon River still have the ritual stealing of the bride, although the marriage has been agreed to. An 18-year-old girl living in the Highlands of Papua New Guinea told me that she likes to go to the river below her village for a swim on a hot day. However, "the enemy," men or youths from another village, try to find a few girls alone, kidnap them, and take them back to their village, thus saving the bride-price. This requires a *payback* or a battle. Youths in her village insist that they always swim with the girls, to prevent kidnapping. Another reason may be that they swim without bathing suits. Girls on many Pacific islands told me they may have sweetheart, but they can't have sex before marriage—that would lower their bride-price drastically. Every member of the family must protect a girl's virginity. In China, a Han young woman is expected to be a virgin when she marries, but my guides said "all youths and girls in the minority groups" have had sex before marriage. Missionaries in Africa where most people follow animistic religions complain that where the bride price is low and either spouse can get a divorce easily, the bonds of marriage are very weak, and either partner may take other lovers.

The knowledge of metal working in Africa developed partly because metal axes, knives, and hoes are superior to those made of stone, but also because some method was needed to keep control of a young bride. They often tried to escape, to run away, usually to their home village. In simple forges with bellows made of goatskin, men made heavy anklets of many coils of heavy brass or bronze, so a bride could not run or walk far. The metal work was slow, at least six men needed 72 hours to make a dozen knives, hoes, or anklets. When a bride runs away in Swaziland, the husband and his friends tie sacred knots in grass along trails so the bride cannot double-back by that route. Attempts of the husband to retrieve his runaway bride are somewhat like attempts of a master to retrieve a slave. In China, from the Ninth Century until recently, the feet of rich girls was bound at age five or six, to keep the feet tiny so they could not stray. On my first trip to China I saw an older woman hobbling on the tiny stubs of her feet.

In Islamic countries a bride usually must be a virgin. If she is tainted she may not be marriageable. Islam permits a man to have up to four wives at a time, so long as he treats them equally. Divorce is usually easy for the Islamic man. Many advanced Islamic countries, such as Tunisia, have a law that permits a man to have only one wife. In other Islamic countries, such as Syria, only rich men or lesser-educated men, such as Bedouins or Gypsies, have more than one wife. I find it difficult to believe that a woman likes *polygyny*, a form of polygamy. However, a woman does have company, and help in child care or doing heavy work, or if she is sick. I have asked several wives how they like to share their husband. They usually shrugged their shoulders and said something like "It's okay." We asked a 25-year-old wife with two children in Papua New Guinea's Highlands how she liked it when her husband took a younger wife. She said "We get along fine. She does whatever I tell her to do. Once when he came home drunk and started beating her she said 'I'll, hold him and you hit him.' " In the Marquesas Islands a man often had a second wife. However, the second wife was often a second wife to many other men—up to 30 men—particularly if she came from a high-status family. Any child born to the second wife was considered to have her primary husband as the father, and the child acquired his status. One Islamic man in West Africa explained to a *National Geographic* writer in 1927 that if a man has more than one wife he must have at least four to have peace in the family. He said two wives fight; if there are three, two fight the third.

In Prague, Czech Republic, an unfaithful wife was put into a cage and displayed half- dressed, in the busy square near Hradcany Castle. Unfaithful husbands were not punished. In Iceland an unfaithful wife was tied into a sack and thrown into the sea. Unfaithful husbands were not punished. In Riga, Latvia, the bells of St. James Church were rung whenever an unfaithful husband walked by. The almost constant ringing of the bells made neighbors mad, they threw the bells into the river. In Parnu, Estonia, a sailor's home had an unfinished wooden floor. When the seafaring husband sailed he pushed the bed together so it was only a single. If the lonely wife opened it to entertain a friend the bed left telltale scratch marks on the floor. In Germany, when the husband left town for a few days he fastened a chastity belt onto his wife and locked it. Some wives are said to have acquired a *pass key*. Immoral wives in Germany and several other European countries had their hair cut off. In France at the end of World War II, men cut off the hair of women who had fraternized with occupying German soldiers.

The Dowry

A young woman in much of Europe, India, and many other countries must bring a dowry to the marriage. If she has a big dowry she can get a man even if she is not pretty. In Ireland, a baby girl begins to acquire linens and other household items, and to have an elaborate chest of drawers built for her. Carved wooden pregnant female dolls represent the babies she will have. Parents of the bride and groom negotiate the amount of the dowry. Parents of an educated man from a rich family require that the bride bring a big dowry. The dowry is often paid on the installment plan—part upon engagement, part upon marriage, and the balance within a year or so, or upon birth of the first baby. India has many disputes over the payment of the dowry. In Delhi alone some 400 new brides have died in a year from severe burns. The groom typically claims that she died accidentally while cooking. Others claim that the groom or his friends burned her because the agreed-upon amount of the dowry was not paid. On some Pacific islands a dowry is expected, but in Papua New Guinea, the Melanesian Islands, and most of the Pacific the dowry has far less value than the bride-price. A dowry was common among many of China's minority groups until the "liberation" by the communists in 1949 or earlier. Now formal dowries are not paid but it is still customary among many minority groups in southern and western China to make "gifts" to the family of the groom or the bride.

Coming-of-Age Customs

Many cultures have a "coming-of-age" ceremony for boys and girls. Boys are circumcised, either shortly after birth or by age eight. Girls are circumcised in fundamentalist Islamic countries, and on some Pacific islands, usually by age 13 or 14. Mali, Tunisia, and some other countries have a law prohibiting female circumcision, but I was told in Mali that it is common there. When missionaries told the Kikuyu tribe in Kenya and Tanzania that girls should not be circumcised, the Kikuyu pointed out that the missionaries had taught them that Mary, the mother of Jesus, was a circumcised girl. In Indonesia, boys and girls are often circumcised at age six or seven. On Tanna Island, Vanuatu, boys at age four or five are circumcised; girls are not circumcised. However, a school principal complained to us that girls are required to dance often during the two-to-four weeks' circumcision ceremonies for boys. The girls are required to skip school classes. Circumcision in Africa, Asia, and the Pacific almost always requires a ceremony, except for a baby. The procedure is often done in unsanitary conditions by people untrained in medical procedures, so there may be infection. In Bali, to prevent lust, the teeth of boys and girls are ground into sharp points at age 14.

In the "Eastern Girls' Kingdom" of the Mosuo minority group near Lugu Lake in China's Yunnan province 13-year-old girls have the "Rite of Putting on A Skirt." She stands by the "female pillar" on the right of the hearth in the main room of the home. Her little ponytail is changed, and the mother or grandmother takes off her little girl's dress. She then wears a long white skirt and a red blouse, usually with an elaborate hat like a turban and a long tassel. She is now encouraged to have many boyfriends, who come to her bedroom at night by a gate near the stairway. Many girls select one main boyfriend when she is age 20 or so. Mosuo boys age 13 have the "Rite of Reaching Manhood." He stands in front of the "male pillar" supporting the roof, to the left of the hearth, putting his left foot on a sack of grain and his right foot on the dried carcass of a pig. His uncle shaves the boy's head, takes off his boy's clothes, and dresses him as a man. He is now encouraged to have many girlfriends, sleeping with one each night, returning home by dawn. If a pair of men's shoes is outside a girlfriend's door, he is too late that evening, so he goes to another girlfriend. Either the man or the woman can end the relationship.

In more primitive cultures girls and women having their period are segregated. They may be required to live in a separate area for weeks, especially for a girl's first period. Primitive man had and still has a great fear of menstrual blood. Two women in Papua New Guinea told us that a woman having her period cannot touch a boy or prepare his food, "by law." They said the boy would be killed in one of the many payback battles that Highlands tribes fight. On many Pacific islands, women must stay in a dark uncomfortable hut with a low roof during their period, they are considered to be unclean.

Men and older boys in the Highlands of Papua New Guinea live in a house or houses separate from the women. One of the reasons for the separation is to enforce the taboo against a brother and sister having sex. Boys at age 14 have an elaborate training procedure for up to six months. They must stay in the *Haus Tamboran* or men's spirit house. A high wall is built all around it so villagers can't peek in. The mother brings the boy to the enclosure. A cut is made on the boys arm, which signifies that woman's blood and influences are gone. Now he must learn to be a man. [The Dogon of Mali have a somewhat similar belief—that when a youth is circumcised the female soul inside him is rejected and the man's soul enters.] The Papua New Guinea boys swim or are bathed early in the morning when the river is cold. Some 20 to 50 deep slashes are then made in the back of each boy, usually with sharp bamboo, and ashes or red clay are rubbed into the wounds. This makes welts, so the skin is rough like a crocodile's skin. The "croc" is a symbol of strength and power. Any infections are washed in salt water. The boys are given a particular betel nut to chew, it causes hallucinations. Men in big masks representing evil spirits scare the boys, often in the dark night. Boys are taught how to be brave and fight, how to hunt and fish, how to send and interpret at least 10 types of messages on a slit drum, and the ritual secrets of the tribe's men. The youths are kept isolated from women and girls during the initiation. A similar but shorter initiation procedure is common on other islands of Melanesia, for boys age eight to 14. The men's spirit house is often called the *Haus Tamboran* or the *Nakamal*. In some villages, such as Yekel on Tanna Island, Vanuatu, youths in isolation are kept in a tree house in a big banyan tree. On Polynesian islands initiation ceremonies are often conducted on the *marae* or stone platform in the village. A few Melanesian islands also have a platform, a *natsaro*, for the ceremonies.

A Zulu youth in South Africa, upon reaching physical maturity, is kept in seclusion. He must eat only special food; sour milk, a common food for children, is forbidden. After a period of instruction about duties of men the youth is welcomed back with a feast. He is washed in a river, given herbs to make him stronger, and is given a new name. He is considered to have become a man.

Kenya's Kikuyu have an initiation ceremony for boys age 13 or 14. Each must have an older man as a sponsor. Early in the morning the boys bathe in the cold river. Each is circumcised without an anesthetic, it is painful, but he is not expected to cry. He is kept in isolation for three weeks or so while he heals. When he reenters village society he is welcomed by all. He is treated as a man, he no longer lives in his father's house, but in a house for older youths. Few Kenyan girls will marry a man who has not been circumcised, it is taboo, as in much of Africa. Many girls are also circumcised in Kenya and throughout Africa. Girls have an initiation ceremony much like boys. Kenya's Masai have a somewhat similar coming of age ceremony, boys often have a cold shower instead of a cold bath. Elders build a smoky fire, symbolizing new life. Warriers dance, up and down with their spears. Girls and women dance around a vertical pole nearby, with wide bead necklaces and beads in ears swaying. After the ceremony the boy is promoted to junior warrier, he can't eat meat inside a hut, and he lives with other junior warriers, separate from his parents. When he gets enough cattle and kills a lion he becomes a senior warrier (*moran*) and can marry. With the population explosion and a shortage of lions, five or 10 youths together may kill a lion.

In Western Europe, the U.S., Canada, and a few Latin American countries, couples often live together without marrying. Shortly before the first child is born the families expect them to marry. A middle-age waitress in Scotland complained that "young people aren't marrying anymore. They are only *loving* together." In the U.S., a couple may live together without marrying because one would lose health insurance obtained through marriage with the previous spouse. Also in the U.S., a man or woman often refuses to divorce because he or she would lose health coverage obtained through the spouse.

Men in many cultures believe that sexual contact with a female weakens or contaminates them. Men in Tahiti and the Marquesas were among the few men on Pacific islands who did not believe that sex weakened them. Men in much of the world fear and try to avoid menstrual blood. Tahitians were among the few men in the Pacific who did not fear menstrual blood. A few isolated villages in Papua New Guinea are only for young men who grow long hair to sell as wigs for rich men. The youths must agree to avoid females and to live a strictly pure life, to avoid women, for at least 18 months. I have watched young men in several countries walk barefoot through thick red coals of a fire. They are told that if they have contact with a female they will be burned. Some must also agree to avoid coconut milk. These include Buddhists in Sri Lanka, and Hindus in Bali and India. Each group of firewalkers had a ceremony first, praying to their god or gods, to get into a hypnotic trance. I examined the deep red coals, they were hot. The firewalkers stood briefly in damp sand at each end of the fire pit to absorb some heat. My wife, a physician, examined their feet. They had little blisters between the toes, but apparently felt no pain.

Latin American countries typically have a ceremony for middle-class and wealthier girls on or near their 15th birthday. Local newspapers have photographs and stories about the "coming-of-age parties" for *lindas quinceañeras*, who are now available for social relations with boys, and for later marriages.

Finding a Partner

In Papua New Guinea, a boy (or girl) who wants a particular person as a girlfriend (or boyfriend) cuts off part of a particular vine. A little of the sap is drunk, while the person wishing says "I would like to have (name of the person) as a girlfriend (or boyfriend)." The rest of the sap is saved in a container, hung above the mosquito net covering the bed of the person wishing, so the wish may be granted. In Japan, a girl writes the name of a boy she wants as a boyfriend on a bandaid and sticks it onto a hidden part of her body, often under the upper arm. Her wish may come true in three days. If a Fijian youth wants to marry a girl, and his father agrees, the father takes a *tabua* (whale's tooth) to the parents of the girl. If they keep the tabua the couple are engaged. The girl's mother can veto the marriage. In Korea, a man gives a wooden duck, symbolizing faithfulness, to his prospective mother-in-law. Duck pairs are usually faithful to each other.

In South Africa's University of Stellenbosch, Afrikaaner women students in dormitories hang a strong string out of their window. Male students pull the string. If she likes the guy they get better acquainted. Until recently, men on some Micronesian islands, including Truk (Chuuk), carried a carved "love stick" three or four meters long. A man poked it through the thatch wall of the hut of a girl he liked, to awaken her. If she identified the particular love stick and wanted the man she pulled the stick inside or jiggled it. If she pushed the stick out she meant "go away." In Latvia, a ballad tells of a girl who gave her boyfriend instructions as to how to find her sleeping in the summer shed, without awakening other members of her family. On isolated Tristan da Cunha island, if a young man repairs a girl's shoes and she knits him socks, islanders expect a marriage soon. In China's southern provinces a boy of the Zhoung minority group throws an embroidered silk ball to a girl that he likes. If she keeps it he is invited to get better acquainted. If she doesn't bother to catch or pick up the ball he must look for another girlfriend. A girl may also throw a ball to a boy she likes. A couple go off and take turns singing songs to each other. They often write the words in advance, like a poet. It is common in Guilin in the evening to hear a boy or girl sitting on the bank of the Li River, quietly singing a song to the other. For entertainment, Zhoung family members sing to each other, making up four-line verses.

The Butterfly Festival is celebrated by the Bai minority group near Dali, Yunnan province. If a boy meets a girl he likes he throws a stone from a nearby mountain into the spring. He waits patiently for a year. At the next Butterfly Festival he takes gifts of brown sugar, tea, wine, and a red rooster to the girl's parents. They ask him many questions to determine how well he would treat the girl. If they agree the parents serve three kinds of tea to the boy. If they do not agree they throw a banquet and serve eight kinds of fish.

Newspapers in India such as the *Hindustan Times*, and others in Sri Lanka, have many pages of ads for a groom or bride. They are often listed in columns with headings such as "Grooms Wanted for Working Girls," "NRIs, Others," and "For Brides and Grooms." Many ads are placed by relatives of a girl approaching age 30 and the possibility that she may never marry. The ads list the girl's age, height, education, employment, and background—especially her religion and her father's occupation, and listing the type of husband sought. Girls often state their color—*honey* or *wheatish*, plus *virgin*. There are almost as many ads placed by "boys" or their relatives, under their occupational heading, usually engineer, doctor, or businessman, describing the type of bride sought. Newspapers in many European countries, the U.S., and Canada have "Personal Ads" listing male singles looking for a girlfriend or wife, and female singles looking for a boyfriend or husband. In Germany the ads often have a photograph of the person seeking a lover. Girls in poorer East Germany sometimes run an ad with a photograph in a West German newspaper, seeking a wealthier man. West German bachelors often drive their expensive cars on weekends to East Germany, or to the Czech Republic or Hungary, seeking a girlfriend, permanently or only for the weekend. Australia has many ads that specify a lover is wanted only for a short time. In Perth, in a full-size newspaper I counted 28 columns of ads, many placed by males and females specified that they only wanted a friend for a night. The newspaper also had the usual ads for escort services, aimed at business men.

Many cities have a statue, tree, or other place that signifies marriage. In Palanga, Lithuania, girls lead a boyfriend to a statue of Birute, a beautiful nun who broke her vows and married. Other girls lead a boyfriend to the "Ladies Bridge." At either place the boyfriend is expected to propose marriage. Scandinavian countries and others on the Baltic Sea have a Midsummer Night festival, usually on June 22 and 23, the eve of St. John. Houses are cleaned, and decorated with green boughs and flowers. Girls jump over a fire or throw a wreath onto a tree limb. Their boyfriend is then expected to propose marriage. Leaves of an evergreen pole are stripped off, but limbs are left on, and flowers, eggshells, and other things are attached to it. It is set up as a maypole and young people dance around it. Few single people waste time sleeping that night. After dances that get wilder as darkness falls, couples disappear into the woods. Until recently a maypole was also set up before May Day, May 1. In Tegucigalpa, Honduras, weddings have been held for centuries in the shade of a "maternity tree" planted by the Spanish near the cathedral. In the past women also went there to deliver a baby.

In Syria, a man "must" marry by age 30. If he or his parents have been unable to find a suitable bride by age 29 they go to a match-maker. The matchmaker performs a useful function in many European, Asian, Pacific, and other countries. She is nearly always a member of the wedding party. The prospective groom and bride are often not permitted to know the name of the person selected or to see each other until the wedding. The boy and the girl each typically asks a friend to scout and spy to determine who is the person selected to become the spouse, and what he or she looks like? In Malaysia, the matchmaker typically hides the face of the bride with a big fan, then reveals it suddenly when the marriage is completed. The marriage is like "buying a pig in a poke." In Bulgaria, a common saying is that "an unmarried man is not a man." A Hindu man has a *religious duty* to marry.

Choosing the Day for the Wedding

It is often difficult. A fortune teller or shaman must be consulted to be sure that all of the signs are in accord. Many countries require that a couple register a few months ahead for a wedding, so they must plan ahead. A big area may have no weddings for several weeks. Then, when the signs are right, dozens of weddings will be held on the same day or weekend. In Cambodia, my guide was excited when we saw five wedding parties, of both Cambodian and Chinese couples, in the city park in one day. He said "When I woke up this morning I thought all of the signs were good for weddings." In Buddhist countries, the 20th day of the 11th month of the lunar calendar is usually considered to be a good time for weddings, or to begin a new business venture. In China, May Day, one of the few public holidays, is a popular time for weddings. In the Czech Republic, May is considered to be an unlucky month for weddings. In the Americas and Western Europe, June is considered to be a good month for weddings.

Wedding Ceremonies

They vary from simple civil ceremonies to expensive parties with hundreds of guests dressed "fit to kill." In Russia and other socialist countries where religion was discouraged, there was only a simple ceremony in the city's "wedding palace." Today there is often a second ceremony in a church. In weddings in Orthodox churches, a religious crown is held over the head of the bride and groom, indicating the church's approval of the wedding. In Latin America, a poor or middle-class family may spend as much on a daughter's wedding as the family earns in two or three years. In Islamic countries such as Tunisia and Syria, the bride often stays in seclusion, with her girlfriends, for a month or more before the wedding. She tries to lose weight, her skin is painted with reddish-brown henna, and her nails are painted red. She wears clogs with thick soles that make her look taller and make a lot of noise when she walks, so she will be noticed. North Africa's Berber girls stay in the shade for six weeks to lighten the skin color, and they eat to gain weight. The man pays more gold and silver for a fat girl. Brides were also weighed in Sumatra. In Morocco many women lighten their hair color with henna. In old Russia, on the wedding day the bride sat in the place of honor in her parents' home, the "red corner," under the icon. In the U.S. it has been considered to be bad luck if the groom sees the bride on the wedding day before the ceremony, or if anyone except the bride's close friends see the wedding dress before the ceremony. In the U.S. the bride's father "gives her" to the groom. Among the Naxi minority group in China the bride's father puts butter on her forehead, signifying happiness.

In Japan and Eastern Asia, the bride and groom perform a tea ceremony to unite their two families. Each dish served at the wedding banquet represents a wish for happiness or many children. In most of Europe and North America the groom puts a wedding ring onto the bride's finger, but the finger and the hand used varies from country to country. She may also put a wedding ring onto his finger. In many tribes in northern Thailand the wrist of the bride is tied with a thread to the wrist of the groom. Chinese believed that a man and wife are bound together by an invisible silk thread. In Buddhist Thailand and nearby countries, the couple kneel, they are tied together with a silk cord, and holy water is poured over their hands while they bend over a table. In Cambodia a Chinese groom traditionally gives the bride a flower. In Jewish weddings the bride and groom drink from the same cup of wine, a symbol of their union. In southern Asia, a cloth representing the threshold is placed on the floor and the couple cross it. In the U.S., the groom carries the bride over a threshold, representing the entrance to the bedroom. Australia's Aborigines had a practice of the girl bringing a fire log to the boy's home, to signify their marriage. In some Australian tribes, the boy twirled a vertical fire stick inside the softwood board held by the girl—symbols of the penis and the vagina. In Tahiti, when a boy and girl who liked each other sat or stood together, the boy's father put a *tapa* cloth over his head, and the boy's mother put a tapa cloth over the girl's head; the two cloths overlapped. The wedding was then announced. In New Caledonia, local *Kanaks* had a simple marriage ceremony—the man and woman sat together on a mat, ate a meal together, and joined in a festival. Parents often gave the couple a case, or thatched house. In Hungary, the bride, groom, and young men and women in the wedding party jump over a bonfire. But in Papua New Guinea, it is "unlawful" for a woman or girl to step over a fire, it will bring bad luck to the family. The bride and groom in the Czech Republic step over a ribbon, a doll, and pacifiers, representing the babies they will have. In Latvia, the bride and groom jump over a doll to ensure that they will have babies. In India, a pot is broken ceremonially at a wedding, and at the birth of a baby, or a death. A couple take seven steps together, symbolizing their walking through life together. The bride puts her foot on a stone, showing her rock-hard devotion. In a traditional wedding in Malaysia a ceremonial cloth is suspended above the couple to ward off evil. Ornamental trays have flower petals and scented leaves, and uncooked yellow rice. Relatives and friends scatter the contents of the trays on the couple. Pillars of the *dais* (raised platform) often have carvings of betel leaves. The dais has an uneven number of steps: three for a commoner, five for a royal wedding, and seven for a ruler. Guests are given a hard-boiled egg with a flower attached. In China, balls of sweetened rice served at a wedding indicate a life of unbroken harmony, sugar cane indicates a sweet future, and fish indicates abundance. The groom provides the food and drinks for the wedding, and often gives the bride a watch, bicycle, and clothes. She usually brings a dowry. During a wedding of the Yao minority group of southern China the groom removes the bride's veil, and they drink from the same cup, called a "happy cup."

The Bai minority group near Dali, in China's Yunnan province have a three-day wedding celebration. On the first day, the boy gives the girl's parents money, always with the number "6": 666 yuan, or 6,666 yuan, etc. On the second day, the groom gives the bride her wedding costume, with many balls on the headdress. Each ball represents one of her friends. On the third day, the girl is expected to cry, to be leaving her family. If not, she is considered to be cruel and ungrateful. The bride's mother serves her rice, she spits out the first bite onto the stove, signifying "I left some rice for my parents." She spits the second bite of rice onto her palm and gives it to the groom's family, so they will treat her well. During the banquet, friends and relatives tease the bride by twisting her arm to congratulate her; they are expected to twist it hard until she feels pain. They tease the groom by slapping him with the palms of the hands. They tie the bride and groom together, back to back, with a red scarf. There is a dance in the courtyard of the house, wet wood is burned to make smoke, and pepper is put into the fire to make guests sneeze. To sneeze at a wedding is a sign of happiness. The groom throws wrapped candy to guests, then they leave. When the bride and groom approach his house the groom, his father, or brother is expected to carry the bride into the house on his back, so they enter it together. They then race to sit on the bed, the first to arrive is considered to be the boss. The bride is expected to let him win. I heard that friends of one bride helped her beat the groom, and it almost caused a divorce. Among the Yi minority group in southern China, a bride is expected to fight her new husband, to show that she is a virgin, and her virginity must be protected. China's Naxi minority group have many weddings in the shade of two intertwined "10,000 camelia trees" at the Jade Peak Temple, Yufeng Si, in Yunnan province.

In much of Asia rice is a symbol of fertility. Rice is thrown at the couple in Asia and the U.S., it signifies a wish for fertility, happiness, and prosperity. In the U.S., the bride throws a bouquet of flowers to a group of bridesmaids. The girl who catches it may be the next one to marry. The bride cuts the wedding cake. It is usually in many layers, smaller at the top, with a small statue of a bride and groom. Until recently girls took a piece of the cake home, put it under the pillow, and were expected to dream of the man they would marry. Throwing old shoes after a bridal couple, or tying old shoes or "tin" cans to their car, means good luck in the U.S.

Girls of some tribes along the Sepik River in Papua New Guinea often live with the boy in the home of his parents for some months, unmarried. His mother prepares the food. When the boys' mother believes they should marry she has the girl prepare the boy's food. After eating it the boy is told that his girlfriend, not his mother, prepared the food. He is expected to complain that the food was not so good, to honor his mother. The marriage is then considered to be final. In Europe, Canada, and the U.S. the man and the woman may live together some months or years without marriage. However, before their first baby is born they are expected to marry. Many Pacific islanders do not consider a marriage to be final until a baby or the first son is born, even though all of the bride-price has been paid.

In the U.S., Canada, and most of Europe the groom rents a limousine for the wedding. In Luang Prabang, the couple rent one of the 100 or so remaining elephants in Laos. They ride the elephant, with a mahout, to the former national palace and to important Buddhist temples. In the former Soviet Union, and other former socialist countries, the wedding party visits important monuments and tourist sites in the area. It is common for tourists to meet the bride in a white dress, the groom in a suit and tie, and others, at tourist sites. In Lithuania's Hill of Crosses, the bride usually leaves a small cross or necklace of amber at the statue of Mary. Some days bridal parties must wait in line for their turn at the statue. On Tristan da Cunha, a mid-Atlantic island, the newly-married couple visit all of the island's elderly. In Islamic countries the bride must receive a gift from the groom or his father. In India's cities, it is common on weekend evenings to see a wedding procession with many people carrying lights while walking in the street. Sometimes the bride and groom ride a horse with a jeweled blanket. An Indian woman wearing 10 red bracelets is a recent bride. A married woman often wears a red *tika* or *tilak* dot in the middle of her forehead, a symbol of the "third eye of knowledge."

Kenya's Masai have a big celebration after the bride-price of cattle has been paid by the groom. His mother paints his face and decorates his hair with red ocher. He can have up to six wives. Village elders bless the bride and groom with a calabash containing milk and honey. A particular kind of dry grass is stuffed into the bride's shoes. Females in the bride's family are expected to cry. Women and girls sing, warriers sometimes dance. The bride's family and others give the bride gifts, usually goats. She is taken to the groom's home, often carried by the best man or groom. The mother of the groom pours milk on the bride's head to welcome her—the hair of Masai girls and women is kept shaved.

In Ireland until recently, a married couple were expected to drink *mead*, a drink made from honey, for a moon-cycle of around four weeks. The period after a wedding became known as a *honeymoon*. Married women in many cultures are expected to dress more conservatively than singles. Many cultures consider long hair to be very sexy. Married women cut their hair or wear it in a tight bun or use some other system to make it less noticeable. In the U.S., many men are attracted by a girl's long hair. After she gets her man she often has it cut shorter. In Islamic countries a married woman must cover her hair. In some Islamic countries any girl age 10 or so must hide her hair with a shawl and the face with a veil. I have watched girls in Yemen at the awkward age take off the veil for a few minutes, then realizing that they are old enough to attract males, they quickly put it back on. The fundamentalist Islamic countries expect a woman to wear a veil anytime she is in public. In parts of some countries she must also cover her eyes, a woman looks like a black tent, even in hot weather. In Uzbekistan I heard a legend, that Tammerlane (Timur the Lame) in the Fourteenth Century first ordered women to wear a veil, after an architect fell in love with his beautiful Chinese wife. However, women in the Middle East wore a veil long before the Islamic religion arrived in the Seventh

Century. *Bas relief* carvings in Palmyra (Tadmor), Syria show veiled women in the First Century. The Temple of Bacchus at Lebanon's large Balbak complex has bas reliefs of veiled dancers, with the child Bacchus riding a panther. They were probably made in the First Century AD. Married women may be required to wear a hat in some European and Latin American countries, and their hat is different from the hat worn by single women. In Germany through the Nineteenth Century, married women in villages were expected to wear a bonnet when they left the house. In Fiji, only virgins are permitted to plait their hair. On Malakula Island, Vanuatu, a woman of the Small Nambas tribe upon marrying was expected to have her two front incisor teeth knocked out. A rock was used to hit a sharpened stick to loosen the teeth. They were usually pulled out by hand and a heated stick was used to stop the flow of blood. It is still common in several Pacific countries to knock out one or two front teeth of a recent bride, it is considered to be an honor for the woman! Some men in Vanuatu wear the curved tusk of a pig on the upper arm, like a bracelet—one for each wife. A man wearing three tusks has three wives.

In Martinique, the home of Napoleon's Josephine, many women wear a hat with sharp knots on the top. One knot indicates that the woman is single, two knots that she is engaged, three knots that she is married, and four knots indicate that she is married but looking for a man. I saw a few with four knots. Local women on Costa Rica's Atlantic coast stare into the eyes of a man they like, conveying an unmistakable message. In China's Yunnan province, unmarried girls in one minority group until recently wore tall black stovepipe hats on dressy occasions. In another minority group married women with at least one child wear their hair in a tall conical shape. Unmarried girls in the big Yi minority group wear a red cap on top of their headdress, a red scarf, or a red cap like a turban. When they marry they wear a huge black headdress that also serves as an umbrella. Many young women in the area near Kunming wear a big headdress with two "horns," indicating that they are not married. If a young man touches one of the horns he is asking her to "marry me." A woman with one horn is engaged, if there are no horns, she is married. In and near Dali, Yunnan, Bai women wear a pretty headdress in a half-moon shape, with a white tassel some two feet long. In the past a young man could not touch the tassel unless he wanted to marry her. If she accepted he was required to work three years for her father. If they marry and live with her parents she cuts off the lower one-third of the tassel. If they live separately or with his parents she binds up the tassel, signifying that she is bound to her husband. Women in and near Toluca, Mexico wear a red rose. If single she wears it at the left ear, if married, at the right ear, if undecided whether she wants to be married she wears the rose in the middle of her hair. If a man or woman in New Caledonia wears a flower on the right ear that person is married or engaged. If a flower is worn on the left ear, the person is available. On the far side of the Pacific, Tahiti, the signals are reversed: a flower behind her right ear signals that she is looking for a boyfriend. In the Marquesas Islands, both men and married women wear a hibiscus flower behind the left ear, but on Hiva Oa Island unmarried women are not permitted to wear the flower. A Zulu girl in South Africa begins to wear her hair in a top knot when she is engaged or married. In old Estonia a married woman wore a hat trimmed in lace, but the hat of a girl with an illegitimate child could have no lace.

CHAPTER 2:
THE FAMILY & WOMEN'S RIGHTS

Segregation of the Sexes

Boys and girls go to separate schools in many Islamic countries. In the more advanced countries, such as Oman, they may attend the same classes in a university. However, girls sit at the back of the classroom, boys sit in the front. They have separate paths between buildings and separate entrances to buildings. Is this treatment of men and women somewhat like the "separate but equal" rights of Whites and Blacks in the U.S. until the 1950s? Some Islamic countries have mixed classes in primary schools but in higher schools, boys and girls nearly always separated. In Yemen, a girls' primary school is often adjacent to a boys' primary school. Older boys and girls are usually not permitted to be alone together in Islamic countries, even if they are engaged. However, they may talk with each other for hours on the telephone. It is not unusual to see a female, covered from head to foot in a black tent, talking on a cellular phone.

It is common in villages in lesser-developed countries or in native reserves in developed countries to have places reserved for males or for females. Ayers Rock, or Uluru, Australia, has long been a sacred place for Aborigines. It is believed to be a major home for their ancestors, the Anangu. Certain caves and niches are reserved for females, others for males, and non-Aborigines are prohibited from entering many. A stranger in a village is usually escorted by a local person, who will be sure that taboos are not broken.

On many of the Solomon Islands, in the Highlands of Papua New Guinea, and on parts of other Melanesian islands, men and boys gather or grow their own food and cook, eat, and sleep apart from females. Women sleep with the pigs, not the husband. The mother breast feeds the baby for at least two years. A man is not permitted to have sex with a wife until the baby is at least two or three years old. This helps to keep the population down. The taboo against sex while the mother is breast feeding was strong in Europe through the Eighteenth Century. Among Africa's Masai a woman does not have sex with the husband until the baby can walk. The taboo against sex for at least six months after a baby was born is common on Pacific islands.

I asked a man in Papua New Guinea how he manages to have sex with any of his wives. He said he usually finds her working in the garden, with her pig tied by the leg to a bush. He kicks the pig, it squeals, she investigates, and he leads her into the bushes. If she is having her period she leaves a big red leaf at the edge of the garden. During mating a man must say protective words to prevent his being weakened by contact with a woman. In Papua New Guinea's Lowlands some families now live in the same house. Youths and men of the Mosuo minority group in China's Yunnan province live with their mother, and older girls and women continue to live with their mother. In ancient Sparta of Greece, men and youths also lived apart from women, and they ate in a communal kitchen and dining area. In rural Korea, until recently, each farmers' house had separate areas for men and for women and children. A boy up to age seven may visit the women's area, with permission. In warm weather a man slept with a "Dutch Wife," rather than a real wife. They are used in several tropical countries—they are a big bolster made of woven fibers that permit the air to circulate under bedclothes. Men in Mali's Dogon tribe do not live with a wife until she has born at least three of his children. A Miao man of southern China and southeast Asia usually does not live with his wife until the first baby is born.

In the small thatch or adobe houses and round huts without a partition, found in much of the world, custom tells where each person should sleep. Throughout Southeast Asia, the Pacific, and sub-Sahara Africa all males and females are often required to sleep in opposite sides of their small home. For example, in Thailand and many other countries it is common that females sleep on the left and males sleep on the right as you enter. In Samoa a newly married couple first make a partition of tapa cloth, made by beating the inner bark of mulberry. I learned how to beat the bark with a hardwood club and to connect small pieces together by beating. Geometric designs are usually drawn with black paint. The partition gives them a little privacy in one end of the parents' home. Most of the Samoan homes or *fales* have only a floor and a roof, with open walls—no shades or drapes. People walking down the village street learn not to stare as they observe the neighbors dressing, undressing, and in various other daily acts of living. When my wife and I stayed with a family in Samoa we learned to lean low when changing clothes. Privacy is unknown in much of the world. Japanese homes have folding screens to give privacy within a room.

In many tribes in Togo and Ghana, such as the Anlo (Ewe), males and females live apart. A wife does not have a conversation with her husband unless he invites her to talk. The father and older sons eat in one room, but wives, daughters, and young sons eat in the kitchen. A man who shows affection in public for his wife is ridiculed and called a "kitchen man." A woman remains a member of her father's clan and is not absorbed into her husband's clan.

On islands of Polynesia and Melanesia, it is common that a family wanting a girl select the youngest son and raise him as a girl. The child is dressed as a girl and begins to look and act like a girl. I noticed that one in Tahiti used the women's toilet. Many of the *mahu* transvestites become prostitutes. Today in China, a family is sometimes given permission to have a second baby if the first is a girl, since every Chinese couple wants a son to support them in their old age. Many families have a third child, which is given a girl's name even if it is a boy. The third child, male or female, is often raised as a girl. In much of the Pacific and Africa, where a child lives with several families in the village as it grows up, parents wanting a girl may casually trade a son for the daughter of a neighbor.

Fertility Symbols

Drawings or carvings often show a female with exaggerated breasts, hips, and genitalia, or a male with exaggerated genitalia. A woman wanting a baby in Ghana carries an *akuaba* or wooden doll on her back for months. In much of the world, including Indians in North America, little girls were given a doll as a fertility and motherhood symbol. In Kenya many tribes give a teenage girl a doll as a fertility symbol. A fat woman doll is a fertility symbol in many cultures. They include the 25,000 year-old Willendorf doll found in Austria, and the fat woman who sat on a stone pillar in the world's oldest above-ground temple, in Malta. A phallic stone was nearby. The National Museum of Aleppo, Syria, has many ancient fertility dolls. Some, nearly 7,000 years old from the Halaf culture, emphasize the female genitalia and breasts, but are otherwise realistic. The serpent and scorpion were then symbols of fertility and the continuity of life in the Middle East. Snakes shed their skin, apparently renewing their life. Clay figures more than 4,000 years old were made from molds. Many of them show naked women. The Central Bank Museum in Quito, Ecuador has pottery fertility dolls believed to have come from Japan around 2,500 BCE. There is considerable evidence of trading long ago. The spirit house in the Lowlands villages of Papua New Guinea often has a large carved statue of a woman with her legs spread far apart, and many statues of men with an exaggerated penis. A common petroglyph drawing by ancient man in Zimbabwe is of a woman, spread-eagled, with zigzag lines leading to a man. In Egypt and other countries bordering the Mediterranean the bull is a symbol of fertility. The Greek God Zeus is said to have changed into a bull. He carried Europa to Crete, where he fathered cruel King Minos. Celts, as they migrated across Europe to Ireland some 3,500 years ago used bulls' head with horns as a fertility symbol. Bulls' heads and bulls' horns were erected along roads throughout ancient Spain. On Crete, men and women held up both arms, forming a symbol like a capital letter *U*, signifying a bulls' horns and fertility. Young Cretan men and women liked to run at a charging bull, vault onto its back, then land on their feet behind the surprised bull!

Inca priests in Cuzco sacrificed animals and old men at an altar like a phallic stone. A nearby stone has a snake—a sex symbol—carved on top. In Luang Prabang, Laos, a Buddhist temple, Wat Si Muang, is dedicated to Si, a pregnant woman who committed suicide under a big rock. Women wanting a baby leave offerings for her. I was surprised to see at least 30 women bring flowers and food to the temple each morning. A truck often takes some of the offerings to another temple that gets fewer offerings. In Hangzhou, China, women sit on the lap of the stone "Lucky Buddha" at the Lingyin Temple to become pregnant. In China's Shandong province a man and his wife sometimes leave a stone on sacred Mt. Taishan, so she will have a son. The Goddess of Mercy is considered to be more important than Buddha in much of China, she is considered to present a baby to a woman. Women wanting a baby pray to the Goddess of Mercy. In Ninglang, Yunnan, women wanting a baby pray to the Buddhist Goddess of Birth, "who has 1,000 eyes and hands," and can stop suffering. In Delhi, India, women wanting to become pregnant tie a rag to the gate of the Shrine of Pots. Other believers leave a pot of rice. Many Hindu temples in India have a stone statue of Nandi, the bull that often carried the god Shiva. Women wanting a baby touch the statue of the bull. In Tahiti, Moorea, and other Polynesian islands women guests at a wedding are expected to grab the erect penis of a carved statue of a man, so the bride will have babies. Ancient Druids, the priests of the Celts, believed that mistletoe from an oak tree would make any animal or person give birth. Italians believed that if a woman carried a sprig of mistletoe she would have a baby. Some Chinese want a *girl* baby. Those women are advised to eat fish, dark chicken meat, tomatoes, apples, and citrus fruits for several weeks before becoming pregnant. A man wanting a daughter is advised to eat potatoes, cucumber, eggplant, lettuce, mushrooms, and seaweed before impregnating his wife.

The Family

The family is strong in many Asian, Pacific, southern and eastern European, and Latin American countries. Grandparents, even uncles and aunts, often live with the "nuclear family." Children have a strong duty to care for parents. A married couple wanting to have a long life together go to China's Mt. Emei in Sechuan province, buy a padlock with sayings engraved on it, lock the padlock onto the handrail to the temple at the summit, and throw away the key. The couple will then be locked together. In countries with a high unemployment rate, a wage earner has a duty to share earnings with everyone in the extended family. They usually agree to a fixed percentage for each group. If a woman is earning money, a brother may make repairs on her home, her mother may care for the children, and a sister may mend clothes for the family. One of my guides in Thailand complained to me that, with a wife and three children to support, he also had to make monthly contributions to his wealthy parents. However, he would never complain to them. He said they give the extra money to the temple. Several of my Asian guides said they would like to go to the university, but they must work until the youngest sibling is through school and all of the sisters are married. In Asia, nursing homes, such as Taiwan's "Evergreen Homes," are necessary only when an older man or woman have no children to live with. My wife worked in a hospital in Agra, India. The owner had immigrated to the U.S., established a successful carpet business, then gave away nearly all of his money when he was around 70 years old but in good health. My wife asked him how he would live. He said "My sons will take care of me. I don't have to worry." An older son must also care for younger brothers and sisters. In Arab and other Islamic countries a father is often proud of his young children, especially a son. Many men have gone out of their way to exhibit a son to me, usually named *Mohammed.*

When a man has more than one wife each wife has her own hut, garden, and granary. He also has a hut and granary. Among Africa's Masai the hut of the first wife is usually immediately to the right of the enclosure's entrance, the second wife's hut is to the left of the entrance, the third wife's hut is to the right of the first wife's hut, the fourth wife's hut is to the left of the second wife's, etc. Children of each wife live in her hut until they become youths or adults. Small calves are brought into the alcove of the hut at night, they bring flies. Cattle are brought into the enclosure each night. A fence made of thorny brush discourages wild animals. The mud huts are built over a framework of sticks (wattle), the low roof is also mud. When missionaries told the Kikuyu men in Kenya and Tanzania that Christians should have only one wife the Kikuyu pointed out that the Bible, in the Epistles, limited the men who should have only one wife to deacons, priests, and bishops.

Rituals have been developed to insure that a baby will be healthy. Pregnant Zulu women in South Africa are warned never to cross the path in front of certain animals. They also cannot eat many types of food because it will cause the baby to have long ears and blue eyes. In New Caledonia's traditional villages an aracuari pine tree (a symbol of the nation) is planted when a baby is born. If the tree dies the "baby" or its oldest descendant cuts it down and must plant a replacement. The aracuari pine tree, yam, and taro symbolize the Kanak culture. The father or grandfather of a new-born baby among Yunnan's

Naxi minority group bury several jars of *yinju* wine, made of barley, wheat, and sorghum. When the child marries the wine is dug up for drinking. In northern Thailand women walk under the belly of an elephant to have an easier pregnancy. I hope they don't get stepped on. In Indonesia the mother of a woman seven months pregnant ceremoniously bathes her daughter. At that time there must be seven kinds of fruit in the house—one for each month of pregnancy. Women in Papua New Guinea are told that they must work hard and carry heavy loads after seven or eight months of pregnancy "so the birth will be easier." She also takes baths in cold water. In the mountains of Austria's Tyrol a woman awaiting childbirth must not take off her wedding ring, for witches and spirits will then have power over her. In the Marquesas Islands, a pregnant woman makes offerings of food to stone tikis that are shaped like a pregnant woman, to have a healthy baby. Pregnant women in China's Sichuan province eat a soup made of pigs' feet, peanuts, chicken, and/or squid, to provide better food for the baby.

In Bulgaria until recently, a new mother was required to stay quarantined in a room with the baby for 40 days. She could not leave. Was that too much togetherness? In Yemen's villages women must also stay quarantined with a new baby for 40 days. She burns myrrh incense, native to the area, "to kill bacteria." In China, a mother traditionally is isolated for 30 days with the new baby, and she is expected to avoid weddings and funerals for a longer period. Thirty days after the birth of a baby in China, and again a year after birth, a party is held and presents are given. In the latter party objects such as books, money, clothes, and toy farm animals or toy farm implements are put onto a table within reach—the object that the baby grabs is said to predict its future occupation. Some Vietnamese believe that a new mother should eat only white rice with salty foods, avoid brushing teeth or washing hair for a month, and sleep on warm surfaces. In Tahiti, a new mother was considered to be unclean and she was forbidden to touch food until the baby was three weeks old. Someone else had to feed her! Ancient Jewish people, like Mary, the mother of Jesus, were considered to be unclean for 40 days after the birth of a male child. When the 40 days was up Mary is said to have had a ritual purification ceremony. In Papua New Guinea it is a taboo for a mother to have sex while the baby is still breast fed, until it is at least two or three years old. Local Pacific Islanders, like most Asians, rarely drink cows' milk. In Ninglang, Yunnan province, China, a woman of the Pumi minority group nursing a baby eats lots of eggs, saves the shells for a month, then dumps the shells in a pile on a busy street. Villagers will then know that she is taking good care of her baby.

A crawling or walking baby is often confined to a safe area on Pacific islands by a large wicker basket, turned upside-down over the baby. Market women in the South Pacific sometimes keep a small child in the security of a big basket right-side-up beside the mother. In Europe, many babies, like William Shakespeare, were fastened to a vertical pole near the center of a room. In other homes, particularly in France, the baby was fastened to a ring that slid along a horizontal pole. Both methods of restraint are now illegal in most European countries. In the U.S. a baby is often confined in a playpen. When I climb up to cliff houses in the U.S. Southwest, I wonder how babies survived, with no wall to prevent them from a fall of several hundred feet. When I see children too young to swim playing on houseboats on the Amazon, I also wonder how they survive.

In some Pacific islands, such as Tonga and Samoa even the youngest daughter has authority over all of her brothers. In New Caledonia's Kanak culture, the mother's brother automatically becomes a child's guardian, with more authority over the child than the father. In Tonga, a sister names the children of her brothers or has veto power over names she doesn't like. If a child is poorly behaved, Samoans say "a rat ate its umbilical cord." Among Africa's Masai, if a child misbehaves it can prevent punishment by an angry adult by snatching a handful of grass, which is considered to be sacred by the cattle-herding tribe. In poor countries, little girls only seven or eight must carry baby brother or sister all day. Children grow up fast. Mothers in the Pacific and Latin America have told me that they were looking forward to when the baby would be around five years old, it could almost take care of itself and the little daughter could start school. On Pacific islands, in Africa, and among Indians of the Americas, a child becomes independent at an early age. Children observe what adults are doing and often do the work of an adult, cleaning the home, gathering, preparing, and eating food, or caring for baby sister or brother, without being asked to.

Children in lesser-developed countries often make their own toys. Naturally, they copy adults by making toy boats, bows and arrows, spears, sling shots, fishing lines, houses, cars or trucks, and animals. Both boys and girls play marbles, roll round hoops of metal or a bent limb pushed by a T-bar, and make things with string. In West Africa, boys make a push toy by attaching a round watermelon to a stick-axle, connected to two long sticks for pushing it. Spinning tops are sometimes a foot in diameter and spin for several minutes, especially in the Burma-Thailand area. In East Africa, youths often use a whip cord to throw a top and start its spinning. Boys usually play with kites, and in Southeast Asia they glue sharp glass to the string and try to cut the string of their opponents in a kite fight. A version of hopscotch is played by girls and boys, especially in Europe, North America, and villages along the Amazon. When our old boat stopped at Caballo

Cocha in Peru's upper Amazon, we watched the youngsters play a game something like "drop the handkerchief." Our Spanish couple recognized it as *patio de mi casa*, a game often played in Spain. We joined the friendly children in their game. Girls are taught to play with dolls, a symbol of the babies they are expected to have later. In Austria and other countries of Central Europe, a doll house may be more than four feet long, with furniture and fixtures in each room like those in a real house. Children and adults often have amazing mechanical skills. I walked several kilometers across the desert in Mali while a small boy walked with me, pushing a truck he had made of heavy wire, with wheels that rolled, by the long shaft of a steering wheel that turned the front wheels. Men and women in West and Central Africa may see only one truck, bulldozer, or crane in their life, or only the photograph of one. But with scissors they can quickly cut a "tin" can and fold it to make a toy truck, bulldozer, or crane that looks exactly like the real one. Perhaps the favorite game in towns and villages in most of the world for boys and men is football (soccer). Playing catch with a ball, or hitting it with a bat, is popular in most of the Americas, Japan, and elsewhere. In former British colonies cricket is still played. In France and French Polynesia, men play *boules* by rolling a steel ball around three inches in diameter, trying to knock out the ball of opponents. The game began in France in the late Seventeenth Century. The loser had to "kiss the fanny" of a doll or kiss a painting of a fanny. Men and women in villages in French Polynesia, not plagued with television, talk with friends or play bingo. Each player may handle 16 cards, quickly putting a marker in the proper square of each card. The French government has wisely built a covered open-wall community building in most villages in French Polynesia. It has also paved a small ball court and the main street of nearly all villages. In Guayaquil, Ecuador, men play checkers on the sidewalk, using the lid of pop bottles for checkers. In southern China men play cards or *mah jong* on the busy sidewalks. Vendors in Dali, China, sell lots of little pottery boy dolls by demonstrating how they are realistic, by pouring water in the open top. Water then comes out below as the doll "urinates."

Women's Rights

Women and girls have acquired more rights in many countries in the past 50 years. In Tokyo I saw groups of young salaried women carousing after work, but they are usually gone by 9:00 P.M. Groups of young *salarymen* are seen after midnight. Japan is one of the few countries where young women work as hotel bellhops. Japanese usually do not expect tips. In most countries, people would be concerned as to how young women bellhops earn their tips. Korean young men have not been taught to help a young woman. Men are considered to be superior. I have seen young women help a young man put his coat on and open doors for a man, but I never saw a man help a woman with her coat or a door. In Papua New Guinea, men have large ceremonial pig kills and eat a lot of pork. Women get only the entrails, which they must share with children. Only 150 years ago many Pacific Islanders were cannibals. In the Marquesas Islands women were not permitted to eat "long pig" or human flesh that the men liked so much. It was also taboo for women to eat real pig or to eat the better fish—bonita and squid. Women and girls in the Marquesas were not permitted to go out alone in a canoe, for fear that men from another tribe would steal them. In Albania, Turkey, Bulgaria, and much of Eastern Europe, women and girls were not permitted to join men in serious discussions, while the men drank tea and smoked. Women and girls could peek down upon them through a small window, and bring more hot tea. In Orthodox churches throughout Eastern Europe, men traditionally stand on the right side, women stand on the left. Today some churches have a few seats along the walls. In traditional China, when a girl married she separated completely from her family, and became attached to her husband's family—even after the rare divorce.

In China, women now do almost all types of work, as in Russia. In India and Bangladesh it is rare to find a female employee working in a hotel, although a few work in restaurants, including hotel restaurants. In most of Southeast Asia, including Islamic Malaysia and Indonesia, women may do almost any type of work. In Vietnam, women wearing a scarf over the nose and mouth and a conical straw hat do much of the work of repairing roads and streets. In fundamental Islamic countries, females don't work in restaurants or hotels, there are few in offices, and married women do not work outside of the home. Men in many Islamic countries told me that married women can work outside the home if the husband consents, "but most women don't want to." Many young unmarried women work in hospitals and clinics. A hospital director in Muscat, Oman told me they always had trouble recruiting nursing students, male or female.

Afghanistan's Talibans prohibit all women and girls from working or going to school. Women who show more than their eyes and feet in public are beaten. Men are beaten for trimming a beard, taxi drivers who transport a woman passenger are beaten. Movie theaters are closed, music is banned on radio and TV. Also in Afghanistan, paper shopping bags are prohibited because they may be made from recycled paper that once had the printed words of the Koran. Most Moslems consider these restrictions to be repugnant to Islam. In Turkey, Egypt, and Tunisia, many women work in offices and professions, even after they are married. Berber women in North Africa and the Middle East have retained much freedom, many refuse to wear a veil. A few years ago, my wife worked as a physician in an Afghan refugee camp near the Afghanistan border and Peshawar, Pakistan. Her female Afghan interpreter said "men are naturally smarter then women." My wife suggested that if Afghan girls and women were permitted to visit and travel freely the way men do, perhaps the females could be as smart. Her 22 year old interpreter thought awhile, then said "that might make a difference."

I have discussed the status of women with men in many Islamic countries. They consider a female to be a "diamond," precious, to be put onto a pedestal. She must be protected, by being covered from head to foot to hide her feminine charms. She can then wander in crowded *souks* (markets) without being molested by men. In the days of chivalry, European knights also protected young women, but "nice women" were not permitted to leave home unescorted, nor to work outside of the home. Many Islamic men believe that a woman's place is in the home, with the family. Fundamentalist Islamic countries are not adequately using an important national asset—their women. With equal education and work experience they can contribute as much as a man to the national economy.

In Syria either the man or the woman may get a divorce. The mother usually gets custody of a boy until he is age nine, and of a girl until she is 12. The father pays child support but no alimony. If the mother remarries the father gets the children, and he gets a boy older than nine and a girl over 12. Some women work as hotel maids or clerks. In Iran, the father automatically gets custody of a boy age two or more, or of a girl age seven or more. In countries that follow the Islamic law of the *Sharia*, a woman marrying must promise to obey her husband at all times. In old Korea, women were required to avoid the "seven sins" by obeying the husband's parents, having a son, avoiding lust, jealousy, serious disease, talking too much, and stealing. However, one of the brightest women I've ever met was a 20-year-old Korean in my class in Madrid, Spain. In traditional villages of the Pacific the chief decides which divorcing parent gets each child. In Pacific villages where the chief makes and interprets the law, many chiefs discourage a girl from going to school beyond the "Standard Six" years of school. In some *kastom* (traditional custom) villages in Vanuatu, the chief prohibits anyone from going to school, to preserve old customs and traditions. In Vanuatu a man wore a cap reading "Ex-wife for sale. Take over payments."

In most of Europe women have many rights, as in the U.S. and Canada. But in the southern tier, Greece, Italy, Spain, and Portugal, they are more limited. Those countries have few waitresses, most restaurant employees are men. Men in Sicily believe that a woman's place is in the home or in the fields. Our teacher in a language school in Florence asked whether we thought the father or the mother made the main decisions for the family in Italy. My first reaction was that men do, as in *macho* Spain and Latin America. After observing our family and others for a few days I found that women are the boss. She agreed.

Some primitive societies were and still are matrilineal—ancestors are traced through the female line. A new husband in some tribes, such as North America's Cherokees, and the Yukon's Southern Tutchone, had to leave his clan to live with his wife's clan. Women make the major decisions in other tribes, including Africa's Tuareg. Women work together on some Pacific islands to decide how the village will be run. In most villages in the Pacific, women operate a small store, open several hours a day, to sell food and small household things. An individual local family would lose money by selling food and other things, for all of their many relatives would expect free food. Some isolated tribes in China's Yunnan province, such as the Mosuo, in the beautiful Lugu Lake area, rarely have a formal marriage. The Mosuo have axia marriage, which means that it is easy to change a partner or to have many partners. Children automatically stay with the mother, fathers have no descendants or property rights. Women of southern China's Naxi minority group do most of the work, earning a living, planting rice and other crops, and handling the money. Men often baby-sit.

On many of the Pacific islands, such as the Marquesas, either a man or a woman could change partners easily. Little attempt was made to identify the father of a baby. A baby stayed with its mother. Local children call all men in a typical Pacific Island village "uncle," all women except the real mother is an "aunt," and all boys and girls are "cousin." Sometimes a small child decides to live with an "aunt" in the village, for weeks, months, or years. In Fiji and other islands a child may have lived with several families before it becomes an adult. In Vanuatu and islands of Micronesia, inheritance is through the mother, not the father. On the Solomon Islands men were more likely than women to be killed in tribal wars or headhunting, so land is still allocated to the woman and her descendants. Our guide in Malta said that when a few boatloads of people first arrived from Sicily around 6,000 years ago there was need for a larger population. Women were more important than men because only women produced babies. The people did not associate men with babies. Much later, when unfriendly invaders arrived, men became more important, to fight the invaders, so men became the head of the family. Anthropologists believe that long ago in Zimbabwe a man moved to his wife's village when they "married." Property passed from the mother to the daughters. Women grew the food, men made pottery or were metalworkers. As population increased and animal herds led by men developed, hostile invaders tried to steal animals and growing food. Men became more important and property passed from father to the sons. The large Yi minority group in southern China was once matrilineal, and women have retained many rights, but they usually have only one lover or husband. My guide said "women are the boss" among Yunnan's large Naxi minority group and its offshoot, the Mosuo.

On many Pacific islands it is taboo for women to enter the men's spirit house or to see the initiation ceremonies for youths. Recently, female tourists have been permitted into spirit houses to see the wood carvings, woven goods, and other handicrafts for sale. In Papua New Guinea, the Haus Tamboran or spirit house usually keeps the more valuable statues upstairs in the loft. The spirit house or Nakamal in Vanuatu and some islands has only one floor. Carved or woven statues are kept in a back room, men use the front room for chatting with friends and drinking kava. On many islands a female may not stand higher or taller than a male, and she must slouch or bend down when entering a meeting. It is taboo for a woman to pass in front of a man. A female cannot step over a fire—one reason given is that its smoke may rise higher than a man. A man may not be in a position lower than a female, he cannot walk under a woman's clothesline or swim under a woman's canoe. A female is required to isolate herself in a low hut during menstruation and childbirth. On some of the Solomon islands, a menstruating woman must have a friend bring food to her, and any clothes a woman wears during childbirth must be purified in a ritual.

Most of the countries in Europe, like the U.S., have recently amended their law so that a daughter has the same rights of inheritance as a son. However, in the more traditional societies of Latin America, Africa, Asia, and the Pacific, a daughter does not have the same rights to inherit property as has a son. A male poorly-educated village chief considers himself to be far superior to any female, even a well-educated woman tourist, executive, or government official.

Women in New Zealand and Australia do not have equal opportunity with men. However, they are seeking changes. My wife reports that graffiti in a Christchurch ladies room read "Women of the world unite, make him sleep on the wet spot tonight."

In Africa, Asia, and the Pacific men have been the traditional hunters and warriors. Hunting is now often illegal, except with a license. Tribal wars are prohibited and are quickly stopped by the central government in most countries. Women have tended the garden, fetched the water and gathered the wood or other fuel, and have taken care of children and the home. Men have little to do, except to drink alcohol, tea, coffee, or kava, chew *khat*, build and maintain the house, and care for the livestock. In the Pacific and some African societies, men have elaborate social rituals that fill their time—dances, initiation ceremonies, religious or spiritual rituals, and ceremonial feasts. Men, youths, and even women in many traditional villages have much leisure time. They can gather or grow their food or other necessities in only a few hours a day. If they do not want town or city luxuries there is little need for them to work hard. If they have reasonably good health they can enjoy life, but they must always respect and honor *kastom* (custom) and those with more authority in the village. They rarely have thoughts about the future, except as it affects their religion or their family.

CHAPTER 3:
THE PLACE WHERE PEOPLE LIVE

Housing

In lesser-developed countries many people live in a round hut made of mud daubed over a framework of sticks and boughs (wattle), or made of mud bricks with a little straw, grass, or lime mixed in, or in a rectangular hut made of the same things. Wattle was used in much of Europe until a thousand years ago. Some round huts are made of bundles of straw or grass tied together. Similar round huts were used in much of Europe 4,000 years or more ago. Athens' Tradition and Folk Art Museum has a rebuilt local ancient round hut made of straw, almost identical with some used in Africa today. Mayans often build oval-shape adobe, stone, or wattle huts, not round. Most of the fales in Samoa and the homes in Tonga, far away in the Pacific, are also oval-shape. Cherokees in the hills of North Carolina built oval-shape houses of wattle until the White man arrived with steel axes. They changed to cabins built with horizontal logs, like Abe Lincoln's. Log houses are common among some African tribes, and in the mountains of China's provinces of Yunnan and Tibet. Most of the buildings are two-story, with log partitions and roofs of boards like shingles, or of clay tile. There are often log buildings on three sides of a courtyard, and a fence on the fourth side. The lower floor is for storage and animals, plus the main living room. Above the entrance to the living room there is often a drawing made by Buddhist monks, to keep out evil spirits. Smoke from the open fire drifts through meat to preserve it, and some of the smoke finds its way to an opening on the roof. There is no chimney. Among the matrilineal Mosuo the head of the household, the grand-mother, sleeps and sits to the left of the hearth fire, the "uncle" sits in front of it. Buddhist symbols for the sun and moon decorate the roof.

Adobe uses little precious wood. Sometimes layers of logs or boards are used in the walls to reduce damage in case of earthquakes. Yemen has many villages filled with adobe buildings up to eight floors high, often more than 300 years old. It has similar stone buildings 800 years old. Horizontal squared logs are used on every floor to absorb earthquakes. In the dry climate, houses often use basalt stone for the ground floor, it absorbs moisture and is said to be healthier. In the Middle East and Albania the ground floor is used only for storage. After a heavy rain men add more mud to the walls in Yemen, the mud mosques of Mali, and elsewhere. Downspouts that jut three feet out do not completely protect mud walls from rain. In Uzbekistan, each corner of adobe houses has a buttress to help it withstand earthquakes. In the Middle East, corners of buildings bordering passageways in busy souks (markets) are protected by concrete buttresses.

Many rectangular huts have a thatch roof of palm leaves and walls made of woven thatch or vertical bamboo sticks, those in Latin America may have vertical corn stalks stripped of their leaves. A wood or grass hut often have a ledge of stone or mud so termites can be found more easily if they attack the house. Granaries are usually built high on rocks to keep out termites and rats. In hot areas or places subject to periodic flooding, the huts are raised high on posts, above many of the insects, and they catch more cooling breezes. The floor, made of springy limbs stays cleaner—anything small, like dirt, falls through the cracks. In forested areas primitive people learned to cut down trees with stone axes, or by pressing many rocks heated in the fire into the trunk all around, to burn down a tree. They learned to peel off the bark of some trees, for house walls or roof, boats, utensils, etc. With stone axes they split some trees, like cedar, to make planks for the walls, roof, and floor. People living in cooler forests made horizontal log houses. Many primitive people lived in a *longhouse*, especially in cold climates. They had as many as 50 families in a building, each separated by a partition. Sometimes the partition was only symbolic. In a forested area with low population density houses made of wood may still be the most practical. But in crowded places like part of the Philippines, too many trees are being cut. The government encourages people to build with mud—adobe. Pueblo and cliff dwellers, such as the *Anasazi* ("Old Ones") and Hopi in the U.S. Southwest had buildings or cave-like structures where many families lived together. Large cities, such as Pueblo Bonito, did not have enough water, cooking fuel, and land to grow crops in a dry year. The villages were abandoned in the late Thirteenth Century because of drought and overpopulation.

Adobe huts dissolve when flooded. One of our trips to Madras, India, was during the monsoon rains. Several thousand adobe homes of squatters dissolved when the river rose. In an earthquake or monsoon rain, mud or tile roofs used in part of Latin America and the Middle East kill many people beneath them. In New Caledonia, where it is not so hot and danger of flooding is low, round *cases* or homes covered with grass and the bark of the *niaouli* tree, are often built on the ground. A hut built on the ground gives better protection during a cyclone. The cooking hut found in many Pacific villages is usually built on the ground, where it is easier to maintain the cooking fires for several families. A threshold one or two feet high keeps pigs, and some of the chickens, out of the hut. The sleeping hut, a traditional thatched *leaf haus*, sometimes with woven walls, is usually on stilts—cooler, and with fewer insects. In much of Africa, older children sleep in a tree house. In the evening the ladder is removed to discourage wild animals. In cold climates huts are built low on the ground, and are sometime half-underground. In a cold climate, such as Alaska and Iceland, some have a sod roof. A half-underground house covered with sod is cool in hot weather and easy to heat in cold weather. They were used by Indians in much of the U.S., by pioneers on the U.S plains, and by Chinese 6,000 years ago in Pangpo Village near Xi'an. A partition to give some privacy was a big improvement. Later Pangpo homes had a partition. The chief's house among Zimbabwe's Venda tribe often has a partition. I saw one that even had a bathtub made of clay. In the U.S. Southwest, Indians often put the fire pit in front of a big vertical flat stone, which reflected the heat in homes, and in a *kiva*, used for ceremonies. Some of the smoke escaped in an opening directly above.

Farmers in the Americas and Europe often use only the rear door, which typically opens onto an easily cleaned linoleum floor. The front door is used only for special guests. One family that my wife and I lived with in Quebec, always used the rear door. Some 15 pairs of shoes were usually piled just inside the door. Two families that I lived with in Germany placed all shoes neatly in a *Schuhschrank*, just inside the front door. We never wore shoes in the house, they were too dirty. On some Pacific Islands even a small home has three or four doors. Each door was used by particular people. On Fiji only the owner or chief could use some doors of the *bure*. Fiji is one of the Western Pacific's more affluent areas, and many houses are built on a platform of earth surrounded by a stone wall. Older homes in the Marquesas Islands were built on a stone platform. In the hills of Zimbabwe, terraces were leveled, protected by stone walls, and the typical round huts are built on the flat terraces. In the Pacific, many traditional homes have a rectangular shape, like the *hale* in Hawaii. In Fiji, walls are usually made of wood, not woven fiber; most roofs are now metal. Thatch only lasts a few years, and typhoons (hurricanes) blow the thatch away. In the Caribbean's hurricanes, metal roofs blow away, many homes now have a concrete roof. Early thatch homes in the Marquesas Islands were also built on a stone platform, the rear roof extended down to it. In Sanai, capital of Yemen, the ancient "skyscraper" buildings usually have a fan-shape window above the heavy wooden door, to let in light. The fan-shape reminds me of the fan-shape windows above the door in Dublin's Georgian-style houses, but in Yemen the glass is brightly colored—red, green, and blue, with some yellow. Many Yemen homes have a sign near the door stating in Arabic "Blessings to Allah."

Squatters moving into a city build with anything available—a tarp, cardboard, plastic, sheet metal, or whatever. In Ireland, laws permitted anyone to build a cottage on unused land, and it was legal if it was completed before the landlord discovered it. Walls were usually of mud mixed with lime for strength, the roof was thatched or made of cattails, floors were packed earth. Smoke from the fireplace filtered through the roof. Smoke helps to keep unwanted insects from making a home but it is bad for the eyes and lungs of those who are exposed to it. The inside of thatch roofs were often scraped in the spring, the soot was used as fertilizer. The box of salt was kept near the fire to stay dry. In windy places the thatch roof of a cottage is often covered with wire to keep it from blowing away. In Australia, birds carry away little sticks used to build fences unless they have a strong cap on top. In windy parts of Scotland a *blackhouse* was built, with inner and outer walls of stone, and sand between. Animals at one end of the house, kept out of the family area by bunk beds, helped to heat the house. Some people say it was called a *blackhouse* because everything inside was covered with black soot. Nearly half of the six billion people in the world live in housing built wholly of local adobe, thatch, stone, or scraps, without electricity or running water. Ugly neighborhoods are beautified before visits by royalty. Belfast built a fake wall to hide ugly backyards and clotheslines before Queen Victoria arrived.

In a warm climate the contents of a hut are little more than sleeping mats, hard pillows, a few extra clothes, a spear and throwing stick, a digging stick in the Pacific, a simple hoe in Africa or Asia, a few pottery dishes for cooking and eating, and a few big pottery jugs to store grain and water. Sometimes gourds and woven watertight baskets are used instead of pottery, especially by nomads. Pottery is heavy and it breaks easily. Bushmen of southern Africa carried water in the shell of an ostrich, plugging the hole with straw. Sometimes they stored emergency water in an ostrich shell, buried in the sand. If the shell broke they made jewelry of it, which they traded to other tribes. Hottentot women of southern Africa made pottery but it was carefully carried by hanging straps. Wooden digging sticks, spears, arrows, and shields are hardened in the fire. Some sharp points are made of stone, bone, sharks teeth, or seashells. The dirt floor is often packed and smooth. Many African tribes pound animal blood or fresh manure into the dirt floor. I have seen many polished dirt floors as smooth and clean as the best concrete. However, the dirt floors do not wear well and need re-polishing after a few months. In Africa the cooking fire is usually outside. In Africa and tropical America, there may be a few hammocks outside in the shade of a roof or tree. Stools usually have three legs in Africa, or four legs in the Pacific and Latin America.

In traditional cultures pottery was made only by a particular village that owned a good source of clay. The skills to make good pottery is still handed down from parent to child. Pottery was so important that taboos developed around it. In New Caledonia pottery was only made by naked women who met in a secret place each year. They had to abstain from having sex during the period they made pottery. Usually only one village in a large area has the right to make pottery. Bilbil Village on the north coast of Papua New Guinea makes beautiful red pottery without glaze. Women shape each soft ball of clay with a round stone. It is put under the house to dry for two weeks, then is put into a small fire to test for bubbles. Finally, it is put into a big fire, but no kiln. More advanced cultures use the coil method or a potter's wheel. In Laos, far up the Mekong, the pottery-making village of Sanghei decided to switch to making alcohol from rice, it was more profitable. A village three miles (5 km.) away, Ban Jhan, was given the right to dig clay from the site, build two underground kilns, and begin to make pottery. Allsaints Village on Antigua in the Caribbean makes practical pottery "coldpots," with a fire underneath—a cheap stove and pot. Guellela, in Tunisia, makes beautiful glazed pottery of many colors—common in Islamic countries, from Morocco to the Middle East. In Meissen, Germany I toured a factory that has made beautiful porcelain since 1710—a skill they, like the Dutch in Delft, learned in China.

When it gets dark, traditional village people go to bed—the light from the cooking fire, candles, bundles of dried grass, or kerosene lamps, is not good for reading or talking with friends, and insects are bad. In Amman, Jordan the evenings are so pleasant that "no one wastes time sleeping until midnight." Indians of southeast Alaska stuck an oily *candlefish* into each hole on the building's rafters, and lighted the fish for light. In the Pacific, candlenuts or chunks of dried coconuts, each on a sharp stick, are burned as a torch. The oily seeds of the *temanu*, a tree in the mangosteen family, is also burned in the Pacific. Insects don't produce enough light to help. During summer in the U.S. South lightning bugs or fireflies glow intermittently. In the Amazon *lanternbugs* are up to six inches long, they produce a much brighter light. Argentina has a *tuco tuco* white crawling "worm" but it can fly. The two bright green eyes glow continuously. Children like to play with them. Toadstools on Uepi Island, Vanuatu, have a green glow continuously, they are eerie in the dark. Caves and well-shaded banks along roads in New Zealand have millions of tiny glow worms in the late afternoon or evening. Their greenish glow continued even when I shined a flashlight on them.

The cooking fire is usually in the building where people live, in cool climates. However, some older buildings, such as Mount Vernon, home of George Washington, kept the cooking fire in a separate building, to reduce the risk of fire, and to keep insects, smells, and heat away from the living area. Along the Amazon and in much of the Pacific and Africa, the place for the fire is outside, or in a cooking hut, so the home for sleeping will not become overheated. On Pacific islands, the home of several generations in an extended family often has separate buildings for cooking, eating, and sleeping, plus a place for bathing and two outhouses. Some tribes in hot climates, such as Papua New Guinea, have the cooking fire inside the building, but it is often at one end to reduce smoke. In huts built on high stilts to protect against flood water or insects, each hearth fire is built on a large pottery plate or on an enclosure filled with sand. The middle and lower Amazon rises 20 feet or more during the rainy season, so all buildings, including the walkway or porch with the sandbox for the fire, are built high on stilts. North American Indians consider it to be bad manners to get between a warming fire and anyone else. The Cherokee Indians, and many other peoples in Asia and Africa, put out individual fires once a year. After a religious ceremony all fires were then relighted from the eternal fire in the council house. It is taboo to step over a fire in many cultures, especially for women and girls. When several generations or closely-related families live together under the same roof, each woman has her own hearth fire. In huts built on the ground each fireplace has three hearth stones in Africa and much of the world, but four hearth stones in the Amazon area, Pacific Islands, and Southeast Asia. Ancient Romans used three folding iron rods that opened up to form a tripod to support a cooking pot over a fire. Thin pots of clay were developed long ago for boiling things in liquid over a fire. There are still some villages without pottery or metal cooking pots. They still half-cook food by putting several stones heated in the fire into a basket with liquid.

Nomadic peoples have also learned to build very practical housing. Australia's Aborigines and several tribes in Southern Africa build a lean-to or small round *witlia* of brush. North American plains Indians dragged five or 10 long poles and skins from place to place. The squaws erected the teepee. The poles were set up wide apart but were tied together at the top. Animal skins were placed outside, starting at the bottom. In the northeast, Indians put big strips of birch- bark or other bark around the outside of the poles, to make a *wikuom* or *wigwam*. Furs were piled along lower walls and on the floor, except for the fire pit near the center. Much of the smoke escaped at the hole near the top. In stormy weather a flap closed the hole. In Central Asia Mongols and other nomads erected a *yurt* (also called a *ger*). First they expanded an *X* framework of sticks some four or five feet high, in a circle, for the wall. They erected a center pole, and a roof wheel plus limbs extended all around from it to the wall. The yurt was covered it with animal skins. I have often drunk sweet tea and eaten dates in the tent of many

Bedouin herders. They make a guest feel welcome. In winter they use a black tent, in summer a white tent. Many of the big canvas tents with a partition are made in Saudi Arabia. With blankets on the ground they can be quite comfortable.

Before Zulus in South Africa build a hut a witch doctor is consulted to help choose a suitable place to build. He also decides which direction the door must face. He must treat the entire area with special herbs and medicines to protect the people who will live there from evil spirits. A similar procedure is followed in much of Africa, some Pacific islands, and parts of Southeast Asia. Zulus, like many other Africans, like to build homes on a hill so they can see an enemy coming. In China and other parts of East Asia influenced by the Taoist religion *geomancy* provides guides as to where a building must be located and how it must be oriented. It must not conflict with other buildings, mountains, water, or anything else. A curved roof line or curved wall surrounding a building may be necessary for it to fit in. A builder or owner usually consults a fortune teller before finalizing plans. A *geomancer* or *fengshui man* tries to find the perfect balance of lines of energy, called *qi*, said to exist in the earth and in living bodies. Chinese consider that a bird in a cage or fish in an aquarium in a home is a sign of prosperity. Older men often take the bird in a cage out for a walk early in the morning, while others are doing *tai chi chuan* exercises.

Older buildings in Amsterdam and several German cities, such as Dinkelsbühl, have a roof beam that extends several feet out in the front or rear. A pulley is easily attached to lift heavy furniture. At least one large window on each floor can be opened to put in or take out furniture when a tenant is moving or buying something new. It saves a lot of effort, and the possibility of damage to furniture and walls. Some houses in Maribo, Denmark have a triple mirror outside windows that abut onto the sidewalk. A person in the living room can see the entire sidewalk. In Italy, the family that we lived with had two cabinets with a lower shelf of steel racks. Washed dishes were put there, they drained into the sink below. I visited a few apartments in the former Soviet Union. In the bathroom it is common to use a long faucet that swivels over either the bathtub or the sink, saving some money in construction. It is considered acceptable to have only a stairway, no elevator, in an apartment building up to eight floors high. Many European homes still have a baby's crib suspended above the parent's bed. A cord is pulled to rock the baby to sleep. Early radios for homes in Europe did not display the frequency on the broadcast band dial. Instead, they had the name of the city that broadcasted in the frequency shown. As more broadcast stations were built in some cities, using different frequencies, manufacturers had to change to show the frequency on the dial.

Fewer families even in poor countries now have a maid, as the standard of living has risen, and women can get other work that pays more. Tropical Latin America has a slowly developing middle class who like to live in a bungalow in the edge of the city or in a suburb. They do not have a maid. Typically, the newer homes are made of hollow clay tile, with painted stucco on the outside and plaster inside, almost-flat roof, and carport behind a small fence. They have three bedrooms, a living room with dining area, kitchen, bath, and fully enclosed small patio. Any other yard is minuscule. The bungalows are very practical for the climate. In more crowded suburbs, such as around Oaxaca, Mexico, most new homes have two floors, built with concrete blocks. New homes in Chinese villages usually have two floors to save valuable space. In Lebanon, once the granary of the Roman Empire, big, new two-floor homes are using the flat rich-soil fields; older villages in the Middle east were usually built on less-valuable hillsides. Orange County, south of Los Angeles, was one of the most important agricultural counties in the U.S. until 50 years ago. It still has orange groves, but the fast-growing "crops" are homes and shopping malls caused by the population explosion. In Israel and the West Bank, very old Palestinian villages with winding streets were built on the side of the hill near their fields and orchards in the valley. Hundreds of large Israeli settlements have recently been built on the hilltops, each with a private access road that uses land traditionally controlled by Palestinians. There is much friction, as Palestinian youths throw rocks at the new Israeli settlers, who shoot the Palestinians. One early Israeli settler who immigrated from Russia told us in his apartment that he has a difficult time getting the new immigrants to do their share of rotating guard duty.

One problem in lesser-developed countries is the absence of zoning. In Belem, Brazil, a large modern home with beautiful ceramic wall and floor tiles was surrounded by vacant lots and slums. Older colonial homes in the tropics were fairly comfortable. They had high ceilings for the heat to rise to, a porch on at least three sides on all floors, opening windows to let in breezes, louvered shutters for the night and to close in case of a storm, and sheet metal roofs. After electricity arrived, a fan in the ceiling of each room made it less uncomfortable. Homes on high ground had a basement that stays cool in hot weather and may be safer during hurricanes. Until the 1940s, most homes in parts of the U.S. South and Midwest where tornadoes are frequent, had a storm cellar. Most small towns had at least one storm cellar. Today, few homes have a storm cellar, but there are just as many tornadoes. For protection during a storm, many Pacific islanders use a heavy wooden container that ships used to carry containerized cargo. They plant a few banyan trees near a village, if the trees are not already there. A banyan with dozens of trunks and a wide root system provides good protection during a cyclone. An entire village can hide in a big tree. Trees have long been planted by farmers and city people for shade, beauty, to protect against strong wind, and to provide a home for birds and friendly animals, as well as fruit and nuts for man, birds, and animals. In Lithuania, farmers plant a linden tree in the front yard— a symbol of a friendly family. Its blossoms also make good honey. In Romania, most farmers plant a grape arbor beside the home, for shade and fruit. On Easter Island (*Rapa Nui*) many of the oval-shape reed homes had a stone building used to protect chickens from thieves, and a rock wall to protect a small garden from the strong winds.

Downtown tropical buildings, from Panama to southern China, have buildings that extend over the sidewalk, providing shade and rain protection for the sidewalk. In the U.S., modern glass boxes—motels, hotels, homes, and office buildings—often have windows that cannot be opened. They use expensive drapes at night or to keep out sunlight, and expensive, unhealthy, energy-consuming noisy air-conditioning. During most of the year a properly-designed building can be comfortable without air-conditioning. Also in the U.S., the large picture windows usually have only one thickness of glass or two glass panes with little dead air space, so there is a great loss of winter heat. Lawns are frequently large, requiring irrigation and a power mower.

In dry climates, such as Yemen, a big jar of water is often placed in windows, for evaporative cooling. A waterfall coming from a ceiling tank, flowing in front of a window, cooled the Sixteenth Century's Hall of Pleasure in the Amber Palace in Jaipur, India. Four thousand years ago visitors waiting to see the king "cooled their heels" in a shallow pool in the Diplomatic Room of the royal palace in Ugarit, Syria. We still "cool our heels" while we wait. When the British occupied India they escaped from summer heat in the mountains in the north. In Jammu and Kashmir the maharaja would not let the British own real estate, so they had elaborate houseboats built, floating on Lake Dal. Some are "Five-Star Deluxe," others are simpler. All are long and narrow, made of wood, decorated in the style of the 1930s or earlier. Guests pay a *shikara*, a small taxi boat, for transportation to and from shore. Electricity is usually on only a few hours in the evening. On our houseboat, a boy built a fire in each bedroom early in the morning, it was cold in November. Damp quilts didn't keep us warm, although they were so heavy that I thought an Indian elephant had crawled onto our bed.

In many old cities of Central and Eastern Europe, the second and higher floors of homes jut out over the street, almost meeting the neighbor's house on the other side. The area was long under Turkish rule, and they based taxes upon the size of the ground floor, so big upper floors were untaxed. Later Turkey, England, and several other European governments began to tax each window, so most were boarded up and artificial windows were painted on.

North American Indians living near the Pacific, from Washington State to Alaska, made totem poles with carved animals or birds, honoring their ancestors. In Papua New Guinea's Lowlands, and on many other wooded Pacific Islands, men carved figures on the poles supporting Haus Tamboran—spiritual or men's houses. The figures are usually of ancestors, spirits, or a fertility symbol. Korean villages had two carved totem poles near the entrance—a male and a female, representing *yin* and *yang*. The top of each pole is flat, men try to throw small stones onto it. Among the Naxi minority group in China's Yunnan province, the entrance gate of some homes has a beautiful carving representing the female yin on the left, and the male yang on the right. Carved totems were not common until metal axes were available—in northwest North America, less than 200 years ago. Beijing's Forbidden City has two totems at the Meridian Gate, with mythical creatures and symbols representing clouds at the top. In New Caledonia, a traditional thatch round case or house has a carved wood totem with a face to look for strangers, on each side of the doorway. The chief's *case* has a tall center pole with a *flèche faîtière* carving on top. There are usually carvings on at least three posts inside the chief's case, and a fire pit lined with stones is inside, between the doorway and the center pole.

In Latin American homes and hotel rooms it was rare to find a wastebasket more than 40 years ago. Trash was thrown into a corner. Maids were plentiful to clean up the mess. My aunt who lived in Africa for many years said that colonialists regularly threw trash on the floor, to provide more work for maids. Wastebaskets are common now in Latin America, but in public places they often have advertising. In Sao Paulo, many advertise *Marlboro* cigarettes. City homes in Argentina and Paraguay have a small trash holder on top of a metal post about four feet high. Trash and garbage is set out, out of the reach of animals, and picked up at least weekly. Homes in wealthier parts of North America, Europe, and Asia use a garbage can that is set out for garbage pickup, usually weekly. In poorer countries trash and garbage are dumped, often in piles, along the street or in vacant lots. Rats, cats, dogs, birds, and wandering cows eat part of it. A smoldering fire burns part of it. Spain has piles of trash along roads. In Spain middle-class women rolled down the window of a railway car to throw out trash, although there was a trash can in the car. In Albania our university-trained guide regularly threw trash out the bus door. In Belem, Brazil, and much of Latin America, men and women drop food and candy wrappers onto the ground, although a trash can is within reach. In

Moenjodaro, one of the cities of the Indus River Civilization in Pakistan, 5,000 years ago most homes had a garbage chute and regular pickup. Dry windy countries like Tunisia and Albania have millions of deteriorating plastic garbage sacks, caught onto weeds and bushes. Oman, a prosperous country with some money from oil, has many trash cans, a law prohibiting littering, and little trash of any kind.

Some housing projects in Europe are still in good condition after many years. Screening of those entering, training them on caring for the property, keeping the total size of the project small, and eviction of tenants who don't follow the rules are necessary. The *Fuggerei*, with 144 brick units built in 1519 in Augsburg, Germany is still in excellent condition. A new male tenant must be at least age 55, and the waiting list is long. The project's gates are closed at 10:00 in the evening. Late comers must pay a fee.

In Europe, doors usually open inward, even in hotels and theaters—it is difficult to leave in a hurry. In the U.S. laws require that doors in public buildings open outward. Many hotels in the former Soviet Union, Eastern Europe, and Asia block the exit from the fire escape at the ground floor to prevent people from leaving without paying a bill, and to keep out undesirables. In case of fire it may be necessary to break the door.

Boats

Pacific islanders and people living along rivers in Latin America and Africa still shape the outside of logs into canoes, and burn the inside away by fire, controlled by wet sand to leave the necessary wood thickness. On many Pacific Islands, the surface is then smoothed by brain coral—it looks like a wrinkled brain—used as sandpaper. The metal ax and adz made the building of a dugout much easier. Other Pacific islanders made canoes of several big planks, lashed together with plant fibers, fastened to handcarved crosspieces, sealing the cracks with sap from trees. Some dugout canoes, like the larger ocean-going canoes of Sri Lanka, are made more seaworthy by adding planks above the dugout portion of the canoe. In eastern Canada and northeastern U.S., a few Indians still make canoes of birch bark, carefully peeled off, and sewn together. After fastening it to a frame and sealing the seams with tree sap the canoe is lightweight and seaworthy. Polynesians learned to make a canoe more seaworthy by adding an outrigger, made by fastening a log to one side of the canoe with several cross-poles. Later they made double-hull canoes by fastening two canoes together with cross-poles. They learned that a double-hull is easier to maneuver if one hull is shorter than the other. Melanesians, Micronesians, and other islanders apparently copied the outrigger from Polynesians. A clam shell was used to bail out water. "Pig trough canoes" made from a big hollow log with extra planks are used on big

Lugu Lake in China's Yunnan province. They look like a feeding trough for pigs. The big boats that Vikings made of planks were often 70 feet long and very seaworthy. They were equal to the magnificent dugout and plank canoes used in the Pacific. British sailors were surprised when New Zealand's Maoris in a big war canoe could run circles around a British ship under sail. Women did most of the fishing in canoes in the lowlands of Papua New Guinea, but on other Pacific islands, such as the Marquesas, it was taboo for a woman to be in a canoe, or for her shadow to fall on a canoe. However, women could ride in a canoe on a long-distance trip. Solomon Islands war canoes have a *nguzunguzus* carving, often a human head, at the waterline to look ahead, and a *papa papa* carving high on the prow and stern to scare away evil spirits. In Bolivia's big Lake Titicaca, boats are made of a hollow reed, bundled and bound together. It becomes waterlogged and sinks. Each fisherman must have at least two—he uses one while the other is drying out.

The museum in *Clos-Luce*, the home in Amboise, France for Leonardo da Vinci's last few years, displays some of his inventions of nearly 500 years ago. One was a ship with double hulls, like new tankers, to reduce the risk of leakage and sinking. He designed a ship with a bulbous bow to reduce water resistance, not used until the last 30 years or so. Other models include a boat with side paddles for propulsion, first successfully used in 1803.

Sleeping & "Borrowing"

Many people sleep in hammocks in Mexico, part of Central America, along South American jungle rivers, and on a few Pacific Islands. Anyone who spends much time in Mexico becomes acquainted with the local family that weave hammocks, usually of sisal or nylon. They are either single or *matrimonial*. In West Africa hammocks are often made of animal skins. In many tropical countries people relax during the day in hammocks but sleep at night on a mat or in a bed, usually with a woven-fiber platform and no mattress. Mosquitos are worse at night, it is easier to use a mosquito net with a bed than with a hammock. In a typical one-room cottage in rural Argentina children sleep in a hammock, parents sleep in a bed. In Hanoi, Vietnam, a girl selling hammocks, age 11 or 12, told me "No mama, no papa, buy a souvenir." In Sri Lanka a hammock is sometimes fastened under a heavy freight cart pulled by oxen. The second driver naps in the hammock, something like the second driver of a cross-country sleeper truck in the U.S. On many Pacific Islands a hammock is never left up, it would soon disappear. Islanders "borrow" anything that attracts their attention on a neighbor's property. They may never tell the owner that they borrowed the thing, but they don't consider it to be stealing. On some Caribbean islands local people have similar practices. When they take another person's property, it is *progging* if they plan to use it, it is considered to be stealing only if they sell it. Many of their ancestors were slaves. If a slave stole something from his master, which often happened, it was not considered to be theft. Why? Because the master owned the slave and was considered to also own everything in the slave's household.

In central Europe, from Austria and Germany to Norway, a typical bed has for a cover, summer and winter, only a comforter in a sack made of two sheets sewn together. In Norway, it was common for two or four children in a family to sleep back to back, sitting up in the same bed. Beds have a pad but no springs. When overcrowding caused warfare on Easter Island families in the reed huts slept sitting up, with weapons nearby. They had to be ready at any time to fight or flee from those who wanted to eat them. Old castles and large homes in Europe and the U.S. formerly used poster beds, with a canopy held some four feet above the mattress. The canopy stopped some of the droppings from birds, mice, insects, and chips from plaster, paint or wallpaper, and in cold weather it stopped some of the draughts. In France, England, and Germany, parents in the one-room homes got a little privacy by enclosing their bed in a cabinet, with wooden doors. The cabinets were originally installed in buildings to separate farm animals at one end from the family's living area. In Ireland it was common, even among rich farmers, that all chickens lived under a sort of table along a wall, and little pigs lived under another cabinet or table. At night a cloth hid them from view. In rural U.S. a century ago most people had a tick or mattress made of two heavy sheets sewn together, filled with straw, corn husks, cotton, or whatever was available and reasonably soft. In New Orleans mattresses were filled with moss. A roller attached to the headboard of a bed was used occasionally to smooth the moss. Children often slept on a *pallet*, typically a blanket or quilt on the floor. In much of southern Asia a typical bed has a wooden frame on four legs, and a bottom made of woven cord which can be tightened. Sometimes a thin pad is used on top of the cord. In Japan a room is measured by how many *tatami* mats it will hold. They are almost three by six feet, used for sitting cross-legged or for sleeping. Many other Asians also sleep on the practical mats, rolled up during the day. Sleeping mats are also found in much of Africa and the Pacific. Many people who sleep on a mat use a small horizontal pillow made of wood or bamboo. They protect the hairdo, which is often carved and elaborate in Africa and Papua New Guinea. Wooden or pottery pillows are used throughout Africa, by many Indonesian islands, and until recently were common on many Pacific islands. Chinese and Southern Europeans also used wooden pillows a few hundred years ago. In India and Pakistan it is common to see a man walking along the road carrying a *charpoy* on the head. When he finds an attractive shady place he plops down the bed and may stay several days or weeks, boiling tea and cooking meals over a little fire.

Insects

During the evening and night in the damp tropics mosquitoes and other insects are so bad that many people sleep in a mosquito tent hung from the ceiling. It is difficult to use such a tent with a hammock, easier with a bed. Many homes and hotel rooms have a coil of punk to light to keep away mosquitoes, in the summer or in the tropics. My wife and I made the mistake of visiting Australia's Outback and the Ayres Rock area one mid-summer. I should have suspected something when we met no Australians there except locals—only foreigners. From sunrise until sunset we were covered with little biting flies, they seemed to like 100 percent Deet repellent. Within seconds after the sun set the flies disappeared. On an expedition through West Africa, for several evenings, big locusts were as thick as snow in a blizzard. Scattered among the locusts were many blister bugs, black, about an inch long. When they land on the skin, usually around the hairline, they leave a blister. Luckily, my wife and I had nylon net bug pants and jacket that covered nearly everything. Rains quickly hatch mosquitos and "*no-see'ums*" in the tropics. In Papua New Guinea's Lowlands, we could not use electric lights when we ate, for we would have mouths full of black gnats with each bite. We turned off the lights and used a bare minimum of candles. In Australia and the Pacific, a smoldering fire is sometimes kept burning under a thatch house on stilts, with a floor of springy limbs. The smoke filters through the floor and discourages mosquitoes and other insects. In a town in the foothills of Argentina's Andes Mountains, the house where we stayed had many large trees in the yard. When we returned in the evening we stepped on cockroaches three inches long. Along the Amazon they are sometimes six inches long. Lice in the hair are a problem among the poor all over the world. In Ho Chi Minh City (Saigon) I saw an entire family searching for lice in the hair of others. When they found one they bit it to kill it.

Fuel

Long ago man learned to use fire to improve the taste of food, to keep warm on chilly days and nights, to keep away wild predatory animals, and to make pottery more durable. In many countries a log was covered with ashes at night to preserve the hot coals, and the fire was started again in the morning by adding dry wood or straw. If the fire log went out a family might have to walk miles to borrow a firelog from a neighbor. Man learned to build a fire by creating a spark and letting it land on dry tender. There are many ways of creating friction to make the spark, including the fire drill—a vertical stick is rotated fast with the hands, or it is twisted by a cord like a bow drill, as it rests in a hole in softer wood. Two sticks are rubbed together to start a fire in Vanuatu—the small stick is pushed back and forth in a groove on the larger stick. In Papua New Guinea I have seen men in several villages start a fire in less than a minute. They rub a strip of strong flexible bamboo very fast on hardwood, it soon begins to smoke. When safety matches were invented in Sweden in 1855 they soon became cheap and were sold in so many places that nearly everyone used them.

Women and girls in poor countries spend more and more time gathering fuel for the cooking fire—sticks, straw, corn stalks, dried cow dung, peat, or anything that will burn. With the population explosion, trees for home construction and fuel are often all gone for many miles from a town or city. In Nicaragua only one large tree remained outside of a village. When I first noticed it several limbs had been sawed off for firewood. A few weeks later a boy had climbed the big stump to saw off the last limb. In the Dachigam National Park in Kashmir, India, our guide-ranger chased four women who each carried a bundle of firewood on the head. After a lot of questioning he let them go, they had only fallen dead limbs, which local villagers were permitted to gather. In the Middle East, villagers and city families store precious firewood for baking bread on the flat roof. Most cooking is now done with gas. Environmentalists try to teach people how to use earth for adobe homes and alternate sources for cooking, such as solar-powered ovens or methane gas generated from fresh cow dung or by toilets. Oxfam and other aid organizations teach people how to make a simple wooden box with a mirror to reflect the sun's heat to cook food. Little metal or pottery stoves use far less wood than an open fire. India has beautiful red sunsets, caused by dust, and smoke from hundreds of millions of cooking fires. But the pollution causes many respiratory ailments. Some villages have a family with a flock of pigeons that live on the flat roof. They are released from time to time, their flapping wings are believed to create air currents that helps air pollution. Even after watching several flocks, I am still doubtful that they clear the air.

Central heat in homes and offices is still rare in most of the world. In Western Europe most city homes now have central heat, burning oil or coal. Rural homes and older city homes have a fireplace with a chimney in each room, usually burning coal. In Ireland, the Falkland Islands, and a few other places men go to peat bogs, make long slices with a machine pulled by a tractor or a horse, or with a special kind of shovel. Peat about four inches square and fifteen inches long is dried and used as fuel, half-way between wood and coal. In Eastern Europe and in village homes elsewhere, a typical cottage has a ceramic stove built in a corner where several rooms meet. It efficiently keeps an entire cottage warm, and children and the elderly in cold weather may either sleep on top of the stove or in the nearby sleeping loft. In most of Asia only little space heaters or charcoal braziers are used. In offices a coal or wood-burning stove may supply some heat. In most of China's villages and cities, vendors with pushcarts or pedal-trucks sell round cakes made by pressing together coal dust. The cakes are used for cooking and heating, but their smoke pollutes the air. Coal carried in big trucks is usually soaked in water to reduce coal dust in the air. City families in China now cook mostly with gas. Central heating is approved only north of the Yangtze River, but winter is chilly in much of China. Factory doorways have heavy blankets to keep out some of the wind and cold. One of my trips through China was in the winter, and it was cold in the north. People dress warmly, shiver, get chilblains, and drink hot tea. My wife spent two winters in Santiago, Chile, shivering as she studied or wrote her lessons for the University of Chile. In Moscow, central heat in apartment buildings has been turned on around October 15 and ends around May 15, regardless of the outside temperature.

Fires were common and more damaging in the old days before cities had modern fire departments. Many European cities, like Chicago, had serious fires long ago. Most cities then required masonry construction and prohibited construction of wooden homes. Until 150 years ago the few fire departments were private. In England an insurance company operated a fire department. Each building had to display a sign showing that it had paid the current premium. If the building did not have the correct emblem the fire department let it burn. Today in the U.S. a few people want to give similar functions to private firms rather than having the government handle it.

Many Europeans like to sleep with bedroom windows open, they believe it is healthier. Air conditioning is rare in European homes. Window screens are rare outside of the U.S., Canada, and housing for tourists. Europe has many flies and wasps in summer. I studied one summer in Weimar, East Germany. It was a hot summer, wasps were bad. All of our meals were eaten outside, and it was sometimes difficult to take a bite without getting a wasp in the mouth. Once in France, a bird flew into the open window of my room, landing on my desk lamp. I quickly grabbed it and thrust the surprised bird out of the window. In a game preserve in South Africa, the couple in the *rondavaal* (round hut) next to ours left their unscreened window open one warm night. The next morning hundreds of big green frogs covered the concrete floor. In the tropics, I am always pleased to find a gecko or lizard in my room, to eat some of the mosquitoes and other insects. Sometimes they make a loud shriek in the middle of the night. I'm not sure whether it is a mating call or it is gloating after having eaten a tasty morsel. I often suspend fresh fruit and other left-over food in a sack with a string. Mice can jump high for food, but some of India's ants can jump as high as fleas.

Water

Women and girls spend much of their time going to a distant stream, spring, well, or fountain for water. The village well is known as the "rumor center," where news is exchanged about everyone in the village. In fundamentalist Islamic countries, women can escape the confines of the home only to get water, wood, or to go to the market. In Old Korea middle-class and wealthy women and girls could not leave the enclosed yard. They stood on a seesaw to see over the masonry fence and the outside world beyond. Servants and poor women and girls could leave the home only to get water, to gather fuel, or to go to the market. In a few countries the well has a pump. During a four-day trek through the isolated Dogon country of Mali we found one village with a pump on the village well, but the pump was broken and there were no parts to repair it. In Eastern Europe and the former Soviet Union each village has a well. In the southern part such as Romania the well has a bucket and windlass or crank to bring it up. In Hungary and farther north the well has a heavy horizontal pole on a swivel, with the bucket attached by a rope or chain. A woman wanting a bucket of water must pull down the heavy pole until the bucket fills with water. The weight of the pole pulls up the filled bucket. Some countries have a bucket and rope or chain attached to a pulley above the well—it is easy to drop the bucket into the water but pulling it up requires a little effort. Not far from Moscow I have seen women each carry two buckets on a shoulder pole to a small lake to get water. They had to break the ice to get water. In Russia, vending machines sell sweet soft drinks, sarsaparilla is one of the most popular flavors. A few glasses are near the machines, they are "purified" by a weak stream of cold water. In Yemen, buckets were made from leather, and markets still sell buckets made from leather or old automobile tires. Old forts and castles in Europe, the Middle East, and Latin America have a combination of deep wells and cisterns, a pulley and bucket was used to bring up water. Some forts and castles stored enough water and food so that they could withstand a siege for several months. Many had an escape tunnel beginning at a well and ending several miles away. In much of the world people buy water regularly from vendors, in tank trucks, pushcarts, burros, or whatever. Markets in Oman sell goatskins to store water, with each of the four legs sewn to be watertight. They are easy to sling over the back of a camel. In Syria, vendors carry a huge bright pot like a teapot and sell water by the cup near the railway station, markets, and parks. Some downtown streets have a fountain with a metal cup chained to it for drinks.

Town and city people in most of the world know that water is likely to be shut off for hours or days at a time, and every night. If the shut-off is according to a publicized schedule, with each part of a city getting water on particular days of the week, people can get used to that. Travelers must ask when water will be shut off, or they learn the hard way. Often the water shut-off is at random. Visitors should keep at least one bottle filled with water in the room. In lesser-developed countries don't expect the water to be pure. I always carry iodine tablets to purify water, and a plastic drinking straw that purifies water. Other tourists buy bottled water. In China and several other countries hotels for tourists provide a pitcher of "pure" water in each room. Electricity, like water, may be shut off at any time in poor countries. Hotels provide a candle and matches in each room. Wise travelers also have a little flashlight handy after dark. Some cities, like Srinagar, in Kashmir, India, normally provide no electricity during the daytime—only at night. Businesses have a noisy little generator so customers in a store can see things for sale. Electricity voltage changes so much in some cities that electric lights change often from very bright to almost off. Motors race or whine and burn out. Electric clocks are called "wonder clocks"—we look at the clock and wonder what time it is. The room where my wife and I stayed in Agra, India had a "swamp cooler" or evaporative cooler. Sometimes when lights dimmed the motor almost stopped. Other times the motor raced so fast that I turned it off, fearing that the motor's coils of wire would be thrown off.

Guatemala and Mexico have tried to provide running water with a faucet in each village, and a wash shed with a roof, running water, and concrete tanks to scrub clothes. Often there is only enough water for one faucet in a village with 1,000 or more people. In Santa Maria de Jesus, a village on the side of huge Volcan Agua, an active volcano, women and girls fasten the handle of several hundred plastic water jugs onto the end of a rope and await their turn at the one faucet. They can often leave for a few hours, and the few who stay in the line kick the jugs ahead of them in line. Our small group met in 1987 with Nicaragua's minister of water and sewers. He said the goal of the Sandinista government was to provide water piped to within 656 feet of any home in a city or village. Sewers were too expensive, a luxury only for rich countries. The socialist government had learned that free water is wasted, so a small charge was made for everyone using water. Each person then helped to police others to see that water was not wasted.

There is no more water in the world now than there was at the beginning of this century, but there are four times as many people. Water will become more valuable. More and more wars will be fought over the rights to water. During our recent trips to Syria people were angry with Turkey for building dams on the Euphrates River upstream, reducing the flow for drinking, irrigation, and power in Syria. Israel shuts off the water to Palestinian Bethlehem for up to three weeks at a time, partly to punish the people because there are a few "terrorists." Bolivia shuts off the water to Arica, Chile, because of a shortage of water, and to punish Chile for not giving Bolivia a strip of land down to the Pacific coast. Bangladesh is angry with India for building dams on the Ganges, reducing the flow of fresh water into the Bay of Bengal, and reducing the water available for a big irrigation project in Bangladesh. Many dry Middle Eastern countries use metal pipes to send fresh water for long distances to most towns and villages. California has a continuing dispute with upstream states over its heavy use of Colorado River water, and California's north is critical of the practice of piping their water to the south, at great expense.

There is a shortage of water in much of the world. The shortage will become much worse as population increases and people become more affluent. People who have running water from faucets in the home use a lot more water than do people who must carry their water a long distance. One possible source of fresh water is sea water. Oman, the United Arab Emirates, and other wealthy dry countries on the Arabian peninsula get most of their fresh water by expensive processes of desalinization of sea water. An iceberg has fresh water, but a big iceberg would be difficult to tow. On Easter Island horses have learned to go to the sea at low tide, drinking from the shore where underwater streams flow into the sea.

Toilets

Public toilets in Europe are often shared by men and women. Little effort is made to hide men's urinals in Europe, Korea, Ecuador, and many other countries. Toilets are shared from Ecuador to France and Italy. The person in the next stall could be either a male or a female. India has built many concrete toilets for tourists, with walls only about three feet high. In Kashmir a sacred cow blocked all four stalls of the men's toilet. I wanted to chase her away, but the patient Indian men said "She also went in there to pee. Just be patient." In each of India's larger cities several thousand families live on the streets or along roads near the city. They have little more shelter than a sheet or a tarp. Men and boys urinate or defecate with little attempt to hide. In China some toilets have a low partition, others have none. Most villages along the main roads have a privy, separate for men and women, marked only by Chinese characters. Travelers quickly learn to identify the male and female characters. Each concrete privy usually has several rectangular-shape holes, and the men's privy has a trough for urine. Naturally, the smell is bad, water for flushing is nonexistent, and there is no paper. Older Chinese apartments did not have running water or toilets. Excrement was dumped each morning into a tank. "Nightsoil workers" pushed tank carts to central dumping stations, where it was hauled off to make fertilizer or was dumped into a sewer. The communist government tried to improve the status of the nightsoil workers by a contest to see who could write the best song about them. For some reason the song selected never became popular.

In ancient Rome, men sat for a long time on one of a row of toilets, chatting with friends. In the U.S. we have rest rooms, but we don't rest there. We have bath rooms, but they often have no tub or shower, so we can't bathe there. We consider the word "toilet" to be too vulgar. In the United Kingdom a toilet is called a *w.c.* (water closet) or *loo*. Throughout Europe more than a century ago people emptied the contents of a pot or "slop jar" from an upper window onto the street. First, they were required by law to shout *garde l'eau*, or *guard your loo*. Any passerby in Britain had to quickly shout "hold your hand" to avoid getting splashed. In 1945 another sailor and I spent a night in Panama City, walking the interesting streets, listening to guitar music coming from balconies and open windows, sleeping on park benches. Several times people poured the contents of a potty from a balcony or window onto the street, without giving a warning. Luckily, they missed us. Until recently, and even today in many poor cities, the center of the street is the gutter, for refuse of all kinds. When heavy rain comes the streets are cleaned.

In Europe and China public toilets are often guarded by a man or a woman, in much of the world they are guarded by a teenage girl. They keep it clean and collect tips. Often the tips are their only income. In Nicaragua, I complained to the lady that there was no water in sinks in the men's rest room. She immediately grabbed my arm and led me to the other room, filled with 20 or 30 women, where the sinks had water. Women clean the public men's toilet while it is in use, even in some conservative Islamic countries. However, it is rare that men clean the women's toilet while there are women in it. Toilet tanks and leaky faucets often run and waste water continuously in countries where maintenance is poor—the former socialist countries and in much of Latin America

The privy or outhouse gives some privacy to a toilet. In villages of the South Pacific one or two privies made of a low wall of thatched or woven leaves or tall grass is often found near the village school. Sometimes excrement is left to accumulate on the surface, since a hole soon fills with rainwater. Missionaries taught villagers to build a privy jutting out over the sea, where excrement is washed away with each high tide. Peace Corps Workers taught villagers how to build and maintain an insect-free privy, using wire screening, like those built on farms in the U.S. in the 1930s. Village guest houses and homes where tourist guests are expected may have a toilet that is flushed with water pumped up into a high tank. In the villages of the Dogon tribe in Mali, where I slept, the toilet with a square hole on the flat roof, was often full. Everyone had to hide in a millet field. We dug "cat holes," like those that backpackers are taught to dig. Around 1935, when hundreds of thousands of villagers in Papua New Guinea's Highlands first saw White men, they thought they were gods—their ancestors. However, they quickly examined any feces where Whites had defecated, and discovered that it smelled just like theirs!

Oriental toilets are common near all shores of the Mediterranean, throughout Asia, and in much of Africa. Typically, they have only a hole and a nearby bucket of water or a hose to flush them. They waste less water than our toilets. Some, in nice buildings, have beautiful ceramic tiles. The user must squat, but they are often cleaner than "Western-style" toilets. Israel, Australia, and a few other countries use toilets that save water by either a major flush or a minor flush. Some countries, such as Greece and China, have small toilet outlet pipes. Toilet paper is put into a waste basket, if flushed it may block the pipe. Germany has many toilets with a grinder that chews up everything with each flush. The handle of some European toilets must be "pumped" up and down to build up air pressure, making the flush more effective with less water. France often has a *bidet* fixture that is straddled to wash the rear end, either by partially filling a basin or by a spray of water. Several countries, including Turkey, Oman, and Egypt, have added a copper pipe and valve to standard Western-style toilets to wash the rear end. In places where water is often shut off completely a few days each week, or every night, local people learn to store a barrel or buckets of water. There is often a bucket or a barrel of water near a toilet, and a dipper to use to flush it. Few public toilets have toilet paper, except in tourist hotels and nice restaurants. The toilet down the hall in our hotels in La Paz, Bolivia, and in Samarkand, Uzbekistan, each had sheets cut from a newspaper, fastened to a wire. Farmers in the U.S. in the 1930s kept last season's Sears or Montgomery Ward catalog in the privy, to read, then use for toilet paper. In much of southern Asia the left hand is used as a substitute for toilet paper. Near the toilet there is either a bucket of water or a sink to wash in. Restaurants in Southern Asia usually have another sink for washing hands, near the tables. Local people eat only with the right hand. One of my guides in an old fort in Oman said that his daughter and son were left handed. I asked him which hand they eat with. He said "They had to learn to eat with the right hand." Herodotus, the great Greek traveler of 2,400 years ago, said in Egypt "women pass water standing up, men sitting down." Today most Islamic men squat to urinate. There are few urinals.

In 1949 the black janitor of a segregated bus station in a small city in the U.S. South told me that he kept busy cleaning the four toilets. He said two were kept clean (for the white men and the black women) but the other two were always dirtied soon after he cleaned them.

In Manaus, Brazil many houses on stilts are built above a ravine. Excrement falls far below, making an awful smell. When the Amazon's rainy season begins it is washed away in the flooded ravine.

CHAPTER 4:
FARMS, COMMUNITIES, & TRANSPORTATION

Farms

In Northern Europe the oldest son usually inherited the family farm. Most laws have been amended to provide that the oldest *child* inherits it. The second son often became a minister, a priest, or went into trade. The third son became a sailor or emigrated to America or Australia. In Austria the farm was split equally among the sons or among all children. After a few generations, with the population explosion, the farms are so tiny that they cannot support a family.

In traditional societies of Africa, Asia, and the Pacific, and among Native Americans, individual families did not own land. It was held in common for everyone in the village or clan, and fields and pastures were distributed or reallocated from time to time. There was and still is little understanding of private and exclusive ownership of land. When Dutch sailors got Native American chiefs drunk and "bought" Manhattan Island for little value, the chiefs had no understanding of what "ownership" meant to the White Man. The meaning of "ownership" of land changes over time in "civilized" countries. Two centuries ago the owner of land in "fee simple" thought he could dig a mine or build an animal stockyard on his land, even if it polluted the air or water of a neighbor. Long ago the owner of a city lot could build almost any kind of structure on it. After terrible fires many cities required masonry buildings. Zoning laws now limit what we can do with land, and environmental protection laws add a further limitation. The constitution of many countries prohibits individuals, or "foreigners" from buying or owning land. They can often lease land for up to a lifetime.

Fences are rare in most of the world, except around a garden, a home, or for security around a factory, warehouse, or military camp. Farmers tether an animal so it can graze only in a circle. Perhaps the hillside is so steep that the rope tether may keep the animal from falling down the hillside? During a hike across England a few years ago we found a few sheep who had lost their footing on a steep hillside, they had tumbled to their deaths. In Nepal, an animal often has a heavy block of wood at the far end of the rope, it can be dragged a short distance, but not far. In the U.S. and other countries with wide open spaces a horse is hobbled so it can graze, but cannot go far away. Other animals are herded by someone hired by the village, usually a youth or older man. Sheep are dumb, they are often led by a goat or cow. Albanians decorate the lead animal with ribbons. In countries with wolves or other predators a mule, guanaco, llama, sheep dogs, or other strong aggressive animal follows the sheep to protect them. In India, white Brahma steers decorated with spots of paint on the side and brilliantly-painted horns, are used to pull carts. They reminded me of women with rouge on their cheeks and lipstick on the lips. In Oman the horns of some cows are painted bright green. In Kashmir, ponies pulling a cart are beautified with flowers on the harness and head.

The barbed wire fence is fairly easy to build, it permits raising animals with little care. When the fences were introduced in the U.S. they were hated by ranchers who grazed cattle on the open range. In Eastern Europe there are few fences. A cow is usually milked by a woman while a man or child holds the animal, or while it is tethered. Water must be carried to a tethered animal, and they drink a lot of water. Fenced-in pastures and water troughs would save a lot of labor. The windmill is a wonderful device to pump water for animals or to grind grain, where wind is reliable. A float in the water tank turns off the windmill when the tank is full. Windmills are used to turn gears and big stones to grind grain in the Netherlands, Baltics, Greece, Azores, Portugal, Spain, many islands, and other countries. In the Baltics, the entire small building with the mill, and the wind vane, can easily be swiveled into or out of the wind by two or three men.

Women do the field work done by hand in Europe's former socialist countries and in Africa and the Middle East. They often bend over to use a hoe with a short handle. Why don't they put on a longer handle so they can comfortably stand erect? A businessman could probably get rich selling long handles or handle extenders. In France, a few hundred years ago, shovels and spades had an adjustable footrest, it could be moved up the handle as the hole got deeper. They were used in Augues Mortes in the ponds where water was evaporated to make salt. In China, a long flexible bamboo handle is often used on a sledge-hammer, helping to deliver a much stronger blow. In Russia and China, it is common to see a man operating a big tractor, while women follow doing work by hand. In 1983 China's communes had some "walking tractors" to pull trailers and agricultural machinery. In 1998 I saw far more of the ugly and noisy but practical and cheap tractors, privately owned by farmers. Most of them now have a seat. In Russia women stoop over to dig potatoes. In 1983 China's women in tarry clothes swung leaky buckets with hot asphalt to put on gravel spread by a man with a tractor along a road. In 1998 modern machinery spreads the tar.

Farmers in most of the world are gamblers and worriers. They invest in time, seed, fertilizer, pesticides, and expensive buildings and machinery. They gamble that insects, blight, a storm, drought, or fire will not ruin their crop, that farm animals will not catch a disease or run away because someone left a gate open, and that they can get a bank loan at a reasonable interest rate. If production is good, the market price may be below their costs of production, due to a bumper crop elsewhere, cheaper foreign products, or a change in consumer tastes. In spite of this, most farmers do not want to make a change, so long as they are making a fair living. Deer are increasing rapidly in many countries, becoming an attractive pest that eat flowers and other crops. Chinese farmers buy tiger or lion dung for fertilizer, they say it keeps away deer. Farming in the U.S. has changed a lot since I grew up on farms in U.S. Southwest and South in the 1920s and 1930s. We grew nearly everything that we ate, buying only spices, flour, sugar, coffee, and a few other foods. In poor countries, most rural people would like to have a few acres of their own and eke out a living by subsistence farming, plus one or two "cash crops" to sell to buy the basic minimum. With the population explosion this century, there is no longer enough land in country after country. Tonga "guarantees" each male, upon reaching age 16, some 8 1/4 acres of land, there is no other social security. However, with the population explosion, Tonga no longer has enough land. In many countries land that should be left fallow is being farmed, resulting in erosion, and permanent loss of the top soil and native wild trees, birds, and animals. Agricultural laborers are still paid less than two dollars a day in some areas, and they even hope to get more work at that low rate. Many give up and take their family into a city slum.

In many countries the rich farmers own most of the best land. They have enough money to buy efficient machinery and equipment, good seed and fertilizer, and to maintain an irrigation system. They should keep the land, so long as they acquired it honestly and are using it efficiently. Big farms often grow things to export to earn money to pay interest on a country's huge national debt. Unfortunately, they don't grow much food for local hungry mouths. In Eastern and Central Europe the big State Farms and Co-Op Farms were split up when communism ended. The land was given back to former owners or their descendants if they could prove ownership. Most of those who got the property do not have enough money to buy seed, fertilizer, a mule or a tractor, and farm equipment. Many have lived only in the city and do not know how to farm. They dismantle the irrigation system on their new property. Agricultural production has been plummeting in Romania, Bulgaria, Russia, and other former socialist countries. The solution is to establish co-ops and government loans, or to sell the land to others. In China under the "responsibility system" a family with several workers can get rich. But a family with only a working husband or wife, or a family headed by a disabled person, earns few "workpoints" and remains poor. Various local subsidy programs are used to help them. China's huge Dujiangyan Irrigation system, some 25 miles (40 km.) west of Chengdu, was so well designed 2,300 years ago that few changes have been made. A dam divides the Min River, the inner flow is used for irrigation, the outer flow is for flood control. The Feisha Spillway also diverts flood water and helps to prevent the system from filling with silt. The Baoping Sluiceway helps to control the flow of incoming water. Syria still has 10 huge creaking wooden waterwheels 12 centuries old, some 80 feet (24 m.) in diameter, to scoop water from the Orontes River and deliver it to fields. I also saw a realistic scarecrow in Syria, of a "man" standing, apparently urinating, with a hose connected to an irrigation ditch.

In Lithuania, I spent most of a day visiting a successful farmer. When the Soviet Union split up he inherited his parent's old small farm. He acquired several tractors, farm equipment, and a truck by "midnight requisitions" from the former State Farm. He complained that most people were lost without socialism. When I told him that I grew up on farms and admired his farming skills he boasted that within a few years he will acquire hundreds of hectares of land from his inefficient neighbors.

Farmers in Africa, Latin America, Asia, and elsewhere need better roads to take goods to the market, and advice from government experts on how to farm better. They need a radio to hear the weather forecast, news, and entertainment, and buses to ride to town for their children's school and to buy necessities. If they are prosperous they need an electric power line, and, perhaps, even a telephone.

There is less agricultural land available now than 100 years ago, but four times as many people live on Earth. Much farm land is lost to roads, towns, soil erosion, poor farming practices that deplete the soil, the climate becoming drier, more competition for scarce water, and salination caused by irrigation. In the early 1930s, I lived on a farm in southwestern Oklahoma. During the "Dust Bowl" a dark cloud often turned day into night. We put goggles over our eyes, a bandanna over the mouth and nose, and rushed for the storm cellar. When each storm ended we crawled out to see what was left of the farm. The government's "New Deal" began a Soil Conservation Program to stop plowing much arid land, to plant trees, to have fallow or always green strips of land, build terraces, and to make rows along contour (level) lines. The government also encouraged some farmers to control water erosion by planting a fast-growing vine, Kudzu. Unfortunately, it soon got out of control. In the South Pacific, the U.S. military planted Kudzu during World War II to camouflage or hide its operations from the Japanese military. The "American Vine" is out of control on many islands, smothering native vegetation. In the Nineteenth Century a plant was cultivated on St. Helena Island to make flax. The plant is no longer cultivated but it grows wild everywhere, like a weed. China has cut so many trees in the upper watersheds of its rivers that floods are getting worse. Much topsoil is lost to erosion, rivers are usually brown from lost soil. Reservoirs fill with silt. The bed of rivers is often higher than the surrounding land, kept in place only by building higher and higher dikes. We were told in a 1998 visit that the Yangtze and the Hwang Ho (Yellow River) each put more topsoil into the sea than the Amazon, Mississippi, and Nile combined!

Terraces make hilly land tillable, permitting a larger population. "Wet" rice fields in China, Japan, and southeast Asia often require terraces to create a water-level paddy. Villages in northern Yemen are often at the top of a mountain. Stone walls or terraces create narrow fields, making the steep hillside usable for two miles (3 km.) below some villages. Terraces are common in many other hilly areas—New Caledonia, Nepal, China's mountainous provinces of Yunnan and Tibet, northern Luzon Island in the Philippines, and the Andes Mountains of South America. Albania has olives growing on thousands of hectares of terraced hillsides, but since the government has become weak the irrigation system no longer has water and most of the olives have been abandoned, they are dying or growing wild. Land that appears to be unusable for agriculture can be coaxed to grow crops. Rock walls protect gardens from wind on many almost-treeless islands, like Tristan da Cunha and Easter Island. Lanzarote, an Island of the Canaries off the coast of Africa, gets only around five inches of rain a year. Some three feet deep, the soil in many areas is burning hot from volcanoes. In other areas, pits some six feet deep and 12 feet across have been dug down to the clay soil. *Lapilli*, or lava cinders and sand, has been put on top of it to preserve moisture. A wall of lava stone is built to stop the almost-constant wind. Grapes, fruit trees, sweet potatoes, and watermelon grow well in the cinders and sand. Grain is also grown, over layers of manure and *lapilli*. Any weeds that come up are cut off—pulling them might disturb the layers. The heavy dew provides enough moisture for crops.

Land that is cultivated can be made more productive, with better seed and fertilizer, irrigation, and by other better farming practices. Modern farming practices often require hybrid seed, fertilizer, herbicide to kill weeds, pesticides to kill insects, irrigation, and expensive farm machinery. However, hybrid plants may become infected with a blight or fungus, fertilizer also pollutes, weeds become resistant to the poisonous herbicides, insects become resistant to poisonous pesticides, and irrigation water often makes the land saltier or more alkaline and eventually destroys its value. In a dry year there may not be enough water for irrigation. In lesser-developed countries suffering from a population explosion, much land is now being cultivated that should always be left in forest, grassland, or any other natural condition. The rain forests in the Amazon Basin, southeast Asia, and elsewhere are being cut and burned to create fields. The thin soil is soon ruined. Steep hillsides are plowed in crowded Latin America and elsewhere, but each rain carries away some of the valuable topsoil. In the past, when there was much land available and fewer people, the best land in a moderate climate was usually settled first. However, in Ireland the northwest coastal area was settled first, it has the most rocks and the poorest soil. Why? Ancient man had only stone axes, making it difficult to cut trees. Most of Ireland was forested, but there were few trees in the northwest.

Villages

A large percentage of the world's people live in villages. People growing up in a village have more of a feeling of security and are likely to be more skilled at getting along with others and making group decisions than those who lived in isolation. Farmers can live in a village and still go to the fields to work each day. Most farmers do not like to walk more than two kilometers (1.2 miles) to get to a garden or field; this limits the size of an agricultural village. The livestock in a village are often combined and are watched by a youth selected for the job. Children have friends nearby to play with, adults can socialize with friends and relatives. It is cheaper to provide water, electricity, telephone service, and public transportation to villages than to isolated rural homes. Countries where many people live in isolated rural homes need private transportation, often expensive to provide. Those people— many in the U.S. and Australia—tend to be more independent.

People in a village have better protection against robberies or attack than isolated people have. Arab villages usually have high walls around each living unit with a home. A stranger walking through a narrow street is surrounded by high walls, often made of mud, plus barking dogs. Most streets wind around in a maze, with dead ends and sudden turns. Arabs were desert people, and in a city they want the protection of a labyrinth that confounds strangers. A protective wall has been built for thousands of years around cities, towns, and villages. Some villages were too poor to build a protective wall encircling the village, so a protective wall was built nearby, often on a hill, so the villagers could escape harm while the enemy destroyed their homes. Esslingen, Germany, is a typical example. In Ireland, when Viking raiders were sighted, everyone in a village or monastery climbed into a tall stone tower and pulled up the rope ladder behind them. In areas where stone is scarce, a deep ditch was dug around the village for protection, as in China's Panpo Village near Xi'an. The doorway on traditional homes was low to make it more difficult for an enemy to enter in a surprise attack. When overcrowding and the cutting of trees caused the people on Easter Island to turn to fighting each other, no one was safe. The survivors often lived in caves, with the entrance made small, and the interior was dark so inhabitants had a defensive advantage over an invader. On Easter Island the traditional long narrow oval-shaped reed houses, like an upside-down canoe, had only one doorway, low, near the middle. The islanders had long used an upside-down canoe for shelter, so it was natural to build their homes that way. Stones lined the lower outside walls, with holes to support poles. Indians who made cedar plank houses along North America's northwest coast also made the doorway low. Some tribes, like the Tlingits who lived near Wrangell, Alaska, required that slaves sleep near the doorway—they would be the first to be killed in case of an enemy attack. In many traditional cultures the chief ate and slept at the rear of the building, he was better-protected. During the many centuries of warfare in Japan the shogun ate at the rear of the dining area, surrounded by old and young samurai warriors. In the U.S. and Europe the person who sits at the head of the table is usually in charge.

On Malaita Island in the Solomons, families build a village at the edge of the sea by putting rocks into the shallow water. They add smaller rocks and sand and build huts. Their gardens are on the nearby land. The villages get more cooling breezes, fewer mosquitoes, and are closer to fishing grounds. Men and youths who have been initiated usually live on one side of the island, women and children on the other.

Custom often dictates where particular huts will be located in a village. Among the Zulus of South Africa, for example, the chief's hut is at the top, a symbol of his high status. The *kraal* for cattle is in the center. Pits in the kraal store grain. In the "Bible Belt" of the Western Pacific—Fiji, Samoa, and Tonga—the home of the missionary or minister is often larger than the chief's home.

In Southeast Asia, Pacific Islands, and South America's jungles each village made a slit drum by hollowing out part of a big tree. The sound usually carries through several miles of jungle. The drum often lies flat on the ground. Youths are taught how to beat the drum to send at least 10 different messages. One call is for the pigs to come to eat. Another may be directed only to one of the extended families in the village to come together, another call brings all villagers together. Another call warns everyone that the village will soon be under attack. Still another call is to a feast or a celebration. Other calls are for a dance rhythm, or the ceremony of initiating youths into manhood. In Africa, drums are often made with a hollow log covered at both ends with the hide of an animal; many tribes have also learned to make sounds that send particular messages. Ghana's Ashanti tribe were considered to be great warriors. They also used psychological warfare, by developing a drum that made a sound like a leopard. In Papua New Guinea's Lowlands the drum often has one end carved like a crocodile's head. In Vanuatu the *tamtam* slit drums have a carved head like a human head at one end, and they may be stood up almost vertically. On some Pacific islands a conch shell is blown, as a warning that strangers are approaching a village, and for other messages. Local men said it had "the voices of our ancestors." On Easter Island a reddish rock more than two feet high has several holes. Some people can make a loud trumpet-like sound by blowing in one of the holes. Near the sea, it was said to be used to call fish to be caught. Petroglyph symbols representing the female vulva were drawn long ago around one of the holes. Nearby big flat rocks have petroglyph symbols of fish hooks, tuna and other fish, and a *birdman*. The buttressed roots of the Tahitian chestnut tree and other trees, when hit with a big stick, was often used as a drum to send messages. A board or flat stone was placed over a hole in the ground, then hit with a stick or was stamped with the foot, to produce a resonant sound. People in Asia, South America, the Pacific, and elsewhere learned to produce a loud trumpet-like sound, or music, by hitting or blowing into hollow tubes, usually made of bamboo. Most local music bands in the western Pacific include a set of horizontal bamboo tubes of various diameters, four or five feet long. One end is hit with a sandal to produce a pleasing sound. In the Marquesas Islands, children showed me how to make a trumpet by rolling a leaf into a cone shape and making a flat slit at the end that is blown. They could make a trumpet-like sound, also said to be used to warn villagers. I never produced a sound loud enough to call fish or to warn anyone, with either the hole in the rock or the leaf. Australia's Aborigines, like some African tribes, swing a *bullroarer* around and around over the head. Its whirring sound warns others to keep away from a religious ceremony that is in progress. The Aborigines often clack two sticks together as they walk toward a religious site.

A stranger wanting to stay in a village in the Pacific, Africa, or in many Lesser- Developed Countries, overnight or longer, should notify the chief or headman, and get his approval. Many villages have a room or a building that can be used by visitors. Payment or a small gift is common. A stranger passing through a village must stay on the road or ask permission to trespass. The gathering of "wild" fruit or nuts, or fishing or hunting in an area that seems to be isolated is likely to be considered to be trespassing unless you have prior permission. A stranger in some Micronesian villages shows a peaceful intent by carrying a green limb or a green plant. Some parts of a village, such as the men's spirit house and places for initiating youths, are only for men. Other parts, such as a hut for menstruating females, are only for women and girls. Some paths are taboo for women and girls, others are taboo for men and boys.

In lesser-developed countries where it may be many miles between villages, each village usually claims the land up to a particular point. The boundary may be marked by particular bamboo, *pitpit*, or other poles. In Papua New Guinea, men from several tribes pointed out the extent of each village's land from a boat on the river. Sometimes there is disputed territory between, a *no-man's land*. In Louisiana, before White Man arrived, tribes erected a vertical pole stained red with animal blood to mark the boundary showing the extent of hunting, fishing, and other rights. French called the red pole a *baton rouge*, which became the name of the later capital of Louisiana. In Costa Rica, our guide pointed out the monument that marked the boundary of the Mayan-controlled land and the Inca Empire before Spanish arrived.

The village chief has been the maker and interpreter of law in many cultures in lesser-developed countries. Even in countries with a European court and law enforcement system, the chief has great power. He hears and decides most legal disputes, including land disputes, domestic disputes, and crimes that may result in a long jail sentence. The chief usually refuses to permit a divorce, forcing a man or woman to live with a spouse that is detested. Women are beaten, men spend time with their mistress or get drunk. The chief usually consults a council of elders or the head of the families in the village. In some countries or islands the chief is elected, in others he inherits the job, usually from his father or a male relative. In Fiji and most Polynesian islands the chief inherits the title, but in Papua New Guinea, the Solomons, Vanuatu, New Caledonia, and other Melanesian islands the chief is often selected by his ability, wealth, or his influence. A woman may be a chief in some places. In villages where the chief does not inherit the job, the wealthiest man is often the chief. Over a period of several years he must acquire supporters by giving them expensive gifts, including feasts for the entire village. In Africa the chief's position is usually inherited. In *kastom* villages in Vanuatu and the Solomon Islands, the chief usually prohibits schools and missionaries, to preserve traditions and the way of life as it was a thousand years ago. The main differences from villages of the Stone Age is the presence of metal knives and axes, and a few pots and pans. During a hike through most of the Dogon villages in Mali we saw little evidence of modern civilization except for a few plastic pans, a transistor radio without batteries, and a broken-down pump at a well. Little boys sat on big rocks only arms-length from us, excitedly pointing to the moving second-hand on our watches. They were also fascinated by scratches and other little wounds on our strange pink skin. Dogon villages, when seen from above, have a shape like a man. The head is the men's shelter, where they meet to smoke, talk, and carve or weave narrow cloth. The roof of some is very low, if a man stands up to argue he bumps his head. Perhaps we should lower the roof of legislative buildings. Pillars of the men's shelter in Dogon villages represent the four men and the four women who are said to be the first people created by their god, *Amma*. The hands are the little houses where women having a menstrual period must go.

Children who leave the village and complete more than the basic six years of schooling often learn new ideas outside of the village. They are half in the traditional village where everything is owned in common, achievers and those who want to get ahead are frowned upon, and the family, the elderly, and the chief have the power. They are also half in modern urban competitive capitalistic society. The police chief for the largest province in the Solomon Islands said they cause the most trouble—by burglary, violence, alcohol, and drugs—in what is normally a society that respects tradition and authority. There are few jobs available for the better-educated even in the capital and larger cities of lesser-developed countries. If a villager is successful in the city and acquires a business or a nice house, people from his village move in, expecting to share his home and food, and to get things free from the business. Many businesses operated by a native go bankrupt, whether in the city or the village. Most successful stores and other businesses in the Pacific and Southeast Asia are operated by hard-working Chinese, East Indians, or Whites. In Africa they are also operated by East Indians or Whites. Port Moresby, the capital of Papua New Guinea, is plagued with unhappy *rascals* who can't find regular work but turn to crime. Young women who leave the village to get a better education have at least as many problems as the youths. Some become prostitutes. Village people who get a job in the city often feel lonely, and, when they can, return on visits to the village. When they admit defeat in the city and return to the village they don't fit in with traditional customs, they are often frustrated. I heard several reports that when educated women return to the village they may no longer respect the chief and elders, who may be illiterate. Young women have even shouted insults at the chief in public meetings.

Tribal land is usually owned in common. In Fiji and much of the South Pacific native villages own more than 80 percent of the land. Each clan or family is allocated part of the village land, and it may be redistributed as the number of people in the family changes. An individual or family only has the right to use the property. In Samoa, the clan or *aiga* may have several thousand people, almost everything is owned communally. In Pacific villages a car or truck is often owned by everyone in the village. One result is that it is poorly maintained and may have an almost-empty gas tank. In West Africa, our expedition had to find the village chief when we needed to negotiate the cutting of a tree or a major tree limb, when we wanted to get our truck through on the narrow trail, called a "road." In South America, villages in the Andes Mountains held the land in common, administered by the *ayllu* system of farming villages. When the lord of Cuzco or Inca became stronger his administrators merely took over control of the ayllu system. In Mexico, agricultural land, under the *ejido* system, is owned in common by the village. Mineral rights are owned by the national government. When land is held in common by a village it is protected from sale to outsiders. When the army in Guatemala chased Mayan Indians from some 500 villages that their ancestors had lived in for centuries, to new combined villages, it created many problems. Tribes who supported the army and squatters moved into some of the empty villages. When a peace treaty was completed at the end of 1996 people began to return to their old village, finding it to be occupied. East Germany and much of Eastern Europe have similar problems, as families return to the ancestral home, taken by the former socialist government, and given to others.

Villagers usually discourage anyone who wants to acquire more wealth. The accumulation of more land or material possessions is considered to be a vice. A chief or headman may have the biggest house, but on Pacific islands the missionary usually lives in the biggest house. A wealthy man in Africa may acquire more wives and cattle, but he is limited in displaying affluence. In the socialist or former socialist countries of Eastern Europe some, "capitalists," acquire more land, tractors, houses, and a foreign car, but they are widely criticized.

Towns & Cities

Nearly every village or town has a place where men, women, and children can go to meet their friends. It may be the village well or the market. Sometimes a church, temple, or mosque is the meeting place. In warm weather benches under a shade tree are the meeting place. Gossips took the place of a village newspaper, spreading news and rumors about what everyone in the village is doing. A park or beach is the place to go in mild weather. In New York and Chicago even the very poor families take the metro train to the beach on summer Sundays. Children, excited to leave their hot tenement, help carry the ice chest, baskets of food, and a portable radio. Swiss and German towns often have a free Sunday concert in the town square. Sidewalk cafes or coffee shops are popular in warm climates, but in Islamic countries women are usually not welcome there. In the evening a pub or tavern is often the meeting place for men, and sometimes women. A pedestrian mall is always a delightful place to walk, stroll, window shop, sit and talk with friends, or to watch the passing parade. Most European cities and a few others, such as "the Paris of South America," Buenos Aires, have learned to bar automobiles from an area and make it people-friendly. In Iowa and other states in the U.S. Midwest, many dying rural towns have been revived by making them pedestrian-friendly, barring automobiles in the downtown area. In Latin America, the plaza is the place to go, especially on Sunday when people are dressed in their best. One or two proselytizing preachers give a sermon in beautiful clear Spanish, waving *la Biblia* to make a point. A one-man band entertains for tips—he may carry an accordion, have a harmonica strapped around the neck, and carry a drum on his back, which he hits with drumsticks fastened to the rear of each foot. In the afternoon a full band is likely to appear, with a singer of folk songs. A magician does tricks, a comedian tells jokes, and a clown attracts children. Vendors push sales of picture post cards, toys, leather goods, textiles, candy, bottles of pop, fruit, slices of watermelons, and almost anything else. Before the noontime siesta and after school, *señioritas*, with a strip torn from the bottom of their school uniform, stroll through in pairs. Boys pass in the opposite direction, *ojeando* the girls. In some cities, such as Oaxaca, Sunday afternoon in a particular park is the place to see and meet the opposite sex strolling. Nearly all European cities had a high protective wall around the old city. In the past 150 years the walls have been torn down. Now they are used for a ring road around downtown, keeping traffic out of the most crowded part. Streetcar tracks often parallel the ring road.

A large public market is a good place to browse in lesser-developed countries the world over, but beware of purse snatchers and pickpockets in some. Many cities have a permanent market, five, six, or seven days weekly. Other cities have market day once or twice a week. Toluca has Mexico's largest Friday "Indian" market. Each product is in its separate area: clothes, sandals and shoes, household goods, furniture, trinkets, paintings, carvings, fruits, vegetables, meat and fish. Most markets have restaurants with rough tables serving soup, tortillas, corn on the cob, watermelon slices, complete meals, and more. The Zegoya Market in Mandalay, Burma, is typical of those in Asia. Under a big tent vendors sold fruits, vegetables, meat, dried fish, textiles, clothes, blankets, tinware, pottery, and hardware. Tee shirts and backpacks with the name of a U.S. city or movie star are popular, and cassette tapes of music. In one of the busiest areas they sold smuggled black market items: soap, lotion, toothbrushes, razors, shampoo, creams, and other scarce toiletries. Near the market are little factories, often on the street, where men make sandals of old tires, tin ware made of "tin" cans, dip cord into wax to make candles, they make pine furniture, and fix flats and repair bicycles and motorbikes. In the Middle East, each product had its own *caravansary*, where caravans of camels or other animals brought in goods, and the animals and their owners had a place to eat and sleep. Vendors of the goods set up shop in the nearby souk or bazaar.

Taxes & Schools

In Europe, uniform taxes began in the Fourteenth Century, when French popes ruled from Avignon. Tithes had begun in the Sixth Century but the French popes began a more efficient system of collecting. The Church and the State were almost the same. Tithes were equal to 10 percent of the income of peasants, land owners, shopkeepers, traders, and almost everyone else. Tithe barns were built in towns to collect the grain of farmers—10 percent of their production. Walled towns typically had a market. At city gates they charged a toll on every sack of grain, animal, or other product entering the town for the market.

Taxes should be designed to reduce or discourage things and activities that are harmful to the public as a whole, and to encourage positive results. Taxes should be greatly increased on activities that pollute the environment or deplete valuable minerals or other resources. In many countries the assessor of property taxes does not have time or authority to enter buildings to determine their value. He only makes a cursory examination from the outside. In Thailand, the tax man often travels by boat on the *klongs*, looking at the ugly water side of buildings. Inside, the Thai homes are often beautiful, with several electrical appliances. In Latin America, the outside of buildings appear from the street to be only adobe or concrete with peeling paint, and a few barred windows. Inside, Latin American homes may have a beautiful courtyard, fountain, tiles, and rooms with nice furniture.

Taxes are either on income, property owned, or on transactions. In the U.S., the federal government, and state, county, and city governments each tax particular things. In Western Europe most countries have a value added tax (VAT) far greater than the sales tax in the U.S. Travelers can usually apply for a refund. Europeans also have stiff income and property taxes. Denmark, Norway, and Sweden are usually considered to have the highest taxes, but Germany is not far behind. Evading taxes has become a fine art in Italy and France, and in large international corporations—they move operations to low-tax countries. In the U.S., total taxes are still far below those in most of Western Europe. Canada began a VAT tax a few years ago, but the government lost the next election. When the U.K. instituted a VAT tax in the mid-1980s there was much talk about setting up the gallows for the government leaders who asked for it. In 1381 the English hung the Archbishop of Canterbury on the gallows for instituting the poll tax.

Many Europeans get far more from the government than do people in the U.S. Europeans have a health-care plan that covers almost every medical expense. Most cover mental illness and some provide long-term care, as in a nursing home. Some cover dental expenses, at least for children and pensioners. Unemployment insurance often continues for two years or more. Housewives are sometimes given a monthly stipend, and parents are given a another monthly stipend for each child. A mother, and sometimes a father, is given up to two years off with pay to stay home with a new baby. This is in addition to a pension plan like Social Security.

European schools have at least one comprehensive exam at around age 12 or 14. Parents often hire a tutor for a full year before the exam. The important results determine whether the child will take an academic program, technicians training, or, perhaps, art training. I have helped with the homework of several children in families that I lived with in France and Germany. Teenagers take a heavy load of tough courses, such as two foreign languages, math, physics, biology, history, music, and religions. School buses are rare except in the U.S. and the more prosperous countries of the Americas. Most children walk, bicycle, or ride public transportation to school. In Vietnam nearly all school children travel by bicycle. In Thailand, pickup trucks with benches on both sides take uniformed children to and from school. Along the Amazon, the oldest child paddles a dugout canoe, taking the other children in the family a few miles upriver or down river to a village with a school. In Fiji, a child beyond the six years of primary school walks up to five miles (8 km.) each way to go to school. Those who live farther away must go to boarding school, which costs much more. Most primary and secondary schools in Asia and the Pacific charge tuition. Large factories in China usually have dormitories for single employees, and schools for children of married employees. Tuition is often free in European, Asian, and Latin American universities for the lucky few local youths and girls who pass a stiff entrance exam. In France, a person who completes the courses at a secondary school must pass a tough exam before graduating or entering a university. Universities have stiff entrance exams, but tuition is usually free for citizens. Books and a monthly living stipend are often paid. All of this costs a lot of tax money. Denmark and Norway have popular "Folk Schools" for adults and for young students who have completed secondary school but are not ready for the university. They are something like the popular community colleges in the U.S., but they have dormitories and give teenagers a chance to become more independent. I have attended classes in two Folk Schools and found that they offer a great variety of classes, for university credit or only for the fun of learning.

In China, more than half of the city children go to middle school, but only about one-fifth of village children attend, they are needed to help work on the farm. Under the "responsibility system" peasant families work much harder than they did under communism, but earning more money is considered to be more important than school. Children of poor peasants usually must do much work before and after school, so they are tired during classes. Poor peasants are often poorly educated and can't help their child with homework. I have visited many schools in China, from kindergarten through universities. In primary schools children often read aloud in unison or sing songs with an educational message. Competition to get a good score on exams, so a student can go to a university, is fierce in China. Students take optional evening classes from primary school through "high middle school." Typical is Yun Li, a pretty 13 year old in Ninglang, Yunnan. She gets up at 6:00, has classes 7 days weekly, until about 6:00 PM. After quickly eating dinner she does homework for half an hour, and goes to evening classes five nights weekly, until 9:30 PM. There are 77 students in her class, but no computers, though the school is considered to be a good school. She takes tough courses: Chinese, English, math, botany, physics, chemistry, and sports. She gets at least two days off each month, plus two months in the summer and six weeks in the winter. Competition to get the best grades in the first 12 years of school is also fierce in Japan, so a student can enter a prestigious university. Many children aged about 10 to 15 go to "cram school" during summer vacation. But when Japanese youths get into a university they often drink and party rather than study seriously.

Post Office

In most post offices a letter or parcel is weighed, the postage depends upon the weight in grams, and whether it goes by land, sea, or air. Post offices have several boxes for outgoing mail. In some countries, such as France, there are separate lines for people to buy post cards, buy stamps, weigh and send letters or parcels, send money orders, send telegrams, pay utility bills, invest money in postal savings, to cash checks or change foreign money, and sometimes for other purposes.

Motor Vehicles & Pedestrians

Drivers in Quebec, along the north shore of the Mediterranean, and in much of Africa, Latin America, India, and Bangladesh, are often wild drivers. In poor countries such as India or Bolivia anyone who drives a motor vehicle is an important person. A pedestrian is poor, of little importance. As Sikh truck or bus drivers in India approach a stop sign or a red light they look first for any nearby vehicles with the right-of-way. If there are none, and there are fewer than six pedestrians, the driver sometimes doesn't stop. Pedestrians must run or jump for their lives. Pedestrians in Asunción, Paraguay, cannot even see the red, green, or yellow light in most of the traffic lights. The lights are aimed at motorists, shielded from mere pedestrians. In Bangladesh, I rented a taxi and a driver to go to ancient ruins east of Dhaka. The two-lane paved highway had narrow high shoulders and on each side the rice or jute fields had water at least three feet deep. Vehicles somehow often squeezed three abreast on the narrow road. The biggest vehicles take the right-of-way. When a big truck flashes its lights, the driver of any other vehicle has two choices: to head for the narrow shoulder or suicide. A bus lost the game of chicken a few minutes ahead of us. It landed upside down in the paddy. At least 30 passengers were crawling out of the bus. Those who had been riding on the roof were probably killed. The next day the local newspaper had a short article about the accident, an everyday occurrence.

China and Russia now have many traffic police who often cruise in a car. A driver convicted of a traffic offense in Kunming, China must work as a traffic policeman a period of time, usually at least 30 days. The convicted driver always works with another police officer, usually directing traffic at a busy intersection. The days and hours that the culprit must work can be arranged to fit his schedule. Kunming also has "spit police" in civilian clothes. They may fine anyone who spits on the sidewalk or in another protected public place. In the past, Chinese men would spit almost anyplace.

My wife and I finally learned not to ride the older "school buses" that ply the dirt roads of Latin America, often going over the Andes or other mountains. However, buses are a good place to meet other sardines—people. But there are pickpockets likely to rob a tourist—they got my wallet in Costa Rica. If anyone walks along the road the driver's assistant asks if they want a ride. He collects the fare, which is cheap. The driver usually has a picture of Jesus or Mary, plus bright-colored cords, cloth, or paper strung across the upper windshield. Before arriving at police checkpoints, the driver or his assistant often asks standing passengers to slouch down so the overcrowding is not so apparent. From time to time, bus companies learn to give nice gifts to the police or military people at checkpoints. Local newspapers have almost daily articles about a *choque* or accident. There are often 20 or 30 people killed, but the driver usually runs away. In Guatemala, local newspapers had a gruesome photograph of the driver without a head. He had asked a passenger to pay the fare. The man swung his machete, the driver's head rolled to the floor, the passenger jumped out of the door and ran away. He was not caught. A passenger managed to stop the bus. In contrast, in Pakistan, the driver of a bus that lost its steering control near Malakand Pass didn't run away. He was still thanking

Allah for good brakes when we arrived. The left front wheel was over an almost-vertical precipice with a drop of 2,300 feet (701 m.). Passengers carefully left the bus through the rear door. Buses and trucks in Pakistan, Afghanistan, and Bangladesh are painted bright colors, many are quite artistic.

Many countries have small buses that are more comfortable, but may be just as crowded. The minibuses packed with passengers have a high-accident rate—even worse than taxis. In Lima, *colectivos* are like a taxi, but they travel only on particular routes. When the driver approaches a stop he holds up fingers to show how many vacant seats he has. Two small children equal one adult. Fares are much less than an ordinary taxi. Mexico City has similar colectivos, usually light-green vans, with a white top. In Panama they are called *chivas*. Istanbul's *Dolmush taxis* ply particular routes. Most of them are Chevrolet cars of 1955 to 1957 vintages. Manila's *jeepneys* began as jeeps left by the U.S. military after World War II. Seats were added to carry more passengers, and they were painted bright colors. Today most of the chassis come from Japan, the bright bodies are made in the Philippines. Each jeepney usually has one, two, three, or four bright chrome hood ornaments, each representing the *macho* owner's wife or girlfriends. Tahiti's *le trucks* run frequently on a regular route, the low standard fare is usually paid upon leaving. They are a wooden bus built on a truck chassis, with padded seats on each side, an unpadded center bench, and glass windows that can be pulled up. In Sri Lanka the minibuses do not leave the station until all seats are filled. They soon pick up many more passengers. In Kenya the *matatu* taxi vans likewise first fill every seat. A woman held her four-year-old in her lap. He opened her purse, holding each of many things up, asking what it was. He held up a package called *Rough Riders*. The woman quickly grabbed the condoms and put them back into her purse.

Africa has large buses that ply the main highways, crossing many borders. They often have exotic names like "Exotic Coach," "Caboose II," and "Space Vehicle." The deluxe highway buses found in Europe and South America are quite comfortable. They usually have air- conditioning, a toilet, reserved reclining seats, and arm-and-foot rests. Many show VCR movies on TV and have a hostess who serves free drinks, snacks, and even meals. Some are double-decker, the upper front seats have a great view. In Latin America, unfortunately, smoking is usually permitted everywhere.

In Ouagadougou, Burkina Faso, our taxi driver stopped to buy one liter—a quart—of gasoline. He then went through all three red lights in the city, driving on the wrong side of the street, swerving back just before he had a head-on collision. The older English lady with us kept saying under her breath "Oh my God! Oh my God!" In Kathmandu, Nepal, we asked our guide what work does a man do who comes from a mountain village where there are no roads or schools. His response was immediate "They drive a taxi." In Calcutta, our taxi almost hit the taxi three feet in front of us when the lead driver surprised ours by actually stopping at a red light. They cursed each other in Bengali while the light cycled to green, to red, and green again while each driver behind us laid on his horn. In Cape Town, South Africa, our driver went through eight red lights on the way to our hotel, although I had told him we were in no hurry. In Madrid, the only people who thought a taxi would stop at a red light are in cemeteries—vehicles often continue through an intersection for a minute after it has turned red. Athens is even worse. Don't expect a vehicle in Naples, Sicily, Guatemala, or in many other countries where most pedestrians are poor to stop at a red light or for a mere pedestrian who has the right-of-way. The three-wheel taxis in Asia are peddled (called pedal rickshaws, pedicabs, *cyclo-pousses*, *samlors*, or *becaks*), or they have a motor (called *tuk-tuks*, *bajas*, *samlors*, or motorcycle taxis). Neither kind is safe, but I often ride them. In Dhaka, Bangladesh, many streets were flooded, so motor vehicles could not operate. My operator's feet were in the water as he pedaled. I had to put my feet up high to keep dry. Most of the open manholes in the murky water are marked by a bamboo pole.

In Beijing it was illegal until 1983 for motor vehicles to use headlights at night. They tend to blind the millions of bicyclists, who have no light on the bicycle. Now there are fewer bicycles but streets are crowded with cars and packed buses. Bicycles in my visits to China in 1983 and 1984 were nearly all black one-speed. In 1998 bicycles are of all colors, and many are 10-speed or more. Bicycles in much of southern China have a metal attachment that fastens onto the front fork or handlebars and clamps around the handle of an umbrella, leaving hands free. China now manufactures many motorcycles. During our 1970 visit in La Paz, Bolivia, drivers rarely used lights at night, they believed they were saving gasoline. But in Finland, Sweden, Norway, Denmark, Iceland, and Canada's Yukon Territory, laws require that if a vehicle moves, its headlights must be on, day or night. Some of Sweden's Volvos (and a few other cars) have a little windshield wiper on each headlight—great when driving in snow or slush. In Europe, many cars permit either the left or the right front and rear parking lights to be left on—safer for parking on a busy street. The outside rear-view mirrors can often be folded back on narrow streets. Many Japanese cars have a plastic rear license plate that is lighted, easy to read. In the Middle Ages, most knights carried the heavy lance in the right hand and passed to the left of the other charging knight. In Great Britain horsemen and stagecoach drivers passed on the left. Today the U.K., Ireland, Japan, Thailand, Suriname, part of the U.S. Virgin Islands, and some 40 of the 54 or so countries in the British Commonwealth drive on the left. Everyone else drives on the right. Sweden and Burma once drove on the left, but in 1962 they changed to the right side. A policeman in the Falkland Islands told me that during the 1982 military occupation by Argentina he gave a ticket to an Argentine soldier for driving on the wrong (right-hand) side of the road. The soldier put him into jail!

Streets and roads everywhere are getting packed by cars, buses, and trucks. Many places have twice as much traffic as only 10 years ago! Much of the planet is close to gridlock. Bangkok, Jakarta, Rome, Naples, Mexico City, and many cities in the U.S. are likely candidates for gridlock, when nothing can move for hours. When a freeway, *autopista*, *Autobahn*, or other major highway is built motorists are delighted. But everywhere in the world they are soon filled with vehicles, except during rare light-traffic periods. The U.S. has only 4.5 percent of the world's people, but it has one-third of the motor vehicles and uses 35 percent of the limited petroleum. Gasoline retail prices in the U.S. are only about one-third of the price in Western Europe and Japan. One French minister said "any country that gives away gasoline, like the U.S., does not have a national debt problem." He thought that gasoline prices should be increased to European levels. In traffic-clogged cities people in a hurry walk. But cities often failed to build sidewalks even on major streets. In crowded cities around the world, desperate motorists may park anyplace, taking a risk that they will get a ticket or that the vehicle will be towed away. French cities must strongly barricade sidewalks to keep motorists from parking there, mere signs and laws won't stop them. My wife and I once had to jump off of a sidewalk in La Grande Motte to keep from being hit by a car racing down the unusually wide sidewalk. In many European and Asian cities pedestrians cannot use the sidewalk because it is filled with parked cars. In Tapei and Jakarta motorcyclists riding and parking on the sidewalk are a hazard.

Trains

France, Germany, and most of Europe have such a wonderful system of trains that an automobile is often only a nuisance. Germany has a system of paths, often paved, for pedestrians and bicyclists, and railway stations have a place to safely store bicycles. The paths connect nearly all towns and villages. In the U.S. groups are converting abandoned railway right-of-ways into wonderful trails. In Europe, a Eurailpass is easy to use, and often cheaper if you plan ahead. On a weekend or holiday it is better to get seat reservations in advance, and the faster trains may require a seat reservation. The extra cost is very little. To determine if a seat is reserved we look for a little card near the seat in open cars, or outside of each compartment. The little card states the two cities the seat is reserved between; if your route does not include those cities the seat is available. Second class is usually comfortable, but on weekends or holidays I go first class. In France, any ticket except Eurailpasses must be "composted" before each trip, by stamping it in a little red machine at the door from the station to the tracks. In Italy, Germany, and a few other countries, but not France, on train platforms you can find a plan of your train, showing the location of your car several days in advance. The French TGV, German express, and Japanese *shinkansen* trains are very fast, and comfortable. They typically travel at 140 to 180 miles per hour (225 to 290 km.). I have ridden many trains in China, they are usually on time, and the "soft-seat" cars and sleepers are clean and comfortable, but not fancy. Passenger trains have a diesel locomotive, but many freight trains are pulled by a coal-burning steam locomotive.

Costa Rica had one of the world's most interesting train rides until around 1989, when a storm washed away much of the tracks. The narrow gauge "Jungle Train" left San José in the late morning. Seats were always filled and many people were standing. Beggars and boys selling fresh fruit, sweets, cold drinks, and almost everything else squeezed by passengers carrying big baskets, sacks of things, chickens, and even pigs. In eight hours, the train made 56 stops in perhaps 150 miles (241 km.), climbing to the Continental Divide, then descending from it to sea level at Puerto Limón. Coffee trees grew nearly everywhere except in fields of vegetables and berries in the highlands. As the train descended the air was hotter, with growths of banana plants, coconut trees, and cacao. Highlands towns have adobe or concrete buildings. In the lowlands brightly-painted wooden houses rise on stilts above swamps and at the edge of jungle streams. The black Creoles of the Caribbean lowlands were brought in to work on the railroad and the banana plantations. Many came from Jamaica and they were more resistant to malaria. It was unlawful for them to live in the highlands until recently. Most of the banana plantations left the Caribbean due to a blight, and were reestablished on the Pacific side. Today the railroad is gone and passengers ride a bus on a paved highway on roughly the same route. The narrow-gauge passenger trains in Guatemala, Peru, and Bolivia were also a delight for those who liked to watch the fascinating men, women, and children, with their loads of chickens, pigs, textiles, and sacks of produce. Vendors and beggars often came aboard trains, somehow finding a way through the aisles. Buses also have vendors, or they hold things for sale up to windows for passengers to take and leave money.

CHAPTER 5:
FOOD, DRINKS, & HARMFUL DRUGS

Food

Men eat first in much of Africa, Asia, and the Pacific. When they are full, women eat. Children are often the last to eat, and there may be little food left for them. Typical is Ghana's Ashanti tribe, where men eat first. Each member of the family has his or her dish, and cannot eat from another person's dish. My wife and I have been guests of several families on Pacific islands. Guests are always served first, they have the first choice of whole roast pig and other delicacies, while the hungry family watch. I finally learned that the husband, then the wife and children, get to eat only what we leave for them. In much of the world anyone with food in public is expected to offer to share it with others. It is also considered to be bad manners to eat while walking or standing.

In Africa and the Pacific local people often eat with the hands. Most Arabs eat with the right hand and its fingers. Japanese and Chinese eat with chopsticks, either flat wooden or rounded plastic. Chinese talk little at meals—eating, avoiding bones, is hard work. The bowl or plate is always close to the mouth, they often sip soup from the bowl. A pottery spoon is sometimes used for soup and some other liquids. They spit bones onto the table or floor and often belch loudly. We should never use our chopsticks to get food from a serving dish, it passes cold germs and other "bugs" to others. Japanese often turn the chopsticks around and get food from the end normally held in the hands. Special chopsticks used only for serving are better. Food should never be passed from one pair of chopsticks to another—this reminds Asians of the custom by Buddhist priests of passing the cremated remains of a body with chopsticks to an urn. Chopsticks also should not be left sticking vertically into a food dish—they look like sticks of incense in ashes, a symbol of death. In much of southern Asia people shovel food in with the right hand. In Europe for centuries people speared food with a knife, until someone invented the fork. They used a wooden spoon for soup.

In many cultures each person who wants to eat, other than a small child, must cook and eat his/her own food. There is no set meal schedule or place to eat. I have slept in several villages of the Dogon tribe in Mali. Each morning little children, with a bowl in the hand made from a gourd, waited patiently while their mother pounded millet in a stump, with a hardwood pole, to make meal. After it has boiled the children get something to eat. A teenage girl sold me little cakes made by frying millet dough. In another village, a girl not more than five years old efficiently pounded millet and did a variety of chores, unsupervised. *Goho* or *gofio*, made by roasting ground corn and mixing it with hot milk, is a favorite food in the Canary Islands. Dessert in Yemen is often *haraj*, a mixture of honey, butter, and wheat boiled together.

In places where men and women live segregated, such as the Highlands of Papua New Guinea, each man must gather and cook his own food. In one village we noticed that there was no food, no place to buy food for many miles, and mealtime was approaching. We asked where the family would get food—what would they eat? The man said "We have a little garden. We'll gather more in the forest." In the Lowlands during the rainy season local people cannot grow a garden, most land is flooded. They eat fish and pulp of the sago palm. A mature tree is cut down and towed to the village behind a canoe. Men chop it up. Women gather the soft wood fiber, pour water over it, the starch is caught in a container, using a bamboo strainer to keep out the fiber. Women cook the starch into pudding or pancakes that stretch like sourdough pancakes, but taste surprisingly good. In the dry season most families have a little garden. The yam and sweet potato in the Pacific and Southeast Asia are nutritious, like the white or red potato in Europe and the Americas. The big yam came from Asia long ago. The sweet potato probably came from South America to the Marquesas Islands and Easter Island in the Fourth Century AD. It spread from the Marquesas to the western Pacific, Asia, and elsewhere.

Breadfruit is a staple food in Southeast Asia and the Pacific. Captain Bligh, famous for the mutiny on the *Bounty*, stole breadfruit plants from the Pacific, to be transplanted on Caribbean islands for food for plantation workers. However, it is too bland to be popular in the Caribbean. In Vanuatu, islanders put breadfruit into the sea for a week to "ripen," then it is slowly heated, becoming hard like a stone. It can be carried in a canoe for weeks. Also in Vanuatu, men learned long ago to mash bananas, wrap the mash in big banana leaves, and store it in a covered pit. It is usually mixed with water, grated copra from coconuts, and roasted. I ate some, said to be 15 years old. It tasted like "blue cheese." My village guide said it is edible for 25 years. We also ate fresh mashed bananas, mixed with fresh copra, and toasted over the fire—it was delicious! Taro toasted over the fire can also be delicious. It is usually eaten as the main ingredient in *poi*, a paste-like food. When mixed with water and wrapped in leaves it ferments and last for several weeks. In the Marquesas Islands, plagued with occasional droughts, an important duty of each chief is to store food for bad years. A hole perhaps five feet deep and up to 20 or more feet long, is dug. It is lined with banana and *ti* leaves. A young village man, known to be wholesome and a virgin, mashes fresh breadfruit with his feet, by walking on it for hours, like crushing grapes for wine. The pit is covered with leaves and dirt. The fermented breadfruit lasts for many years. Breadfruit is a wonderful tree. Its inner bark is used to make tapa cloth, the wood is used to make canoes and houses, and for wood carvings. The sap is used to waterproof cloth and to caulk canoes. Breadfruit is a symbol of life in Southeast Asia and the Pacific.

During an expedition through West Africa in a truck, our small group slept in pup tents every night and cooked our food over a camp fire. Sometimes we stayed in small campgrounds with Africans. A family often brings a dog, and six or eight chickens with them, to provide fresh eggs. They build a small cooking fire, and use pottery jars to hold water. Each family had a little teapot to boil water. They spread mats on the ground to sleep. When my wife worked in a hospital in Agra, India, a family member of each patient usually camped in a corner of the hospital grounds, protected from the busy street by an adobe wall. They cooked most of the meals over a small clay stove and bought more prepared food in a little restaurant near the street. In much of the world, family members are expected to provide any food and nursing care for hospital patients .

Bananas are a favorite fruit in much of the world, there are many varieties. I have eaten tasty bananas toasted over an open fire in the Pacific. A family that I lived with in France had a barbecue on the beach in Cannes. They had a gas cooker, the flame was spread by volcanic rocks. They slit banana skins in several places and toasted them over the fire. In Vanuatu, a weight, usually a piece of coral, is tied to the lower part of a stem of green bananas. It then develops a U-shape curve on the stem, so a ripe bunch can easily be carried by draping the loop over a shoulder. I have seen beetles or blight on the end of green bunches of bananas on Pacific islands. In Vanuatu, leaves of the Madonna Lilly are twisted, and the sap is rubbed on green bananas to keep away the banana beetle. In Latin America and parts of Africa and Asia, a fruit similar to banana, the plantain, is cooked, usually by frying; it is not eaten raw. The delicious tropical fruits include the mango. It is usually eaten ripe, but on Pacific islands green mangoes are dipped into the sea to get the salt, then they are quickly eaten. Taro is a staple in the Pacific, usually eaten as a paste. Toasted taro makes a good snack food. When taro has a blight, as it recently did in Samoa, people go hungry.

Rice is a staple food in much of Asia. Sticky rice is usually served in a woven canister and is eaten like bread with the hands in Southeast Asia. It is often served with meals in Burma and Laos. The Miao people of southern China and southeast Asia often color their sticky rice yellow so the "little demons" or mischievous gods won't know it is rice and steal it. Rice and beans have been the staple food in much of tropical America, but rice is becoming too expensive for many families. For many centuries maize (corn) has been a popular food of Indians in the western U.S., Mexico, and Central America. Manioc (also called *mandioc, cassava,* or *yuca*), "sour" or "sweet," is a staple food in much of tropical America. Tapioca is made from the tubers of the sweet kind. Sour manioc is put into a fiber strainer about five inches in diameter and seven feet long, hung from a tree. It is twisted at the bottom with a pole to wring out all of the liquid. Many Pacific islanders use an identical type of strainer to get the juice from fruit. In the Americas the remaining fiber is pounded like flour, and eaten several ways. I never learned to like it, but it is edible with garlic and sauce. Sometimes the red juice of a type of sour manioc is used to put on the tip of arrows as a poison, like curare. In one home in the Venezuelan jungle little naked children played near the pan filled with deadly poison.

Native peoples in the Pacific, Indians near the northwest coast of North America, and other places have long given a feast to celebrate particular events, as part of their culture. I have participated in many of the feasts, which are often given with traditional dances and demonstrations of skills and athletic ability when outside groups visit the village. These feasts were given long before White Man arrived. Only people with leisure time and stockpiles or other supplies of sufficient food can give a big feast. People from several nearby villages often come to the feast, and children may get out of school early to eat the leftover food. Local leaders and politicians use the feasts to strengthen their group of supporters and followers. The banquets usually include a great variety of local fruits and vegetables, plus fish and meat, including the exotic kind, like whole roast pigs. Women are expected to do nearly all of the work of preparing, cooking, and serving the food. Sometimes they refuse to do the work unless the men agree to make certain concessions or to do certain work. In Fiji and Samoa, I have seen village women enhance their power by refusing to prepare a banquet—a refusal that seemed reasonable to me. The Kikiyu of Kenya and Tanzania have many occasions when they slaughter cows and goats as a sacrifice to their ancestors or to *Ngai,* their god. However, they wisely eat most of the meat themselves and leave only a little for the spirits. The Kikiyu say their ancestors are not hungry and eat only when it is dark. Pork is popular in China, most of Southeast Asia, and on Pacific islands. However, many villages in Laos are growing turkeys instead of pigs. The meat is said to be better for health and turkeys are easier to grow. Farmers in Ireland call the pig "the gentleman who pays the rent." Pigs are often sold for cash, potatoes are eaten.

Both salt-water and fresh-water fish are becoming scarce nearly everywhere. Many Pacific and Caribbean islanders said the sudden scarcity happened fast, in the last 20 years. Newfoundland fishermen told us that cod in the western North Atlantic is almost gone. Salmon and other fish in the eastern Pacific is only a tiny portion of a typical annual catch 40 years ago. Over-fishing, big nets, and the population explosion made fish scarce. Hatchery or pond-grown fish make only a dent in the scarcity. On the Amazon, the crew of our old boat bought big fish from lucky families in dugout canoes. Local people smoke a big fish over a smoldering fire for two days. It won't spoil for several weeks. Indians of the West Coast of North America smoked extra salmon. They double-smoked it to make tasty hard "squaw candy," eaten like candy. In Oman men catch kingfish, sharks, and sardines in big wooden *dhows* (native boats) still made locally with hand tools, and no plans or blueprints. Today dhows are still handmade but most have a 485 horsepower diesel engine rather than the sails Sinbad the Sailor is said to have used 12 centuries ago during trips to China. One family that I visited in Oman live on the coast of the Arabian Sea. They said at low tide they can gather all kinds of fresh sea food on the beach. In Fiji and other Pacific islands, men build a low wall of stones in a half-circle near the shore. The rocks are covered with water at high tide, but at low tide fish are trapped behind the dam. Fijians catch shrimp in a snare made of strong coconut cord. The shrimp backs into the loop and is snared when it tries to get out. In North America, Indians used the water wheel, secured near the shore. The current turns it slowly, trapping fish. I have never seen a fish-trap water wheel in other areas. In Papua New Guinea's Sepik River area women do most of the fishing, in dugout canoes. A legend is that a cormorant showed them how to fish. Local woodcarvers often make carvings of a woman fishing with a cormorant on her head. Markets in China sell live carp and other fish with a red cord tied through the upper fin, so the fish can easily be carried home by a bicycle rider.

On China's Li River near Guilin, men in canoes use a cormorant to catch fish, usually at night, with a light. At first a ring is tied around the bird's neck so it can't swallow them. Near the end of the workday the ring is removed so the hungry bird will be rewarded with food. In Vanuatu men put a kind of vine under rocks at reefs to poison and stun many fish. Local men said the vine's poison is usually not harmful to humans. If they eat poisoned fish they eat the bark of a particular tree as an antidote. Wiser men give a little of the fish to ants; if they live it is safe to eat. In some of the islands of Vanuatu and the

Solomons men fish, usually at night, burning torches of coconut limbs or wood with a lot of sap to attract flying fish. They are caught in nets. It is usually taboo for a female to see them fishing at night. Vonavona Island has an ancient shrine, with the skulls of some 15 local chiefs, protected by wooden covers on a stone mound. There is also shell money, in circular form like a big washer. Fishermen still go to the nearby shrine to leave an offering of taro and pray for a good catch. Hawaii and other Pacific islands still have ancient fishermen's shrines. Polynesians looked for sooty terns circling just above the water, indicating a school of fish. Another method to find fish, less effective, used by Marquesans, was to carry a small stone *tiki* (statue) balanced on the prow of the canoe. When it fell into the water there was believed to be a school of fish. Tongans, Samoans, and other Pacific Islanders export canned fish and buy frozen chicken or canned meats, a habit they acquired during World War II when the U.S. military gave them canned meats. Among some tribes in Zimbabwe, the Venda (Bavenda) and the Ndebele, in the past it was taboo to eat fish. Some Africans refused to eat catfish. We were told in Luxor, Egypt, that for thousands of years Nubians (in today's Sudan) refused to eat catfish because of a legend: The god Min was killed by his brother Set (Seth), god of evil, war, and storms. Min was later put back together, except for his penis, which a catfish had eaten.

Indians of the high cold *altiplano* in South America learned how to preserve potatoes long ago by freeze drying. They leave them on top of the ground, it freezes nearly every night, forcing out some of the moisture. The *chuños* are sold in local markets and are often put into soup. Several of us went on a five-day backpack trip on the coast of the State of Washington. The national park ranger who went with us carried no food, only condiments and a little salt. He gathered his food. Mussels pulled from big rocks at low tide are great when grilled over the campfire. Nettles, vetch peas, and seaweed "lettuce" make a good cooked salad. New tips of spruce trees make good tea. The rhizome of licorice fern tastes like licorice. We traded some of our food for his. In Brussels I once ordered mussels and was served a huge plateful. I ate fast for nearly an hour but finally finished them. Belgians like to eat and take long lunch periods.

Man has learned to eat almost anything that he can chew if it is not poisonous. Chinese say they eat "anything with legs except table legs." They grind up poor quality pearls and feed it to the baby, for the calcium "and shiny eyes." Poor Indians in the Idaho panhandle lived mostly on the roots of the camas plant. Some types are poisonous. When Lewis and Clark first arrived in 1805 they were almost starved. They ate too many camas roots and had stomach problems for days. In Iceland many people almost starved in winter until recently. They ate lichen, called *mountain grass*, mixing it with milk or water. The Spanish brought many great foods from the Americas to Europe, including beans, corn, cacao or chocolate, tomato, potato, squash, peanuts, avocado, and chili peppers. Europeans at first believed that tomatoes and potatoes were poisonous. The Spanish learned the frying method of cooking from the Mexicans and brought it to Europe. In general, in the north the Spanish cook by stewing, in the center they roast, and in the south they fry. The Spanish eat a lot of fish and pork. When I attended a school in Madrid the professor took our class for a field trip in the big market, explaining in Spanish how the many meats and cheese were used. Like the French, Chinese, and others, Spanish like odd parts of animals—the heart, brain, testicles (called "Rocky Mountain oysters" in the U.S.), kidney, and eyes. In Argentina we often ate *chinchulines*— broiled beef testicles. They taste like liver. Beginning with Columbus, the Spanish, Portuguese, Dutch, and others raced to the East Indies to begin trading for spices. Columbus had sought a new route to Asia but he only found the Americas. Before the days of refrigeration spices were even more important, to disguise the taste of spoiling food. Today, spicy food is popular with Mexicans, Thais, Laotians, Koreans, Chinese in Sechuan and Yunnan provinces, and a few other peoples who live in hot climates where food spoils quickly. Spicy food is not common in South America. Peanuts, originally from Brazil, soon spread throughout the Americas. In Europe, they are often called *American nuts*, in Africa and Asia they are *ground nuts*. Peanuts are put into many foods in the Shanghai area. In Africa, boys sell roasted peanuts in the shell, wrapped in a conical-shape piece of newspaper. They are often either burned or raw. In Oman vendors sell shelled peanuts and chickpeas, toasted in sand cooked over a charcoal flame. The sand is sifted out, the remaining nuts or chickpeas are evenly cooked.

Where cannibalism was practiced in Africa, tropical America, on Pacific islands, and elsewhere, a body (or parts of a body), was usually eaten in a ceremony, to get strength from the victim, after a revenge killing, or to preserve the soul of a relative who died. However, in times of hunger it has been common to eat human flesh, like any other meat. When overcrowding and warfare caused starvation on Easter Island it was common to kill another person in order to eat the body. Many archeologists, including Christy Turner, have found human bones that cause them to believe that some of the Anasazi Indians in the U.S. Southwest killed and ate men, women, and children. Perhaps warfare or terrorism caused the Hopi Indian cities to be built in almost inaccessible cliffs, and warfare or terrorism, as well as drought, may have caused the cities to be abandoned in the Thirteenth Century. In times of extreme hunger "civilized" man has eaten other humans, who may not have died before they became food. Examples are the Donner Party of pioneers who got caught in snow in the Sierra Mountains in the winter of 1846-1847, and the survivors of the crash of an airliner in the Andes Mountains in October, 1972. In Hangzhou, China, in the Twelfth and Thirteenth centuries human flesh, called "two-legged mutton," was served in restaurants. Human flesh and blood was thought to be good for health and to cure several diseases.

When a particular seasonal food is an important part of the diet of a group of people there is usually a ceremony in honor of the first appearance of that food. Thus, American Indians celebrated when salmon returned in the stream, or when camas roots or a wild fruit was ripe. In much of the world the harvest time of an important crop, such as potatoes in Ireland or South America's altiplano, sweet potatoes or taro in the Pacific, yams in the Azores or much of Africa, or the return of migratory game animals in Africa, is recognized by a ceremony.

The *horno* or outdoor oven is common in Latin America and parts of southern Europe and western Asia. A fire is built in a big round stone, concrete, or clay oven. When the fire goes out the ashes are removed and bread or other foods are put in, cooked by the residual heat of the masonry. In Yemen, women cook a ball of dough in the fire, after putting small stones in the center to cook the inside. In the Pacific, hot stones are sometimes put inside pigs being cooked over flames to speed up the process. In the Pacific, it is common to cook meat, fish, and vegetables in a pit in the ground. Big leaves or aluminum foil is put over the food, then a layer of dirt, and a fire is built over it. After a few hours the coals are raked away and the tasty food is pulled out. In Tahiti it is called a *heman* or *ahimaa*, in Hawaii a *luau*, in Samoa an *umu*, in Papua New Guinea it is a *mumu*. In Vanuatu, local people make *laplap* by putting grated manioc, taro, or yams, plus meat or fish, into dough. It is wrapped in big leaves and tied. The package is put on top of pre-heated stones in the ground, and more hot stones are put on top. It is quite tasty. Meals are cooked in a heated *motu* in the Solomon Islands by a similar method. On Easter Island, each long low reed house had a pit for cooking, protected from wind, several steps from the entrance door. In New Caledonia, vegetables, meat, and seafood are mixed with coconut cream, wrapped in banana leaves, and the *bougna* is cooked on coals or in an earth oven. In the Marquesas Islands, men used damp burlap bags, as well as big leaves and dirt, to protect suckling pigs and vegetables from the hot stones used in the underground oven. A banana or hibiscus leaf, or another big leaf, is often used as a plate in the tropics. A small mat woven from a local plant is also used. Cooking in a pit is also common among the Berbers in North Africa. Our mutton, potatoes, and other vegetables were delicious, with fried bread, wine, and sweet cakes made of honey or dates. In the Azores, our dinner of meats and vegetables was cooked in a big kettle, put into a bubbling hot volcanic mud hole.

When Sir Walter Raleigh brought the potato from the Americas to Ireland the population increased from a million in 1800 to eight million in 1840. However, a few years later a blight hit potatoes. A million people starved and another million left Ireland. In Alaska, I learned to like *muktuk*, the thick skin and fat or blubber of whale. It is chewed a long time and tastes good. A whale, caught after the ice breaks up in late spring, can feed a village of 200 people for a month. Food keeps a long time in Alaska's winters. Local people dig a hole in the permafrost to store food. Others build a *cache* or little log storehouse, on four strong tall poles, out of the reach of hungry bears. Some people plant a vine with thorns near the ladder to discourage bears from climbing. Zulus and other tribes in sub-Sahara Africa dig a hole four feet or so deep, three feet in diameter at the bottom, narrower at the top, to store food. They coat the inside walls with fresh cow manure, and build a fire to bake the sides, like clay. The hole is hidden by a flat stone, covered with dirt. Some 4,000 years ago it was common in Syria to store vegetables in a deep, cool pit in the ground. The Mosuo people near Lugu Lake in China's Yunnan province store "pipa pork" in a dry room or porch for 10 or 20 years. They kill a pig, then take out the internal organs and bones. They rub it with spices—salt, garlic, ginger, or prickly ash. Before using it is cleaned in hot water, then soaked until the skin is soft, cut into pieces, and cooked. When I first saw it lying on the upper porch floor of a home I thought it was a burlap bag, half full. However, it tastes all right.

Hearty soups are among the best foods, and after boiling a few minutes they are likely to be pure. Brazilians eat *tacacá*, made of whatever the cook has handy. In Belem, it usually contained egg, manioc, little shrimp, and strange herbs. In Paraguay, I liked *sopa Paraguayas*, with egg, corn bread, cheese, onion, and more. In southern Chile, we liked *paila marina*, a mixture of eel, sea urchins, and *cholgas*, like clams. It equals the best French *bouillabaisse* in Marseilles. *Jambalaya* is a tasty spicy Creole soup, made of shrimp, oysters, potatoes, and whatever is handy, popular in southern Louisiana. Baked casserole dishes containing vegetables and meat or fish are often as good as soup. One of my favorites is *pastel de choclo*, popular in Chile. Typically, it contains corn, eggs, raisins, avocados, olives, ground meat, and spices. In Quebec's Lake St. Jean area, the popular *tortiere* is made with potatoes, ground meat, onions, and other vegetables. Romanians like tasty *mamaliga*—cooked soft yellow corn meal, often eaten with fish. Trinidad has tasty *pastelle Trinidad*—ground beef cooked in corn meal. Most people who visit Scotland participate in the address to the *haggis*, a dish of chopped heart, lungs, and liver of a sheep (or calf), with turnips, barley, oatmeal, and onions, baked in sheep's entrails. It tastes fair but I prefer many other mixtures. When my wife began to eat her seafood salad in Angelmo, Chile, the little crab on top began to crawl away. She learned to eat fast before her food disappeared. We talked in Spanish with the families of fishermen. They live on old sailboats, catch fish and sea creatures near uninhabited islands, and bring their catch to the mainland from time to time. A woman asked if we were from *la capital*, Santiago. We said we were from *los Estados Unidos*, the U.S.. She said "That must be a big empire. They're always having so many wars."

Chinese iron cooking pots used for stir-fry cooking have flared sides, they catch more heat, cook more evenly and faster, saving valuable fuel. Most foods are chopped into small pieces before cooking, they cook faster and are easier to eat with chopsticks. Green vegetables are a common food, tortoise is also eaten. However, if eaten together many Chinese believed, until recently, that they were poisonous. Buddhists are told not to eat meat, it might be an ancestor—animal or human. However, stores in Tibet sell a lot of packages of thin dried yak meat, flavored with little red peppers. For thousands of years vegetarian cooks in China and India have specialized in making vegetables and fruits look like meat, and even taste like meat. A restaurant in Beijing's Diaoyutai State Guest House, where presidents often stay, served us a vegetarian meal. The "crisp fried duck" was made mostly from mushrooms and no duck, and the "sweet and sour shrimp" was made from water chestnuts. In India, Jaipur's Laxmi Restaurant is famous for tasty vegetarian food. My "stroganoff" made from fruit, *rasmali* for dessert, plus a cheese ball cooked in milk, flavored with saffron and pista, was delicious. On St. Petersburg's Nevsky Prospekt, I often passed the former home of Count Stroganov, who "invented" beef stroganoff in the Eighteenth Century—sautéed beef in a creamy sauce, with vegetables. In Stockholm we enjoyed the Swedish smorgasbords. They began as pagan harvest feasts, then as buffet tables with sandwiches. In Bulgaria, we liked the hearty *shopska salad*, with sheeps' cheese, peppers, olives, tomatoes, and cucumbers. However, none of us tried the "tomatoes stuffed with farming products."

Rome's *La Repubblica* reported that Italians spend more money on food than anyone else in Western Europe. France is next, then Belgium, Greece, and Germany. The least money is spent in Ireland, followed by the United Kingdom, and Denmark. The noonday meal is usually the big meal in Germany, Italy, France, and the United Kingdom. Most Italians and French drink a little wine with every meal except breakfast. When I attended schools in France and a school in Florence, each school found a family for me to live with. The family is required to furnish wine with the evening meal. My wife and I spent a week in Bologna, Italy's gourmet center, one spring. Many men went into the country to gather tender dandelion leaves to sell. Restaurants featured *ruccola* sandwiches—dandelion leaves. Italians and French eat many salads, the British eat cooked vegetables, but many Germans eat few salads or vegetables, except potatoes. I lived with four families in various parts of Germany while attending local language schools. Food has improved in Britain in the past 30 years. During a hike across Northern England, and many hikes in the Scottish Highlands, my wife and I usually found good food in pubs in small towns.

In Northern Europe, Germanic tribes used horse meat in ancient pre-Christian rituals. The Christian missionaries taught them that horse meat is bad, so it is no longer eaten there. But French and others in Southern Europe like horse meat. I do too, but it is much more expensive than beef. Few farmers now have horses in Europe. Old horses can be eaten, old tractors cannot. Mutton is also more expensive than beef everywhere, except for tough mincemeat. In Yemen, I found camel meat to be the best, less gristly than goat. In Sri Lanka, we walked on an isolated beach after midnight, meeting a local man who was looking for turtle eggs. Big sea turtles come ashore at night, dig a hole, and bury many eggs. They dig a second hole to lead away egg hunters. The eggs are a good source of protein for hungry people. In Mexico, men insist upon eating fertilized hens' eggs, they believe it makes them more virile.

Africa's Masai get most of their food from their cattle—in the dry season, when there is less milk, blood is drained, a quart or so at a time, from the neck of a live animal; it is often mixed with milk. A moran shoots the animal at close range with an arrow, aiming at the lower neck. The blood is caught in a container, and the wound is said not to hurt the animal. Each morning, my guide in Cambodia's Angkor Wat area found that men, usually Khymer Rouge guerrillas, had built a fire in a hole in the trunk of big trees. They collected the sap to make torches and to waterproof boats. Sometimes they add palm fronds and green leaves to a fire to make a lot of smoke. Bats then drop from the tree and are eaten. "Flying foxes" or fruit-eating bats are eaten on many Pacific islands. In the Solomon Islands a man told me that he usually puts a little poison on the tip of an arrow before shooting the flying foxes. He said it is dangerous—they can catch an arrow and throw it back at the man who shot it. I am still not sure whether he was kidding.

The coconut is one of man's greatest foods in the tropics. The copra can be eaten or processed in many ways, the liquid makes a pure drink, and it is used for several medicinal purposes. Toasted or grated copra is delicious. The husk is usually removed by men who carefully hit it on the sharpened end of a stick in the ground. A husked coconut has two eyes and a mouth. I learned how to open a coconut quickly by hitting it near one of the two eyes with a rock. Coconut hulls are used for bowls, to store money in shops, to cover women's breasts, and much more. The husks are used as a home for baby chicks, for fiber to make tough mats, baskets, or clothes, and as fuel for a fire. Coconut wood is used in much construction, but it is not as useful as bamboo. Copra is dried and sold for coconut oil in much of the tropics, but much labor is involved in cleaning it from the hull and drying it, either over a fire or in sheds protected by rain. The world price for copra is so low that much of it is not processed. Sri Lanka's big king coconut provides only liquid, the copra is not edible. Sri Lanka's jackfruit is such a great free food that a law prohibits anyone from cutting a jack-fruit tree without government permission. It is light yellow, with a slightly sweet pulp, eaten raw or cooked, said to be nutritious. It also grows in southern India and on many islands of the western Pacific.

In Central and Eastern Europe, it is still common to use molds to shape bread or gelatin, so it looks like roast beef, lobster, or other delicacies. People in many countries learned to make food that lasts for weeks or much longer. Peasants in Armenia have long made a rect-angular flat bread like tortillas. They sometimes store it for a year, merely soaking it in water before eating. Norway's thin crisp flat bread, made of rye and oat flour, is baked on a griddle at low heat. It keeps for years. In the Caribbean, New England, and the southern U.S., men going on a long journey took with them a supply of fried flat cornbread called *journey cakes* (also called *johnnycakes*, *ashcake*, or *cornpone*). Indians in western North America made easy-to-keep pemmican by drying strips of meat or fish, adding berries for a better taste. Many French restaurants serve vinegar in a bottle, with a small green pine or cedar bough to preserve it. German restaurants, for *Frühstück* or break-fast, have a cute plastic container on each table for waste. It helps to keep everything neat. In Sicily our ice cream cones had two cones doubled to prevent loss of ice cream on a hot day. In Guatemala and Nicaragua, vendors carry 10 or so ice cream cones in holes on a flat board, fastened to the end of a long pole. They offer ice cream cones to the crowd, and on the board there is a little place to put coins in pay-ment.

I asked a young Frenchman what he found to be most interest-ing during his recent trip to the U.S., his first. He said, in French, "I'm surprised that the 'all-you-can-eat' restaurants don't go bankrupt. In France, we would fill our pockets and bags with foods." He found drivers in the U.S. to be more relaxed than those in France, but he was surprised to find so many foreign-made cars in the U.S. He said that anyone in the European Union would be considered to be unpatriotic if he or she drove a car not made in Europe. But in the past few years, several Japanese and American auto companies have an assembly plant in Europe, and the cars are better accepted. Most of us hate to waste food, but some restaurants serve portions that are far too large, and we may not have refrigeration for a "doggie bag." If we serve our own food at a buffet there should be little waste. In Singapore, if much food is wasted at a buffet the customer may have to pay a stiff fine.

There is often a conflict between the culture of immigrants and local people. During my German school in Stuttgart, the teacher asked us each Monday morning what we did on the weekend. The girl from Thailand said "I cooked a big meal for my family." The teacher asked what she cooked. She said "I cooked a dog and a cat." The teacher asked where she found the animals. She replied "We buy them from a Thai man. He finds them around, in the street." That evening I told the story to the *Frau* with whom we lived. She said "My cat disappeared a few days ago. I'll bet they ate it!"

Men in Cambodia and Laos asked me what I thought of Vietnamese food. I said that I liked it. They said "But they eat *dog*!" I told them that I had eaten dog and it is good. Chinese and Koreans believe that dogs should be eaten, not seen in cities. Lewis and Clark, during their trek across Northwest U.S. in 1804 and 1805, found that many North American Indians considered dog to be great food. Snakes are eaten by some men in Korea, China, and Taiwan. Mexican men buy ground dried rattlesnake in small plastic sacks. They believe it cures many ailments and is an aphrodisiac. As a farm boy in the U.S. Southwest in the 1930s, our county had a rattlesnake drive each spring. We usually filled a two-ton truck with them. Men and boys wearing boots, thick trousers, long sleeves, and gloves, each carried a long forked stick to pin down the snake's head. We sometimes ate the meat, it tasted okay. We tanned the skin and sold it to make belts, wallets, and other things. Some men believe that if they wear part of a rattlesnake skin on the shoes, other rattlers won't bite them—a superstition. Putting whiskey on a snakebite will not cure it—another superstition. My father said that when he was a boy in "Indian Territory," now Oklahoma, the local Indians caught land terrapins and put them into a bonfire. When they tried to crawl out they were pushed back. When half-cooked, the entire terrapin except shell and bones was eaten with relish. In jungles of Peru and Brazil I have often eaten monkey, like the local people. It is usually cut into small pieces and grilled. The meat is gristly but good. Iguanas, often three feet long, like a big lizard, taste like chicken.

My wife and I stayed a few weeks on a ranch in Argentina, a sort of commune. Most of the residents claimed to be vegetarians. But when a hunter shot a wild goat and it was barbecued the vegetarians ate it so fast there were only bones for us to gnaw on. In the Andes Mountains local restaurants serve *carne del altiplano*—often llama or burro, tough, like wild goat. In Malaysia, I ate a plate of sea worms with a wide tail. They were good when hot, but soon became slimy. In Australia's Outback, I ate popular delicacy, crunchy grilled *witchety grubs*. In China I ate grated rat. They eat a lot of grain, so why shouldn't they be eaten? Rats are eaten in much of Africa and by some tribes in India. Pork is not eaten in Islamic or Jewish areas. Hindus don't eat beef. Pork is eaten on ceremonial occasions and festivals in much of the Pacific and Southeast Asia, but Easter Island apparently never had pigs or dogs—people there ate chickens. Most Pacific Islanders do not eat hens' eggs, but Easter Islanders do. Tonga has several hundred pigs that fish for their food. At low tide they rush for the beach to eat all kinds of sea creatures. Tongans claim that their meat is healthier than most pork. In Laos, many villages have stopped growing pigs, they have changed to turkeys. Goats and pigs were often left on islands in the Pacific and Atlantic in the Eighteenth and Nineteenth centuries by explorers, whalers, and other sailors from Portugal, Holland, England, and elsewhere. The animals would provide meat for later visitors, but they have multiplied and become a nuisance, eating most of the native vegetation. Norwegians brought a few reindeer to South Georgia Island, now there are at least 3,000. Falkland islanders, aware of how destructive sheep are, carefully limit the number of sheep that each farm may have.

Koreans like *kimchi*—spicy, smelly, fermented cabbage. I often rode in an elevator with well-dressed Koreans, but the smell of kimchi was strong. Koreans don't eat the peeling of apples or pears. I lived with many German and French families while going to language schools. The French did not eat apple or potato peelings. Germans eat apple peelings but not potato peelings. A French roommate regularly dipped his bread or toast into coffee. A roommate from Switzerland had only thick hot chocolate for breakfast. One of our nice hotels in Rome served only *Milka Slurp* hot chocolate and bread for *prima colazione* or breakfast.

Man has always had a sweet tooth. Men who knew how to make smoke and rob a bee hive for the honey were prized in primitive societies. They sometimes enticed bees to a hollow log by baiting it with sweets, then getting the honey. Australia's Aborigines dug deep to find a colony of honey ants, then bit off their honey-filled abdomens. They sucked sweet dew made by *lac scale* insects on branches of the *mulga tree*. They also sucked the sweet nectar on flowers of the *Honey Grevillea*. In Yemen, families spend a lot of their income by going to a particular village to buy honey made from the blossom of a rare tree. In the past it was sold in leather bags, today it is usually in glass jars. Men consider it to be an aphrodisiac. Local men say pure honey will burn, it won't freeze, when poured it has a steady stream, and dust will not absorb a drop of pure honey. In Romania, hundreds of hives of bees on big trailers are towed to any shady area where a particular plant is blooming. The first white men in Papua New Guinea, and parts of Africa and Asia, found that local people used joints of sugar cane as a standard of trade. It is still one of the best sellers in markets from the Pacific and Asia to Latin America. In cities, an entre-preneur sets up a small hand press to squeeze out the juice, which is sold by the cupful. In Malta, a staunchly Roman Catholic country, during Lent, local people cannot eat candy. They miss it. However, they have many carob trees and eat the sweet pulp of the pods. People in the U.S. eat a lot of sweets, but I believe the English, Swiss, and even the Germans eat more. In Argentina, especially near the Andes, *rama* chocolate is popular. It is either brown or white, twisted like a rope.

Drinks

Man has learned how to make alcoholic drinks from nearly every fruit that ferments, plus many other raw materials. Japan, China, and several other Asian countries make sake by fermenting rice. In Japan, it is usually served warm, in a special *choko cup*. In a dinner meeting a man sometimes stands up suddenly, puts both arms above the head, and proposes a toast by shouting *Banzei!* Toasts are also a problem in China, Russia, and a few other countries. To refuse to stand and take a drink is considered rude. I learned to cover my glass with my hand so others couldn't see how much alcohol it had, and I learned to fake the actual drinking. We should not take a drink until the host/hostess proposes a toast. Sanghei Village on the Mekong in Laos, fer-ments sticky rice for 15 days, puts it into big metal barrels, and keeps a fire burning under each barrel. Cool water from the nearby river is poured by hand on the top to distill the steam. The potent liquid is caught in pottery jugs and sold in the market. In China, tourists are usually served a drink with meals—tea, *Coca Cola*, or weak beer in bottles. The distilled *mai tai* is potent, often 180 proof. Most of the mai tai is given to a public official or to a boss for a "favor." In Sri Lanka and India, *toddy* made from fermented sap of the coconut palm is a popular drink, something like beer. During a storm, a group of shore-bound fishermen in a village near where we stayed had been drinking toddy for days. They tried to get me to buy them the more potent *arrack*, distilled from toddy. In Estonia and other Baltic countries, many men grow barley for homemade beer. Fishermen catch herring, hanging it below the eaves of the house to keep dry, out of the reach of hungry cats. It is delicious with beer. A farmer that I visited in Latvia proudly gave me a drink of the beer he made from barley. In South Africa, *Bantu beer* is usually made from fermented corn or maize. Another popular beer is made from sorghum, like sugar cane. For centuries Mexico's Mayan Indians have made *chicha* beer by fermenting sugar cane juice for some 24 hours. Little shops or private homes in South America's Andes Mountains put out bamboo poles with flowers on them when a fresh batch of chicha is ready. Men and women in the

Andes chew coca leaves to get more energy in the thin air. In Cuzco, I saw a little man trotting along chewing coca while carrying a teak log that I could probably hardly lift. In the high altiplano of Bolivia, restaurants serve coca tea, made with leaves of coca, which can be refined to make cocaine. Even our young sons were served the mild stimulant. In Venezuela's jungle, I drank a little *cacchia*, a reddish beer made from the sweet yucca plant. Indians in Mexico make *pulque*, like beer, by fermenting pulp of the maguey plant, it looks something like cactus. They also make *mescal* by distilling the pulque. West Africa's shops sell *pito* beer in pottery jugs, it is made from millet. Our hotel room in Krakow, Poland, had a practical bottle opener that also had a tight plastic lid to recover the bottle after it was opened.

Sugar cane in the West Indies was made into molasses, carried to New England where it was made into rum, which was traded for slaves in Africa some 250 years ago. Today rum is made either from molasses or from sugar cane juice. Islands where the cost of labor is higher, such as Puerto Rico and Martinique, import the molasses from poorer countries, such as Haiti or Dominican Republic, to make rum. The family of Napoleon's Josephine grew sugar cane and made rum on their Martinique plantation. In Greece, I drank inexpensive *retsina* wine, though it tasted like turpentine. After a few weeks it still tasted like turpentine but I learned to like it. *Ouzo 12* is a potent distilled drink, usually flavored with anise. In Turkey it is called *raki*. Polynesians learned to ferment the root of the *ti* plant to make an alcoholic drink. They also learned to distill it to make a much more potent drink. Governments often put a stiff tax on alcoholic drinks. Men in the hills of Scotland, the U.S. Appalachian Mountains, and elsewhere make illegal *bootleg, moonshine,* or *white lightning* whiskey. The Gaelic *usige beatha* or "water of life" became *uskey*, then whiskey. An old sheepherder in Scotland's hills showed us where local people had set up watchmen to look for the tax man, like Sir Walter Scott, before he became a successful writer. In the hills of North Carolina another soldier and I found an operating still not far from our battalion area in Fort Bragg. We kept quiet about the discovery and did not disturb it.

Europeans and Asians learned to make good wine from grapes more than 4,000 years ago. When the French persecuted Protestant Huguenots in the 16th Century many moved to England or the Moselle River Valley of Germany. They took with them their-grape growing and wine- making skills. Grapes require a change in seasons to grow well. In Guyana, South America, grapes do not produce but local people make a poor substitute, Banko wine. It is sweet, made from rum and several other things. In Europe, Latvia is the northernmost country where grapes can be grown for wines. In China, wine made from kiwi fruit is popular. China also produces some great wine made from grapes. Restaurants and bars often have at least one big bottle of wine with preserved snakes or geckos in it. That wine is much more expensive than ordinary uncontaminated wine. Some Chinese claim that the snakes or geckos make the wine healthier, but I believe that is only "snake oil." In Islamic countries liquor is rare except in hotels and restaurants and clubs that cater to tourists or other foreigners. In Oman I joined a group of local men who drank imported beer in a building attached to a tourist hotel. Three girls in long dresses danced a sort of tame belly dance. When my wife worked as a physician in an Afghan refugee camp near Peshawar, Pakistan we went to the American club for an occasional drink. Many of the other customers worked for either the U.S. CIA or the Soviet KGB. In Islamic Tunisia, local men have learned to grow excellent grapes but Italians are usually hired to make the wine.

Tunisia's national drink is tasty *tai-le-monta*, mint tea spiked with vodka. The French taught many Algerians, and Arabs in France, to drink good wine. Russians, Scandinavians, Alaskans, and many other people who live in socialist countries or in cold northern climates drink far too much alcohol. In Russia the tram operators, train engineers, and crane operators are usually women. Why don't more men do those jobs? Because they are often drunk or suffering from a hangover, they are not reliable or safe. I noticed that our big hotel in Moscow set up a room for a banquet. A full bottle, three-fourths of a liter or nearly a quart, of vodka was at each place setting. Later I saw people at the banquet—one third of them were children! In sub-Sahara Africa, men sometimes have little to do: they smoke and drink much of the day, and in some tribes they herd the cattle or goats. In South Africa many of the highway workers are women, because the men are unreliable.

Sometimes pets are taught to drink. A pig on St. Croix, Virgin Islands, has learned to open a can of beer and drink it. Near the Teotihuacan ruins in Mexico, a burro has learned how to hold an open bottle of beer high and swallow its contents. The parrot of my first ship as a Merchant Seaman drank alcohol and was sometimes drunk, like its owner. It could swear in several languages, it was a true sailor. The Spanish like *sangria*, a mixture of red wine and orange juice. I prefer them separate. The inside of oranges, from Greece to Sicily and Spain, are often red, and their juice looks like tomato juice.

In restaurants in Germany we tried many ways to order ordinary water from the faucet. We finally concluded that it is impossible to get. If you get water there, it will be bottled. Germans believe that water from the faucet is not safe to drink, even though their cities spend fortunes to purify the water. We finally found two drinking fountains in the entire country, the water was good. Most Europeans drink water from the faucet, but they drink more bottled water than North Americans.

Tea is perhaps the most common drink, after water. Green tea, popular in China and Japan, usually has no added milk or sugar. Many East Asian men add dried deer feces to tea, they believe it makes them healthier and virile. In India most people add milk, as do the British. When my wife worked at a hospital in Agra, a house boy brought each of us a cup of cardamom tea with buffalo's milk each morning. We were also served sweet jasmine tea in India. In Pakistan, restaurants serve buffalo's milk with tea. In Yemen's desert, in a big white tent, a young Bedouin woman served us tea with cardamom and cloves. In Mali a village woman brought us a basket of *da* or red sorrel tea. It was very sweet. I have watched the tea ceremony several times in Japan. Women and girls train for years to learn how to perform the tea ceremony properly. In expensive British hotels, High Tea is often a bargain around 5:00 P.M., the little sandwiches, pastries, and other things can be a substitute for dinner. Tourists walking or browsing in Egypt, Turkey, or much of the Middle East or North Africa are likely to be invited by a man speaking good English to have a free cup of tea. The man usually leads tourists to a carpet shop, where they must listen to a sales pitch while drinking tea. In the mountain areas of China's Yunnan province, especially where many Tibetans live, we were served butter tea in a bowl—tea with a little butter, and spices—chopped walnuts, linseed, and egg, stirred until it is frothy.

In Africa, *Bushman's tea* is made from the leaf that also produces *khat* or *qat*, popular in Arabic countries. This tea is drunk in North Africa to get rid of symptoms from a cold. Khat is a narcotic stimulant, derived from a small evergreen bush. In Yemen it is chewed. I found the taste to be pleasant but I didn't chew enough to feel any effect. A day's supply costs the equivalent of at least four to eight dollars—a lot in a poor country. Most local men buy khat around noon from one of the many vendors, and chew it for hours, stuffed into a cheek. In the afternoon most men in Yemen have fat cheeks. Khat makes them thirsty, they must drink a lot of water or coffee. Yemeni farmers have found that khat is a better crop than food to earn money. In the past Yemen exported much food but now food is imported. Khat is illegal in Saudi Arabia and Yemeni men who work there suffer. Before our plane landed in Jeddah, Saudi Arabia (the airport for the holy city of Mecca) announcements in several languages warned us that there could be no chewing of khat and no visible bottle or glass of alcohol. In Arabic countries, plus southern China, and countries long occupied by Turkey, such as Yugoslavia, men sit for hours in a tea house, sipping and talking with friends. Although many of the tea houses are on a sidewalk, in North Africa women are not welcome unless they are accompanied by a man. In the Arabian peninsula, a teapot or coffeepot and a plate of dried dates is often kept on the tile floor under a covering like a huge straw hat, to protect it from flies. A hotel lobby often has a conference corner with carpets, pillows, a plate of dates, and a teapot or coffeepot. My wife and I have visited tea plantations and processing plants in Japan, China, Sri Lanka, India, Papua New Guinea, Georgia, and the Azores. Most tea is picked by machine, but the best tea is hand-picked. In Sri Lanka, dark Tamil women with nimble fingers put tea leaves into a basket they carry on their backs. A blower separates some of the dirt, little rocks, and stems from the tea leaves, which are then rolled and dried. To make black tea, moisture is blown in, the tea ferments, then it is roasted. In older processing plants much tea spills onto the concrete floor, but it is swept up, along with the dirt, to be processed. Poorer quality tea is usually sold in tea bags.

Yemen and Ethiopia each claim to have the first coffee. In the Sixteenth Century, coffee suddenly became a popular drink in Europe. The plants were stolen and re-planted in many countries. I watched women picking some of the best coffee beans, to be hauled by trucks to the port of Mocha, Yemen, on the Red Sea, on a paved road built in the 1960s by Chinese. *Mocha* is still a popular form of coffee. My father called coffee *java*, after the Indonesian island where much coffee is still grown. When the U.S. began an embargo in 1961 against shipping goods to Cuba, the people suffered from the lack of popular U.S. soft drinks. After two years Cuban experts finally produced a soft drink that they thought was passable. I was told during a recent visit that Che Guevara tasted it, and announced in Spanish "it tastes like shit." Cuba for many years has been importing popular U.S. soft drinks from bottling companies in neighboring countries. In Ghana, when I finally tried *Pee Cola* I found it to be quite tasty. Peruvians drink a lot of *Inca Cola*.

In Uruguay, Paraguay, Argentina, and nearby parts of Brazil, shops and vendors sell ground *maté* tea, gourds, and *bombillas* or drinking straws. The *gauchos* who herd cattle often tie up their horse to take a break and drink maté. Restaurants serve maté with each meal unless the customer asks for something else. It is a mild stimulant, with caffeine. In meetings, a gourd and drinking straw filled with maté is passed to each person, like the peace pipe of North American Indians. After drinking it all, the gourd is re-filled and passed to the next victim. I always try to be near the head of the line to reduce my exposure to diseases.

In the western Pacific local people and tourists participate in the kava ceremony. In Fiji, the *yanggona* plant, which is about six feet tall, is dug up, the tubers are separated, washed, put into a hollow log stood on end, and men pound it into powder with a tall pole. It is popular in many western Pacific islands, there are many varieties of the plant used. In Vanuatu men sometimes chew the pulp to grind it. Men put the powder into a big wooden bowl partly filled with water and they strain out lumps with fibers made from coconut husks. For the

Fijian kava ceremony, complete plants with tubers attached are spread out on the floor or ground in a particular manner. The village talking chief welcomes guests and he presents the tabua or whale's tooth to the leader of the visitors. A coconut shell filled with the tan-color relaxing, slightly sedative liquid is presented to guests in a particular order. Each person claps hands once when it is his or her turn for the kava, and claps hands three times when it is drunk in one long gulp. Sometimes a small amount is thrown over the shoulder for the gods. In Tonga the ceremony is slightly different. In Samoa kava is called *avia*. Kava is also common on many other Pacific Islands, including Papua New Guinea's Lowlands. It is muddy, slightly bitter, calming, and relaxing. Some men eat fruit or chew sugar cane with kava. In Vanuatu men drink it in the *Nakamal* or men's house. In some parts of Vanuatu, such as Tanna Island, it is taboo for a woman to see kava made or to drink it. In many places women also drink kava. I found many public markets in the Pacific where small plastic bags of kava powder are sold. In Tahiti and other islands in the Eastern Pacific, kava is also drunk, but privately, without a ceremony. Kava from the Solomon Islands is unusually strong. It quickly made my lips numb. Men in Vanuatu said kava is unsociable, a tranquilizer—after two cups you don't want to talk with anyone. They said they drink kava to communicate with the spirits of their ancestors. On some Pacific islands, such as New Caledonia (according to my guide), it is illegal to make and drink kava .

Harmful Drugs

Betel nuts from the areca palm are chewed by women in Southeast Asia and the western Pacific islands, but rarely in Vanuatu. Few men chew betel nuts, which leave a purple stain, but they smoke tobacco. Signs near airports, public buildings, and stores often state "no betel nut chewing." Airlines make the usual "no smoking" announcement, and add "no betel nut chewing." Vendors sell the little green nuts at markets and along roads and streets wherever people congregate or walk. In Burma I paid a vendor about three cents U.S. to try it. He put chopped dried reddish-brown betel nut—greenish gray outside— lime, and nutmeg on a leaf tasting like camphor. I used the tongue to separate the hard part and the juice, then spat it out. It is apparently habit forming, but it tasted awful. It is a mild stimulant and is said to kill intestinal worms. However, it blackens the teeth, may cause cancer, and the lime wears out gums.

In the past, Africans, Asians, and Native Americans used tobacco mainly for ceremonies, i.e., peace negotiations or big meetings. It was not used every day, as it is today. The Spanish brought tobacco to Europe, which soon had many nicotine addicts. Jean Nicot of Arles made tobacco popular in France, nicotine was named after him. Today, most men in Asia, Latin American, and southern Europe smoke tobacco. In Turkey I watched a father and mother in a restaurant booth try to teach their son to smoke. He was only eight or nine. His father put a cigarette into his mouth and told him to inhale. They boy coughed and pushed the cigarette away, but the father persisted. In several Eastern European countries boys carry school bags with a big ad for *Camel* cigarettes. Few Asian women smoke, except in Vietnam. I have seen a few older women in China and Southeast Asia smoke a thick cigar, but when they saw me they quickly hid it. In Latin America, Spain, and Italy, young women in cities are told that they have the same rights as men to smoke. They do not have equal rights with men, but they do have equal rights to get lung cancer. In the U.S., children are told by tobacco company ads that children do not smoke, it is an *adult* right. What effect does that have on a typical rebellious teenager? "No smoking" signs are becoming common on planes and in public places everywhere, even in Asia and Latin America. They are often ignored, particularly in China, Greece, and France.

Our guide in Malaysia's Taman Negara National Park said that he had heard of the U.S. but he had never before met anyone from that country, though he had been a guide for six years. I asked him what he had heard about America. He said "That's Marlboro country." In Bangladesh, India, the Middle East, and North Africa men and women often smoke a *hookah* or *hubble-bubble* water pipe. I bought one in Bahrain as a gift for my father. In a nice restaurant in Syria, three or four local young women wearing shawls and long dresses each had a tube and pipe connected to the same ornate water pipe. In southern China, men and a few women smoke either a pipe some one or two feet long made from a thin piece of bamboo, or a *bong*, two or three feet long (60 to 95 cm.) and five inches (12 cm.) in diameter. Chinese told me that they smoke to keep away snakes; smoking is a bigger risk. In African villages I often saw a few tobacco plants and a few *bhanji* or marijuana hemp plants growing near the round huts. European countries are putting up "no smoking" signs in some public and private places, but other countries are far behind the U.S., Canada, the United Kingdom, and New Zealand in prohibiting smoking.

I recently visited a large cigar factory in Cuba. Some women pulled the spine from big leafs of tobacco, other women wrapped bits of tobacco inside a big tobacco leaf, and a machine rolled it together. One end is cut off. Women put a band around each expensive cigar, or a band around a bunch of 25 cheaper cigars. They are allowed to smoke an occasional cigar as a fringe benefit. Cuba's health plan is considered to be the best in Latin America, and government officials have mixed feelings about selling cigars, which cause so many health problems. Cuba needs the hard currency from cigars and the millions of tourists it gets, from nearly every country except the U.S. Cigar workers asked for soap, candy, and souvenirs. Many Cubans asked for *un dolar*.

Stronger drugs are common in many countries. Signs in airports in Singapore and Malaysia warn that those convicted of bringing in illegal drugs will be executed. Criminal laws must be combined with a factual educational program, beginning with very young children. Grand Cayman Island schools expel any student found to be using drugs, but they are still used. The Bahamas have slogans such as "say nope to dope, say yes to life," "dope is for dopes," and "use your head, don't crack it." A high school senior in Iquitos, Peru, showed me a one-page summary of the harmful effects of local drugs and how to respond to requests of friends or drug pushers to try a drug. His school provided the sheet, which he carries in his wallet. In Leticia, Colombia, on the Amazon, I saw no drugs but it is a major distribution point. Near Thailand's Golden Triangle I saw a big field of poppys, and visited an opium den in a Meo (Hmong) village. Several of my acquaintances smoked the thick black tar.

CHAPTER 6:
THE GROOMING & APPEARANCE OF PEOPLE

Weight & Beauty

When I return to the U.S. from abroad I quickly notice the great number of local people who are overweight. Around 35 percent of us are 20 percent or more overweight! Residents of no other country are so fat. Even young children, fed on a diet of french fries and quick-service foods, plus sitting before TV, are fat. Other Americans try to eat a healthy diet and exercise regularly. At times in the past, artists have thought that being slim represented beauty. The Sixteenth Century German painters, Cranachs, father and son, painted beautiful slim nudes. In the next century painters showed fat female nudes as the ideal. During times of hunger people wanted to be fat, they were more likely to survive. In poor countries where most people don't get enough to eat, to be fat represents the ideal. Indonesians say that a man with a fat belly "is full of experience and knowledge." Ganesha, the Hindu god of wisdom and a favorite god of children, has a fat belly and an elephant's trunk. Statues of Buddha usually show him with a fat belly, full of experience and wisdom. Chinese say "a broad belly, a broad mind." Until recently upper-class men in Tahiti and some other Polynesian islands preferred a fat bride. Local girls also sought a fat husband. The "Venus of Malta" is a headless chubby buxom woman without a head. She was considered to be the epitome of beauty and fertility some 5500 years ago. One of my skinny guides in Cambodia said they consider that a fat person is beautiful. When a Cambodian is comfortably rich he or she has a plastic surgeon lengthen their short nose, to look more Western. Some Asians go to a plastic surgeon to have the skin around the eyes changed so the eyes are not slanted, they are rounder, more Western. Yet, many Asians are handsome just as they are.

Masai girls in Africa told me that when they were babies a hole was punched in each ear lobe and a small wooden plug was inserted. Every year or so a larger plug was inserted. At age 12 the plugs were something like a big spool of thread without the thread. They also wear many necklaces and bracelets made of red and white beads. When they dance by jumping up and down and swaying the upper body the necklaces bounce up and down in a pattern. In the Marquesas

Islands both men and women wore ivory earplugs. On Easter Island long ago, men also put wooden plugs into the ear lobes, gradually increasing the size. Some *moai* statues show "men" with long ears. In Mali and Burkina Faso, West Africa, some men and women wear a bone in the nose. Men in some tribes in Papua New Guinea also wear a bone, a feather, or a piece of a particular kind of wood in the nose. In Vanuatu and Papua New Guinea, a bone in the nose indicates a person of high rank. Women and girls in India often wear a small round brass or gold ornament on one side of the nose.

Until recently, many peoples thought that a person with a flattened, conical, or pointed head was handsome. The heads of babies were wrapped, so that, gradually, the desired shape was achieved. Tribes on Malakula, one of the Solomon Islands, prized a pointed head, they covered a baby's forehead with a mat and tightly wrapped *sennet* cord made from coconut fibers around the mat. Many Indians in the Americas flattened a baby's forehead against a board; they included the Chinook Indians and some Salish Indians (often called *Flatheads*) of the U.S. Pacific Northwest, plus Olmecs and Mayans of Mexico and Central America. In 1800 BCE Ecuador's Chorrera began to flatten a baby's head.

People around the world try to have lighter-colored skin. One of the best sellers in countries where most people have a dark skin is anything sold in a bottle that may lighten skin color. However, a dark-colored skin can be more exotic and even beautiful. In Martinique and other beaches the French women take off their clothes and sun for several days, to try to become brown all over. Their skin soon looks like tanned leather, and they risk getting skin cancer. The local women wear clothes that cover them and use a hat, an umbrella, a newspaper, or handbag to protect their face from the sun. On Pacific islands and in southeast Asia, women and men may walk for miles, carrying a big folding umbrella for protection against sun or showers. In Burma, Thailand, and Indonesia, local women carry tan-color *tanaka* powder and spread it liberally on the face to avoid the sun. The northern Thais consider themselves to be superior to the southern Thais because their skin is usually a much lighter color. In India, the tan-colored Aryans of the north consider themselves to be superior to the black Dravidians of the south, who have lived in India much longer. In Sudan and other African countries, the tan-colored Moslem Arabs consider themselves to be superior to the Blacks in the south who follow animistic religions. Some Vietnamese believe that if a pregnant woman drinks a bottle of beer each day the baby will have a lighter skin color.

In Africa's sub-Saharan countries, men and women put mud in the hair to control it and keep out insects. They often color it with reddish ocher, so it looks like a hat. At night the hairdo must be protected by a pillow. Typically it is made of carved wood or bamboo, with two low end posts and a horizontal piece. In Fiji, women lighten their kinky black hair with lime. I never saw any Fijian with gray hair, they dye it. In Samoa, women put gum and scented oil on their hair. In China, boys' hair is often shaved, except in the back, where it is made into a pigtail. In many Southeast Asian countries, a boys' hair has a topknot, which is shaved off at puberty. Some Melanesian children in the Solomon Islands, Vanuatu, and children of Australia's Aborigines, often have almost blond color hair. As they get older the hair becomes darker. Hottentots of southern Africa sometimes have yellowish hair.

Women and girls in much of the Pacific paint their lips red with red coloring from the flower of a particular hibiscus. In Arab countries from Morocco to Pakistan, many women decorate their skin with reddish henna. Some of the designs are artistic and may drive the local men wild. In the more fundamental Islamic countries only the hands, ankles, and feet are open to public view, so they are decorated the most. Many primitive people put various types of sweet-smelling oil on the skin instead of clothes. In much of Africa, red ochre is mixed with the oil put onto skin. Oil also discourages little insects from biting. In the past, before marriage in the Pacific islands and parts of Southeast Asia, a youth, and sometimes a girl, were made to smell good by staying a few hours in the smoke of sweet-smelling sandalwood. Many of the sandalwood trees were cut in the Nineteenth Century, for the market in China, but some trees remain. In Polynesia, women and older girls sometimes wear a sweet-smelling sachet in the hair or bosom. It typically contains mint, *tiare* (like gardenia), *ylang-ylang* (a fragrant tree flower), and sandalwood powder. Bushmen women of southern Africa carry sweet smelling herbs in the shell of a small tortoise.

Clothing

In China and tropical Asia, men usually wear the tail of the shirt outside of the trousers. In Latin America, men also wear the tail outside, especially the decorative *guayabera* shirt. China and Vietnam have encouraged women for many years to wear olive drab or blue trousers, they must do most of the work that a man does. Now more Chinese women are wearing bright-color dresses. Young Chinese sometimes wear a miniskirt like Europeans and an almost- transparent blouse, like many other women in Southeast Asia. Most of the bras displayed in shops are padded, but pads are not needed for today's well-developed young Chinese. Some Chinese men and women are even wearing short pants. The men are abandoning the military-style *Mao jacket*. In the more conservative Islamic countries, local women must wear the *shalwar kamis* with long sleeves and pant legs, or the *burqa* or *chador*, like a black tent covering all but the eyes. In parts of Yemen even the eyes are covered with a black veil. When my wife, a physician, worked with Afghan refugees at the Pakistan border she bought several shalwar kamis. In Yemen, Iran, and Saudi Arabia local women often wear a long black "tent" and a thin black veil covering the entire face. Even in more progressive Islamic countries women are expected to wear a scarf on the head and a long dress. School uniforms for girls are a long dress over trousers, and most wear a shawl covering the hair. Women in Europe and North America in the recent past wore a thin white or black veil, and a shawl, hat, or bonnet to cover the hair when they left the home.

Men on the Arabian Peninsula and much of the Middle East and North Africa typically wear a long light-color gown over pants, they are ideal in a hot dry climate. Islamic men wear a turban, often over a white skull cap. They also wear the embroidered flat-top *kuma*, Uzbekistan square *tsibitika*, the North African or Turkish red *fez*, or the white *ghutra* with a cloth to protect the back of the neck in the desert. Islamic men avoid a cap with a bill or a hat with a brim because they must touch the earth or floor with their head during prayers five times a day. In warmer parts of Asia men and women wear a straw hat, of various shapes. Some are conical- shape, some are flat except for an indentation for the head. On the Arabian peninsula, farm women often wear a straw hat at least 18 inches tall, it insulates in the hot sun. But they are usually dressed all in black, in the hot sun they are in a black oven. In warmer parts of Latin America both sexes wear straw hats. As a farm boy I bought a new straw hat each spring, shaping it by first soaking it in the horse's drinking trough. When dry a straw hat keeps its shape. In the Andes Mountains, *Aymara* Indian women wear a white hat, *Quechua* Indian women wear a brown bowler hat. On a cold damp trip through the Andes Mountains local girls put plastic sacks on the outside of their socks, then into shoes or boots. Alaskan Eskimos and early Antarctic explorers put dried grass in their sealskin *mukluks* for warmth. In Ecuador and Peru Indian men leave their villages in the mountains or jungle, move to the cities, cut off their pigtails, and change to *Mestizo*, like many of the other residents.

Men and women on many Pacific Islands and in the forests of South America and Africa traditionally wore little more than tattoos or body paint. Along the Amazon, women in villages may wear only a little skirt; many of the women have tan-colored skin and beautiful features. Women in the lowland villages of Papua New Guinea, Vanuatu, along Africa's Niger River, and elsewhere often still wear only a loin cloth or less. Many women of Vanuatu's Big Nambas tribe wear a small grass skirt and a big headdress made from fiber of the pandanus, usually dyed purple. The fibers often hang to below the hips but leave the breasts exposed. The pandanus is a wonderful plant, the leaves are also used to thatch houses, to make hats or mats, for brushes and necklaces, and the fruit, like pineapple, is eaten. Pollen from the male pandanus flower is considered to be an aphrodisiac, any girl wearing it is likely to attract boyfriends, both wanted and unwanted. Girls of all ages on some of the Solomon islands don't wear any clothes, but when married they wear a tiny cover over the genitals. The missionaries in many areas took off the grass skirts and put clothes on women— a *mother hubbard*—a loose long dress, or a Tee shirt above a dress. Men had to wear trousers.

Tee shirts with the name of a U.S. city, the flag, the letters *USA*, or the name of a U.S. sports hero or musician, are common everywhere. I was surprised recently in Cuba, Cambodia, and Vietnam to find that Tee shirts, jackets, backpacks, and other things with the name of a place or anything in the U.S. were, by far, the most popular, the best sellers. In Manaus, in the heart of Brazil's Amazon, the brown-skinned girls wear a tight Tee shirt and no bra. They outnumber men about 15 to one. Women work in assembly plants and stores of the free-trade zone, the men work in the jungle mines or in cocaine smuggling. In Manila a local girl wore a Tee shirt reading:

God save America. Please hurry.

On holidays and Sundays even the very poor wear beautiful clothes in Latin America and sub-Sahara Africa. Girls and women wear pretty dresses, never blue jeans. In some Latin American countries any woman wearing trousers is considered to be "loose" or a prostitute. Clothes of men and women in Latin America should be conservative. Short pants are frowned upon, except in resort areas. Swedes likewise do not like casual dress. The best thing to wear to be accepted everywhere is a smile. In the Pacific's "Bible Belt," Samoa, Fiji, and Tonga, women must wear long dresses, except in the cities and resort areas. The roads and streets are empty for 20 minutes in the early evening, everyone is expected to say their prayers then. When we stayed a short time with a family living on an outer island of Samoa, television had arrived just two weeks earlier. Only half the usual number of people attended Sunday services in the two churches. The missionaries have tough competition. In many Lowlands villages in Papua New Guinea, and in kastom villages on Vanuatu islands, men wear only a penis shield or *namba*. One Vanuatu tribe is called the Big Nambas because men wear a big penis shield. Another tribe is the Small Nambas. Women wear only a loin cloth or grass skirt. The namba is made of dried leaves and is sometimes dyed a bright color with vegetable dyes. Some villages sell nambas to tourists. Local vendors ask the *wife* what size namba is needed, they believe the man will exaggerate the size.

Indians in the Americas spun wool, cotton, hennequen, maguey, or other fibers to make thread or yarn, long before the Spanish arrived.

Women and girls in much of the world carry a spindle and wool, cotton, kapok, or other material, twisting it as they walk, talk, or sit, to make yarn. They know where to get dye, from plants or insects. They wove clothes long before the Spanish arrived. The backstrap loom is the simplest type, often used by a girl as young as three years. The long *warp* cords or yarn are fastened around a tree or a table leg, the weaver sits facing it, keeping it tight by pushing backwards. The cross threads of the *weft*, of various colors, are woven in, to make a pattern. Mexico City's great Anthropological Museum has ancient elaborate looms with wooden frameworks. On one of my visits to the Mayan section I told a guide in Spanish how much I admired the Mayan culture. He proudly said he was Mayan and spent all day showing me how Mayans lived. China's Panpo Museum near Xi'an shows that local people knew how to weave around 8,000 years ago.

When Roman soldiers first arrived in what is now London they fought local men and women, who wore only oil on the skin. Fighting them was like fighting a greased pig. Poorer Hindu men often wear only the *dhoti*, like a big diaper, tucked up between the legs. In Burma, Bangladesh, Sri Lanka, and India's West Bengal, men wear a *longyi* or *lungi*, often with a plaid pattern. Those men, with narrow hips, often have to tighten it to keep it from falling off. Women in Burma, Sri Lanka, and West Bengal, wear the same type of wrap-around but it often has a flower pattern. Women in Burma and Sri Lanka often wear an *aingyis* or *cambaya*—a sheer blouse. Women in India usually wear a *sari*, made of many yards of sheer cloth wrapped around. Even after being wrapped several times the thin cloth leaves little to a man's imagination. Vietnamese women and older girls often wear an *ao dai*, a traditional sheer pants suit that "covers everything but hides nothing." Vietnamese women must have both traditional and Western clothes, like Japanese women, who must have at least one expensive complete *kimono* outfit plus Western clothes. Colors of indigenous Mayan women in Guatemala are perhaps the brightest and prettiest clothes in the world. Reds and blues predominate. Young women there like to have a complete woven outfit of *huipile* (blouse), *refajo* or *falda* (skirt), *faja* (belt), *cinta* or *tocoyale* (headband). Married women have a *perraje* (shawl) in which to carry a baby. The complete Mayan dress for women costs far more than Western clothes. Locally woven clothes in southern Mexico, Ecuador, and other parts of Latin America are beautiful, but the colors are not as bright as Guatemala's.

Women and girls in the hill tribes of China and Southeast Asia wear clothes in beautiful bright colors that identify tribal members. When a woman marries the colors are often more subdued. Heavy silver jewelry, bead necklaces, or other jewelry also is unique for each tribe. The huge headdress worn by many also protects against cold wind and rain, and may function as an umbrella, even covering a baby in the usual backpack carrier. *Bai* women wear mostly white and red, with a large headdress, embroidered red over white. Mirrors on the chest are to drive away evil spirits. Some women of the large *Yi* group wear mostly black, others wear green or red, usually with a big headdress almost like a hood in front. They like earrings and to pin silver flowers on the collar. *Yao* women typically wear a dark blue blouse or jacket and turban, with much red trim. They wear a lot of black, but a big bright red headdress and a lot of silver. *Miao* (also called *Meo*—"Primitive," or *Hmong*—"Free Men") women wear embroidered red, white and other colors over a dark dress or pants, and a huge headdress that looks like an upside-down bowl. *Akha* (*A-Kha*) women wear a black dress, embroidered red and white waist band, and often have silver coins dangling from their bright headdresses, which have furry red balls attached. *Naxi* women wear dark blue outfits trimmed in red and partly covered with a sheepskin cape. On the back, they wear a cape with seven ribbons, representing the seven stars of the Big Dipper. The embroidery has designs of bees and butterflies, showing that the women "are as industrious as bees and butterflies." *Mosuo* (a branch of the Naxi) women often wear a rust-color blouse and a long white skirt, with a blue turban-like headdress. *Lisu* (*Lisaw* or *Lee So*) women often wear a mint green or pink dress, brightly trimmed with embroidery. Their turban is usually trimmed with beads and sometimes has a long tassel worn on the left. *E-kaw* (*I-ko*) often wear a black or white dress, many bead necklaces, and a heavy bright metal hat with fluffy red or yellow balls attached. *Shui* women like a medium blue dress and a long silver necklace. *Yang* wear a red dress, embroidered sleeves and leg bands, like some women in southern India, with long necklaces, and a small turban. *Karen*, in and near northern Burma, wear a pink-rust colored blouse or a purple dress and simple head scarf, *Red Karen* women often wear dark trousers trimmed in red, and an embroidered red and yellow blouse. *Pumis*, like the Yi, Miao and Akha, often live on poor land high in the mountains. Pumi wear darker colors but a huge turban-like dark headdress with a tassel. *Tibetan* women have a somewhat similar red and black headdress and tassel but they often wear a bright scarlet dress covered by a white and black embroidered apron. Sometimes Tibetan women wear a black dress with red socks.

In Scotland, the plaid tartans indicated the location where the wearer lived. Now clan members living in Nova Scotia, the U.S., or anywhere, wear the same tartan. Each clan had a cap of a particular pattern. When "Bonnie Prince Charlie" was defeated by the English in 1746 the wearing of a tartan was banned for 25 years. When tartans returned each clan had a dull or muted tartan and a bright dress tartan.

Many men in Japan and Taiwan wear silk underpants, they think it makes them more virile. Men on many Pacific islands wear a *lavalava, laplap,* or *pareo* wrap-around. It is a big rectangular piece of cloth, with many ways of using it, and with several names. On many Polynesian islands and in Vanuatu some men wear a skirt made of tapa cloth. Men wear something like a skirt in many countries—the longyi, Scottish kilts, the pointed lavalava or *sulu* of the police and other men in Fiji and Samoa, and Greece's *foustenelli*. In Papua New Guinea men and women in isolated villages still wear grass hanging vertically from the waist, and little more except body paint. Many women on Pacific islands and in American jungles consider themselves to be dressed if they put stripes or geometric designs with paint on their faces, breasts, and backs. Sometimes men and women wear a grass skirt to reduce the area subject to insect bites. Women in the Pacific often wear a *sarong* or pareo. In Tonga, for dress clothes, men and women wear a fine long mat wrapped around the waist, tied with a cord, over regular clothes. Some fine-woven mats are said to be worth several thousand dollars. I attended the Sunday service in the largest church in Tonga. Men and women each wore a fine mat over other clothes, many carried an umbrella for protection against the hot sun. An elaborate belt is used to tie around the mat. Boys and girls fidgeted with uncomfortable shoes, they often go barefoot. At the end of the service, as the word *amen* left the pastor's mouth, little boys were airborne, in the direction of the door.

In Yugoslavia and several other countries of Eastern Europe, men wore shoes with pointed curled-up toes. They sometimes still wear shoes with curled toes. Until recently, wooden shoes were common in much of Europe, not only Holland. In France, during World War II when there was a shortage of everything, I saw men with wooden shoes. Farmers liked them because they were waterproof. One cold day in Le Havre in 1945, two shivering Frenchmen, one with a long "butcher" knife, tried to rob me of my warm sailors' clothes. I noticed that they wore wooden shoes, so I ran away as fast as I could, expecting to feel that knife in my back at anytime. In much of Europe, Asia, Canada, and the Pacific islands everyone takes off shoes at the entrance door. Then they often wear a soft shoe in the house. This keeps a house much cleaner. Several families that I lived with in Germany and in Quebec, while attending language schools, had a practice of leaving shoes at the door or in a *Schuhschrank*. People in some countries, such as Japan, are very particular as to where and in what position the shoes are placed. Store your shoes in the same manner as the others. A smaller percentage of the people in the world go barefoot than they did 50 years ago. However, it is still common on Pacific Islands, in lesser-developed countries, and for children in summer or in the tropics. The owner of our nice houseboat on Lake Dal in Kashmir, India, was always barefoot, even when frost was on the ground. He wore a business suit and necktie, owned several other businesses, and made frequent business flights to Delhi and Bombay.

Affluent teenagers in North America and Europe often tear out the knees or rear pockets of jeans. In Paris' metro I noticed several men looking at something. It was a pretty teenager. The entire seat of her jeans was torn out. After studying her carefully I concluded that she tore them intentionally, she was not a victim of crime. Not yet! Tokyo's metro had a poster showing a pretty girl wearing shorts. When she left the train at an isolated station in the dark, a half-wolf man leered at her behind bushes. In the U.S. the current clothing fad for youths is baggy pants that droop, looking as if they were about to fall off. In southern Europe, from Greece to Portugal, except in France, older women wear black, as if in mourning even when they have no recently-deceased relative. Women in southern Europe wear dresses, not jeans, except in France. In Italy, except Sicily, many young women wear leather miniskirts that fit tighter than when the cow wore it. Women and girls in Poland, Lithuania, Latvia, and Estonia are perhaps the best-dressed in Europe, wearing pretty dresses.

In Iceland, fishermen wore gloves or mittens with a thumb on each side. The reversible gloves wear twice as long. Men and women today are lucky, with permanent-press clothes and electric steam irons. My mother used flatirons heated on the wood stove. When an iron was no longer hot she put it back onto the stove and used the wooden handle to get a hot iron. Later we became affluent enough to buy a gasoline iron that stayed hot. Goethe's wealthy family of wine merchants in Germany had so many clothes that they did laundry only three times a year. They used a linen press to take wrinkles out of clothes. Many poor men or bachelors in the U.S. press trousers by leaving them under a heavy load of books for a few days. In old Korea women beat clothes with wooden clubs to take out wrinkles. In Germany and other European cities before the days of street lighting, anyone out in the dark was required to carry a light when on the streets. Anyone without a light could be arrested. Members of wealthy families like Goethe's carried two lights, and all persons with only one light had to yield the right-of-way to them. In many villages on Fijian islands only the chief may wear sunglasses or a hat. Visitors are also discouraged from wearing them. Shoulders must be covered in Fiji except when swimming.

In countries of the former Soviet Union, and in most of Eastern Europe, guests must check coats at a theater, restaurant, sports event, museum, or other public place. It makes the meal, visit, or performance much more pleasant. However, after the event crowds wait impatiently to retrieve their coats at the checkstand. After 15 minutes I was finally near the checkstand; in the corner of an eye I saw a stocky Russian woman surging through the crowd to get to the front. She shoved people aside like a Russian tank, and when she hit me I thought she must have been at least an elephant. In old Russia wealthy women had sleeves twice as long as their arms, to show that they did no physical labor. Men did not have pockets, they carried papers, a wallet, and other things under their tall hat. To keep a secret, they were told to "keep it under your hat." In Lithuania, men wore a hat made of big oak leaves. In Bulgaria, men wore an ivy plant on the head. In the South Pacific I have seen boys carry the big leaf of a plant, for the frequent noonday showers. Wealthy people sometimes wear impractical clothes to show that they don't have to work. In Argentina more than 150 years ago, wealthy women wore a *peinelone* on the head—a hat more than two feet in diameter, decorated with mother-of-pearl. The hats were a hazard to anyone not wearing one. In Russia and many other former socialist countries, girls and women to at least age 30, wear a huge bright ribbon in the hair. They are very feminine, usually pretty. In Russia and other European countries more than 100 years ago, queens and rich women wore a dress so long that it trailed six or eight feet behind them. A little girl was usually required to follow, holding up the tail of the dress. In a few museums I was permitted to lift a crown that had been worn by a king or queen. If their duties didn't give them headaches the heavy crown certainly would.

In Fiji, Samoa, and other Pacific islands men and women are tattooed. A man's tattoos sometimes cover almost the entire body. Women said their tattoos end at the thighs. Both men and women said it is painful to be punctured so many times with a needle, and requires at least three months of misery. They said "we have no choice, it must be done." The tattoos are usually hidden by clothes. Missionaries told many Pacific islanders that tattoos are a sin because it makes people with tattoos feel proud. However, islanders no longer follow all orders of missionaries. Young women often have the name of their secondary school and the year of their graduation tattooed on an arm. Only some classes of people could have particular tattoos. In the Marquesas Islands only a chief or a warrior was tattooed on the left ankle. A girl's first tattoo, on the right hand, around the age of 10, indicated that she was old enough to prepare the traditional food. Like many other peoples, the Marquesans believed that evil spirits could enter the body through any natural opening, so tattoos were applied around each opening, such as the lips, nose, eyes, ears, and genital area. On Easter Island during some periods only the oldest son was tattooed. Easter Island tattoos identified the clan and valley where one lived, as tartans in Scotland once identified the clan. The designs of tattoos on the back of Australia's Aborigines are uniform for members of the same totem group. Many wear a Tee shirt covering the tattoos. Along the Amazon River some tribes have both tattoos and beads that they have learned to glue directly onto the skin. On some islands of the Solomons, the face of children, men, and women is scraped with a sharp bone, to make a permanent design. Sometimes black or blue pigment is put into the scratches. The designs are sometimes on the forehead, or below the eyes. Women tattoo the breasts or thighs. In the Pacific, blue pigment from the root of candlenut trees is mixed with coconut oil and rubbed into incisions, to make tattoos. Women in Mali's Fulani (Peul) tribe often have tattoos around the lips and horizontally across the face. They claim that it emphasizes their pale skin which many Africans like. Many African men and women make cuts in the skin and rub in ash to make a permanent mark. Bushmen women in southern Africa typically make the marks on the face, thighs, and buttocks. Youths who are being initiated get the marks on the forehead; if they become a good hunter they get the marks on the face. Men and women in the Pacific and Africa sometimes primp for more than an hour before a dance, putting on body paint, jewelry, and clothes, getting everything just right. On a boat near Shanghai the magician had two pretty young assistants. Only one was needed at a time, the other was constantly busy primping before a hand mirror.

Many people swim or bathe every day. In Scandinavian countries it is common to take a daily sauna, by pouring hot water onto rocks heated by a fire. Men and women often take a sauna bath together, sometimes wearing a towel. Many Native Americans in the U.S. took a daily bath in the sweat lodge, perhaps the idea came from Europe's sauna bath. Ancient Romans built baths in all of their cities. They usually had a hot, a warm, and a cool bath. Air was heated by a wood fire, then it circulated through the hollow floor. Turks built public baths in nearly all of the cities they occupied. Men and women bathed at separate times of the day. For centuries Arabians have had a daily habit of going to the *hamam* or public bath. Historians say "Europe went a thousand years without a bath" during the Middle Ages. They bathed at birth and death, sometimes at no other time. Some priests said it was a "sin" to take a bath. Today Germans and many Central Europeans regularly spend weekends or a vacation at bath resorts. Most of the baths are warm or hot and have minerals. Soaking in them is said to be good for rheumatism and many other ailments. Many German towns include the word *Bad* in their name—bath. New Zealand also has many popular baths. Thermopolis, Wyoming, the "world's largest hot mineral springs," has a wonderful system of mineral water baths, but they have never been so popular in the U.S. as in Europe. Polynesian islands in Tahiti, the Marquesas, and elsewhere had "sacred pools," usually near where a stream comes from a grotto. It was considered especially important to bathe there. Grotto Vairoa on Makatea Atoll in the Tuamotus is a typical grotto with a sacred bath. Polynesians were very clean, they bathed several times a day in the warm, humid climate. Even today, Polynesians who work in laundries often refuse to handle the underwear of other people, each person washes his/her own underwear. Tahitians thought the unwashed British sailors smelled awful. Deodorant was rare everywhere until this century. In

New Orleans, well-dressed men and women wore a *tussil mussie*, a clip holding a small bouquet of flowers. Japanese buy machines for the home that check the smell of the breath and rate it from bad to good. If it is bad the testor is advised to brush and clean teeth, use a mouthwash, or see a dentist.

School uniforms are common in Asia, the Pacific, Latin America, Islamic countries, Ireland, the United Kingdom, the former Soviet Union, and Eastern Europe. Most of the uniforms are handsome and practical. They tend to equalize children so the rich don't flaunt expensive clothes. Children are usually proud of their uniform, are better disciplined, and have fewer fights than children without uniforms. I was in Greece when the government decided to follow most of Western Europe in not requiring the uniforms. Many students were very unhappy with the decision, they preferred the uniforms. Very poor families say they cannot afford to buy uniforms, so their children don't go to school. In China uniforms are usually required only in the cities, not in villages. Local people in Vietnam and Kashmir, Gypsies in Bulgaria and Romania, and some families in Mexico said they cannot afford more than one outfit of clothes for each child; consequently, when the clothes are being laundered the child must stay home. However, the very poor children would be needed to sell things, or to work in the fields or shop, to support the family, even if uniforms were free.

Jewelry

Museums are full of beautiful jewelry made long ago, with gold, silver, and precious or semi-precious stones. They equal the best jewelry made today. St. Petersburg's Hermitage Museum has the "Gold Room," with jewelry dating mostly from 3,000 BCE to 200 BCE. There are gold belts, animals, coins, hatchets (to hold a polished stone), swords (for a bronze blade), scabbards, alligators, combs with long teeth, earrings, and more. Most of them were made in Greece, Turkey, Russia, or Siberia. The big Faubergé eggs are gold with precious stones. Lima's Archaeological Museum has a magnificent "Gold Room" with jewelry and pots that the Spanish somehow failed to loot and melt down. We were told that in mainland China the best jewelry made over thousands of years by China's great civilization had been stolen by Chiang Kai Shek and taken to Taiwan. We then went to Taiwan's Palace Museum to see it. Seventeen balls, each inside the other, were carved from one piece of ivory. Seventy-nine cups were carved, each inside the others, from a single block of wood. Several museums and tourist shops in China have a grain of rice under a magnifying glass. An entire village has been carefully carved in detail on one grain! Jewelry factories and shops in Sri Lanka, Johannesburg, and Amsterdam have also brought out the best in diamonds, sapphires, rubies, and other precious stones. Istanbul's Topkapi Palace has the sultan's treasury, with the "world's largest uncut emerald," almost the size of a football, weighing seven pounds. It has the Spoonmaker Diamond with 86 karats, a night light made from a huge diamond with a hole for a candle, the Topkapi Dagger with four big emeralds for a handle, chain-mail armor loaded with jewels, and much more. Bulgaria's Rila Monastery has a wooden cross with 60 scenes from the New Testament and 300 detailed tiny faces—each is the size of a grain of rice!

In Yemen, men in the northern hill tribes wear a *jambiya* or curved dagger on the outside of a robe or other clothes. It is always worn in front, with a wide decorated belt. Local people can tell which tribe the man comes from by the dagger's design. They like to have a handle made of rhino horn, even though this leads to killing of rhinoceros by poachers. In Oman, some men wear a smaller curved dagger, the *khanjar*. In India women often wear a brass or gold nose pin, plus several bracelets. High school girls wear a brass or gold nose pin, earrings, and pigtails. A wedding ring is worn on the right hand in some countries, on the left in others. When a woman divorces or her husband dies, she moves the ring to a finger on the other hand in several countries. In Vietnam men wear a wedding ring on the left hand, women wear it on the right. Some men in Vanuatu wear a curled pigs' tusk or a round shell on the upper arm for each wife. Women in many Asian and African countries wear much of their wealth, in the form of jewelry. It is the only real security for some women. Fulani (Peul) women in West Africa usually wear large gold earrings. I noticed that many are aluminum, painted with gold paint. Women in another West Africa tribe, the Tuaregs, wear a lot of silver jewelry. Tuareg men often carry a silver sword. To keep wind-blown sand out of the mouth and nose they wear a hand-woven cloth dyed indigo blue with dye they make from leaves of a tree. In Latin American countries during periods of high inflation middle-class and wealthy families keep most of their wealth in the form of jewelry or U.S. dollars. Men on Vanuatu's Banks Island wear earrings made of a stick. Some Indian tribes in the U.S. Southwest, including the Navajo, are wonderful silversmiths and jewelers. Women wear heavy silver jewelry with semi-precious stones. In China and Japan parents often give a daughter much jewelry, inherited or bought over a period of many years. In India, Sikh men can be identified by the "five Ks" they wear: the *kesha* or long hair in a turban, the *kangle* or comb, the *kacha* or knee-length breeches—often replaced by a business suit, the *karm* or steel bracelet, and the *kirga* or sword, often small and only symbolic. In the U.S. and Europe women often wear necklaces, including one with the Christian cross. Not long ago many people wore a rabbits foot for good luck. In West Africa many people wear a *grigris* charm around the neck to keep off evil spirits. Some people have several. The *juju* charms they wear are often made of cowry shells. Boys sometimes wear a necklace with leather lockets that have been blessed by the medicine man. They are said to protect the boy against all kinds of bad luck, from snakebite to drowning.

Nudity

Public nudity is illegal in Islamic countries, and most of North America and Latin America. However, the cover of the telephone directory for Manaus, Brazil, capital of the huge state of Amazonia, was risqué. It showed in color many nude women riding horses, calling them "Amazons." The swim suits worn by the *cariocas* of Rio de Janiero covered only the bare essentials when I visited Copacabana Beach as a sailor in 1945. The *tongas*, three little triangles, were worn later. Our hotel room in Istanbul had a painting showing four girls, age about eleven, leaving a bath, wearing tall clog shoes but nothing else. Our family hotel in Perth, Australia had a painting of "schoolgirls" age about 10, nude and anatomically correct. Women tourists visiting beaches or swimming pools in Europe, Africa, much of Asia, many islands, and Australia often are topless. Those wearing a top are usually from the U.S. or Great Britain, countries that still suffer from a puritanical period. It is common to see topless young women sunning themselves on university campuses and in isolated parts of city parks throughout Europe, Australia, Canada, and even in parts of the U.S. Most Europeans, Africans, Pacific Islanders, and Australians are much more casual about public nudity than are people in the U.S.

"Willie," a Highlands' man in Papua New Guinea, dressed like most of the local men: a skirt made of woven *pitpit grass* in front and big leaves of *arse grass* in the rear, a knife made of the leg bone of a *cassowary* (a fowl larger than a turkey), leg bands and arm bands, necklace, no shirt, a decorated woven bilum (bag) on his shoulder, a big wig of hair grown by another man, and a headband made of feathers, including two feathers each more than two feet long, from a bird of paradise. Willie was hired 10 years ago by the government tourist bureau to travel and tell people about his great country. Dressed in his usual clothes he rode taxis and stayed in nice European hotels with no problem. In Orlando, Florida, management in the hotel where he had reservations told him "You can't stay here. You're naked." Willie said he answered "You come to my country, and we'll make war." In the Marquesas Islands the sexiest dance was the *toe heva*, done by a new bride, who took off the tapa cloth skirt made for her wedding. Missionaries banned the nude dance. Argentina's Museum of Patagonia in San Carlos de Bariloche has exhibits about local Indians. They liked to play *chucea*, hitting a ball made of native rubber with a long stick. Men and women played almost nude, while drinking homemade beer. The games usually ended with what the colonial Spanish called "indecent behavior," and the game was banned.

Nudes are common on some beaches in France, Italy, Eastern Europe, Bali, many other islands of the Atlantic and Pacific, and Australia. I was surprised on the busy beach of Nice, France, where I stayed for two months, when a beautiful girl arrived, took off her street clothes, but had no bathing suit. She wore only a necklace and a wrist watch. On the crowded beach at La Grande Motte several more modest women wore full-size one-piece swim suits, but they were transparent. I have seen many nudes in city parks in Berlin, Munich, and other German cities. When I went to school one summer in East Germany, local boys and girls, ages up to eight or nine, regularly played nude in fountains on hot days. When I shopped in a supermarket in Weimar a girl about 11 or 12, wearing only blue jeans, rode her bike in to buy a few groceries. No one else seemed to notice her. In Quebec's Pointe-Taillon National Park I went for a hike on a warm day. I saw at least a hundred young women and men loafing or playing volleyball. They were all nude, near a sign that stated in French, "Public Nudity is a crime." A park ranger sat, watching them. I also sat there awhile, to help him observe the law-breakers. One attractive girl bounced around as she played volleyball. The first time my wife and I stayed at Australia's Gold Coast we checked into a hotel just behind two pretty university girls. A few minutes later I saw them swimming in the hotel's outside pool, without swim suits. I decided that it was time for a swim. One area of Bali's big Kutu Beach often has nudes. When we walked past a woman lying on her back, my wife, a physician, said "She looks 10 months pregnant. Let's hurry. I don't want to have to deliver a baby." I expected the baby's head to pop out at any moment.

In warm Lesser-Developed non-Islamic countries, boys and girls ages six to eight rarely wear any clothes. When African children appear in a color photograph they seem to be only shadows with eyes and white teeth. Along Mali's Niger and Bani rivers women wash clothes and swim without clothes. When my wife and I walked in front of the president's palace on a street in Ouagadougou, capital of Burkina Faso, we met a man without any clothes. He was apparently just in from the "bush," where we had seen many people unencumbered with clothing. In Kenya we returned in the van to warn five or six women and a dozen children, all swimming nude, that a big crocodile just slid into the river, heading their way. They said they weren't afraid of "crocs." A girl about 15 held my hand and asked for bonbons as we walked half an hour in a village of the Bozo tribe on Mali's Niger River. Her bare breasts were longer and more pointed than the tail fins of a 1959 Cadillac. Unfortunately, I had no candy. Girls and women in South Africa's Zulu tribe are taught that if she wears clothes during a dance it indicates a loose moral life. Nude dancing shows that her body is pure, that she has led a moral life. A girl is expected to be a virgin until she marries, but her lover is permitted to thoroughly explore her naked body. They are supervised by older girls to see that there is no actual sexual intercourse. In most lesser-developed countries and tropical islands where missionaries are weak everyone is casual about public nudity. On a flight from Bangkok to Calcutta, the 18-month-old boy next to me had no clothes. When he pointed in my direction I used a magazine as a shield. Many babies in China wear clothes completely open at the rear, diapers are rarely used. Almost anything soft has been used as diapers, including rags in Latin America, and moss or cattails in North America.

Rome's emperors built huge baths to get popular support. At various times men and women bathed together without clothes. Emperor Augustus complained that too much time was wasted in the baths, so he ordered that men and women swim at different times, or in segregated pools. Later emperors again permitted mixed nude bathing. In Germany, *Baden*, hot mineral baths, have long been popular. Wilbad has an exhibit showing that in the 16th Century nude bathing of men and women together in big wooden tubs like a hot tub was popular. Later they had to wear a bathing costume. Men, women, and children of China's Lugu Lake area bathe nude in a big hot pool some six miles (10 km.) north of the lake. The pool looks polluted. When the Christian church was strong in Europe artists could show the nude female figure only in the context of a religious setting from the Bible. If they failed to name the painting after a Biblical man, woman, or setting the painting could not be displayed in public. A layman or priest could then examine at length a realistic painting of a beautiful nude woman, without committing a sin. The Ludwig Museum in Cologne, Germany has a popular painting showing a priest bathing pretty young maidens 11 or 12 years old for their baptism. Germans said the priest did his job slowly and thoroughly.

My wife and I spent 10 days on a boat in the Galapagos Islands with a group of young Europeans. Several times we went swimming, with sharks or fur seals. There was no place to hide to change into swim suits. In tropical French Guiana, my wife and I went on an excursion with a group of young French men and women, we are fluent in French. We traveled in a big dugout canoe on two rivers. After lunch we hiked a mile or so on a trail through the jungle to a stream with a waterfall and a slide. It was hot and muggy. Several people said we should go for a swim. No one had a swim suit. Someone said *pas de problème*. Soon they were frolicking nude in the refreshing water. Being more practical than puritanical, we decided to join them.

In Greece, Romania, the former Yugoslavia, Hungary, other countries of Eastern Europe, Austria, Spain, and more, magazine covers, at all levels in kiosks, display front views of nudes. Madrid's largest newspaper had color comics, one showed a couple coupling. The families that I lived with in France often watched TV. One ad featured an attractive young model. As she held various products for sale, her clothes fell off one by one. When she had completed the commercial and lost all of her clothes the men had forgotten what products she advertised. During one dinner hour two young women and a man frolicked, each wearing only a tiny sign with the symbol of the TV station. My French family were aghast when, in horseplay, they tore away the little signs. TV programs in Italy and Germany often show topless women, and a billboard that I passed every day when going to school in Cologne had a topless woman in an ad. Some hotels in Canada wisely distribute free condoms. Canada, like countries in Western Europe, has a lower rate of AIDS and venereal diseases than the U.S.

Although native people in much of Africa and the Pacific are nude or almost nude, they usually don't like visitors to be nude or almost nude. Women visitors are expected to wear a blouse and a long skirt. African and Pacific islands' men are often "turned on" more by seeing a woman's thighs than her breasts. Women of the Big Namba tribe in Vanuatu often do not cover their breasts, but it is taboo for them to be seen without a long headdress.

Sex

Man has believed that many foods and herbs serve as an aphrodisiac. Many East Asians and some Mexicans believe that snake, in various forms, is an aphrodisiac. In Taiwan, on Tapei's "Snake street" I watched men drink the blood of a live snake, with alcohol as a chaser. They believe it makes them more potent. Mexican men put dried ground rattlesnake into a drink to become more virile. Chinese men believe the sea cucumber or *bêche de mer* is an aphrodisiac; gathering and drying it for shipment provides an income for many Pacific islanders. Some East Asians add deer fetus to the tea of a girlfriend. In Taiwan a package of rare dried mushrooms, claimed to be an aphrodisiac, sells for more than 5,000 U.S. dollars for a few ounces. Tea sold with the flavor of those mushrooms is not quite so expensive. In Yemen most men chew khat, but only married men are permitted to chew clove with it. They claim that the combination produces an immediate erection. The *durian* is a bad-smelling but sweet fruit, common in Southeast Asia. Local men say "When the durians go down the sarongs go up." However, signs in hotels in southern Asia often warn that durian is prohibited, because it smells awful. Chinese use roots of the ginseng plant to relieve stress, and men believe it helps to make sex better. In the past, unmarried Chinese girls were not permitted to use rhinoceros powder, considered to be an aphrodisiac. They thought it would make a girl sterile unless she had a man. Korea, Taiwan, and other East Asia countries buy the velvet on deer antlers, from New Zealand deer farms, to use as an aphrodisiac. As a young merchant seaman near the end of

World War II old sailors told me that if I put "Spanish Fly" into a girl's drink or food she would be mine. I never tried it.

It is common in many mountain villages in Laos, Thailand, and on Pacific islands that a husband and wife have sex only in the garden, to help make the garden grow better. Egyptian pharaohs had sex in temples to help make crops more fertile. The Temple of Luxor has a typical carving in stone showing Ramses II making an offering to Min, god of fertility. Min has an erect penis almost as long as his arm. In Ireland I visited several holy wells. Long before Celts and Druids arrived around 3500 years ago, a king was expected to mate with the goddess of the well to insure good crops. Celts celebrated a three-day Fire Festival at the end of July and early August at the holy wells. Local women still leave a gift at a holy well. In rural County Cornwall, England, May Day is celebrated with a parade, as in much of Europe. A man and a girl often dance together for 24 hours, hidden in a cage designed to look like a horse. If the girl becomes pregnant she says "the horse did it." In Australia's Great Barrier Reef, the sea polyps, sea cucumbers, and other marine animals select one night a year, usually the eleventh full moon, in November, to inject eggs and sperm into the water, like human beings at a big party. Several types of male fish at the Great Barrier Reef, the Galapagos Islands, and elsewhere bite off the genitals of other males, so they will have less competition. The bitten fish then become females. Angel fish, common in tropical seas, can change their sex by eating algae. In the Galapagos Islands big marine turtles are allowed only about 10 minutes to mate. After that, several males waiting in line bite the shell of the busy male to drive him off. The females are larger, they can stay under water longer than males, so they sometimes stay submerged half an hour to drive away a male. During several trips to the former Soviet Union and Russia, young local women approached me and other men in my group in the bar of a tourist hotel. They offered "fun" for dollars or rubles. I was always wary, they may be under-*the*-cover KGB agents.

Mali's Dogon tribe carve masks of their ancestors and make crude pottery figures of ancestors, but they also show a great depth of spiritual feeling. Some Dogon villages that I visited have beautifully carved door panels and door locks, as well as carved wooden bowls. Kenya and several other African countries have similar carvings. Perhaps the most common mask in Africa is carved to look like an antelope head. In Papua New Guinea's Lowlands along the Sepik River men have made beautiful artistic wood carvings for generations, using only primitive tools. Today they use a pocketknife. A big portion of the statues are a male with exaggerated genitals. The men's house in Sepik River villages often has a carving of a nude woman with her legs spread apart—a fertility symbol. In the Solomon Islands wood carvings often show a mythological dog that is believed to have taught the islanders how to fish, hunt, build houses, and to live with nature. Their carvings also show *Kesoko*, a god, with a head and beak like a bird. Ancient man carved pictures of the female vulva or male penis on rocks in much of the world. A typical example is the many petroglyphs on Easter Island, of the vulva or penis. Incas at the Kenco Amphitheater near Cuzco, Peru sacrificed animals near a big phallic stone and a carving of a snake—a fertility symbol—on a flat rock.

In Europe and Latin America few young persons can afford a car of their own. They hug and kiss passionately in movie theaters, parks, alleys, or dark doorways. In the U.S. outdoor movie theaters or "Drive-ins" were called "passion pits," but few remain. In the Nineteenth Century few homes in the U.S. had more than one heated room in winter. When a young man "courted" his girlfriend, they were often permitted to go to bed alone in a room fully clothed, with a "bundling board" between them. Pregnancies and "shotgun marriages" were common, perhaps there were knotholes in the bundling board. On "White Day," March 14 (like our Valentine's Day), a Japanese man often gives a pair of panties to a girlfriend or to a girl he would like to meet. The panties are sold in vending machines, like almost everything else in Japan. They often include printed romantic messages. Tokyo has many brightly lighted *LOVE* hotels where a couple can rent a room for an hour or more, with no questions asked. Near Rome's *termini* railway station many hotels rent rooms by the hour. Guides in Dublin say that sweet Molly Malone, who sold live mussels and cockles, also sold herself. They call her statue "the tart with a cart."

Prostitution is legal and somewhat regulated in much of the world. However, there is still a big risk of sexually transmitted disease. The buyer, or renter, must be wary. Everyone knows the location of the red-light district(s) in Hamburg, Copenhagen, Vienna, Paris, Amsterdam, Bombay, and Bangkok. Tunisia is known by Europeans for the *three s's*: sun, sand, and sex. In the U.S. only a few counties in Nevada have legal prostitution. Thailand and the Dominican Republic are said to have more prostitutes than any other country, but they also have a high rate of AIDS—not far behind central Africa. Many of the girls who work above shops in Bangkok are as young as 12 years old. Recruiters often go to villages in the north where people have a lighter-colored skin. When they find a poor farmer with a pretty young daughter the recruiter offers around 500 dollars cash for the girl. The farmer accepts the offer and signs papers to mortgage the home. The money goes quickly. If the girl leaves the recruiter's place or refuses to work the mortgage is foreclosed and the family lose their home. However, most of the girls seem to be happy, primping, wearing silk dresses, and living in the glamorous city.

Cuba was the playground of the rich and the middle-class men from the U.S. from the 1920s until the late 1950s. The girls were pretty and inexpensive. Since the U.S. blockade of Cuba began in 1962 few men from the U.S. now go to Cuba. However, it is a popular and inexpensive vacation spot for people from nearly all other countries of the world. Most Cubans are suffering from shortages of food and everything else, but those with a few U.S. dollars can live and eat well. Each evening during a recent visit I noticed many pretty *señoritas* looking for a customer, along the busy streets and in or near every tourist hotel. During my first trips to Panama as a sailor, in 1945, Cash Street was the red-light district of Cristobal. When a man walked by, young women held up three fingers, older women held up two fingers, signifying their price in dollars. Prostitution is perhaps the only occupation where a premium is paid for the young and inexperienced. When city officials in Fairbanks, Alaska prohibited the use of red lights, girls grew red geraniums in summer in the window of their establishment. The brothel of a replica of a Nineteenth Century Western U.S. town in Bend, Oregon, did not have a red light. It had a bell to ring to call "Mona." A customer "rang her bell." Girls who worked upstairs above the Red Dog Saloon in Skagway each had a doll hung on the wall above the bar, with her name. The girl took the doll with her when she left. A customer selected one of the remaining dolls. "Dolly's House" in Ketchikan, Alaska, was where the "sporting ladies" worked. However, they were always lying down on the job.

Censorship of novels and other writings considered to discuss explicit sex, or of paintings that were too sexy, was common in Europe and the U.S. until recently. Even in "liberal" France the first public exhibition of Ingres' 1862 painting *The Turkish Bath* was delayed for 43 years because it was too daring, showing a room full of nudes. The Roman Catholic Church in Boston maintained a list of novels and other writings that it considered to be immoral. A book or movie that was "banned in Boston" because of its sexual content got a lot of publicity but often could not be sold. Famous novels that had trouble in Boston or the courts included D.H. Lawrence's *Lady Chatterley's Lover*, Henry Miller's *Tropic of Cancer* and his *Tropic of Capricorn*, and Vladimir Nabokov's *Lolita*. In the late 1950s decisions of the U.S. Supreme Court began to uphold the legality of many writings, so long as the explicit sex did not appeal "primarily to prurient interests" and it had "redeeming social value."

Many of us believe that modern man in the Americas and Europe is too obsessed with sex. Some of the ancients were also. Much of the Greek pottery 2500 years old has clear pictures of a couple coupling. In Hanoi, Vietnam, the museum has a large bronze kettle also 2500 years old. The handles on the lid are molded bronze couples, with the woman on top. Museums in Lima, Peru have pottery of the *Mochico* and *Chimu* cities with drawings or statues of men with women, and men with men, in various positions. The Spanish thought they were immoral and destroyed all they could find. Some were hidden. Many of India's temples have hundreds of *bas reliefs* or statues carved in stone showing the *Gupta lovers* and others making love. The "Marriage Hall" of the Varadarajapermal Temple near Madras, and the Khajuraho Temples in the northeast are best-known. Hindu stone statues and bas reliefs are "anatomically correct," showing every detail. India never had a Victorian period. A carved phallic symbol or *lingam* often represents Shiva, and a voluptuous statue of his consort Parvati represents the *yoni* or female vulva. In Sri Lanka, Sigiriya has many Fifth Century paintings of voluptuous topless maidens. Crete's palaces had many frescoes 3,800 years old of topless maidens in white, and topless men in red. In Lebanon, the Temple of Bacchus at Balbak was dimly lighted, popular long before the ancient Romans arrived. Each daughter of nobles regularly did *bacchanalian* dances there, then participated in orgies, sacrificing her virginity to the first man approaching her after the dance.

The U.S. lags far behind Canada and most European countries in educating children about sex. Some people believe that to educate children will encourage them to have more sex. In France and a few other countries, government notices on TV show in detail how to use a condom. The U.S. lags far behind in the distribution of free condoms. The U.S. also has one of the world's highest rates of teenage pregnancies and of unplanned pregnancies. It has the highest rate of AIDS infections of all industrial countries. Some other countries give even less sex education to children than does the U.S. They include Islamic countries and most Latin American countries. In the "Bible Belt" of the Pacific where missionaries have been strong it is often taboo to talk about sex between parents and children, and between a male and a female.

In traditional societies in Africa, the Pacific, Southeast Asia, and elsewhere, children learn about sex at a young age. A family often lives in one room, and children see and hear their parents engaged in sexual intercourse. They also see brothers, sisters, and neighbor children or adults nude. Farm children who care for animals quickly learn the importance of breeding at the proper time. Traditional cultures do not have the belief that many Christians have, that sex is sinful, except with a husband or wife. To them, sex is natural, like eating and sleeping. If a girl gets pregnant, it will not hurt her reputation or her later chances for marriage. If she has a baby, relatives or other villagers will gladly take care of it. Many girls in Thailand who work in massage parlors, dance halls, and brothels do not feel guilt or shame by earning their living by renting their body. In Java my wife and I stayed a few days in a hotel on the beach near a rural farm and fishing village. Teenage village girls often asked to give me a "massage," especially when my wife left briefly to go swimming alone. Indonesia is officially an

Islamic country, but religion is of less importance than having fun and earning money.

It was not uncommon in traditional societies for a host to offer a guest his wife for the night or longer. Marco Polo was a great traveler who went overland from Venice to China in the Thirteenth Century. He stayed in Asia many years, then returned, reporting the many strange customs he found. Polo reported that in "Kamul, in the province of Tangut" (northwest China) when strangers arrived it was customary for the husband to offer his wife and daughters to them for the night. The "handsome" women were said to be honored to sleep with a stranger. It was also common to have "temporary marriages" along the main caravan routes in Asia. Polo reported that women in Pem (Peyn), now Turkestan, had the right to sleep with any man if the husband was away for 20 days or more. Men gone for 20 days were expected to sleep with any willing woman. The temporary trading of wives with a guest was common in Africa. When Samuel Baker and his blond wife, Florence, explored the upper Nile in 1863 one of their hosts, King Bunyoro (in today's Sudan), was amazed when the Bakers refused his request that they trade wives. When missionary John Harris arrived in the Marquesas Islands in 1797 the chief sent his wife to sleep with Harris. When he refused the amazed woman brought her friends to inspect Harris' genitals, to see if he really was a man. The terrified Harris left the island the next day. When Lewis and Clark explored the new northwest territories of the U.S. in 1805, they spent the first cold winter in a village of the Mandan Indians, in what is now North Dakota. Men in the village encouraged their wives and daughters to sleep with the White men and with Lewis' Black slave. The women were happy to comply. Australian miners in the mid-1930s discovered that several hundred thousand people lived in the Highlands of Papua New Guinea, an area that had been unexplored and was thought to be empty of people. The Stone-Age natives thought the White men were their ancestors, and they were amazed at their technology. Men regularly offered their wives and daughters to the White men, in exchange for valuable steel knives or axes.

Some conservative cultures have a time of the year when promiscuity is ignored or even encouraged. Rio de Janiero, New Orleans, a few other Latin American cities, and many French- speaking areas have a *mardi gras*, usually beginning the last Tuesday before the strict Roman Catholic Lent. The mardi gras is celebrated with a carnival, parades, skimpy costumes, and street dances. When people are disguised, as they often are, there is more drinking and general *iddish* behavior, thus attracting people from far away. The Bai minority group in China's Yunnan province have a three-day annual festival, usually beginning on the 15th day of the third month of the Chinese Lunar Year—often April 15. Men and women are disguised. We were told that it is common for a husband and a wife to leave each other during the festival, searching in disguise for other lovers.

In the Seychelles Islands rain on the day of a wedding indicates that the bride is not a virgin. It often rains there. One visitor described the girls of St. Helena in the South Atlantic as "promiscuous." I found many of the girls to be pretty, with skin colors from chocolate to white. Even the most promiscuous is considered to be a "saint"—all residents of St. Helena are called "Saints." On the Caribbean islands of St. Thomas and St. Croix even the prostitutes are "virgins," like everyone else who lives in the Virgin Islands.

In the Nineteenth Century, whalers and other sailors liked to visit Maui, Tahiti, and other Polynesian islands. Pretty girls without clothes swam to the anchored ships and offered sex for a nail. In the Eighteenth Century, the girls offered their services free, but they soon learned the value of nails in their Stone-Age culture. Some ships lost so many nails they were no longer seaworthy. When missionaries in Lahaina, Maui, ordered the girls to keep away from the ships the disgruntled sailors shot cannon balls at the town.

CHAPTER 7:
FOLK DANCES & PERSONAL PRACTICES

Folk Dances

Folk dances tell us a lot about a culture. Dances depict things that are important in peoples lives: dances of hunters and fishermen hoping for success and to pay respect to the souls of the animals or fish captured, war dances to whip up men's bravery, planting and harvest dances, marriages, births, circumcisions, and deaths. A typical harvest dance of four hours or more in the South Pacific honors the yam harvest. Hunters' dancers often mimic the animal or bird hunted. Sometimes men do a shamans' or medicine man dance. Women show how graceful they are or skills they have acquired in carrying things on the head. Men show their athletic skills and strength, and sometimes show skill at throwing knives, shooting arrows, or cracking a whip. In a dance popular in Mexico, a man and a woman, using only their feet, tie a knot in a big scarf lying on the floor. The hat dance, with one or two dancers circling a big hat on the floor, is also a favorite. In Yukon Territory women do the cancan that gold miners liked—they lift up a long dress and petticoats, kicking the legs high. Around the Fifteenth Century, when the sad Quechuas or "Incas" incorporated the fun-loving Commenchinga and Saraviron tribes of northern Argentina, the Incas ordered a stop to dances of nude men and women that continued for days, getting wilder each day.

In Southeast Asia, women sometimes dance while carrying a lighted candle in each hand. In Cambodia the Khymer Rouge regime under Pol Pot killed anyone they could find who was educated or trained in the arts. However, two middle-aged dance teachers escaped, lived in the hilly jungle a few years, and returned to Phnom Penh to teach traditional dances. I watched the students for several hours. For the examination, advanced students chose to act out stories from the *Ramayana*, a delightful set of stories. Each hand and arm, foot and leg, and the entire body must have exactly the right position to tell the story without words. Most of the graceful dances in Bali come from the Ramayana or the Balinese *Malat* stories. The classical dances of India are just as graceful, women wear a sarong, bracelets, tinkling bells on the ankles, and move the hands, arms, feet, and entire body in motions learned only by years of practice. In China and other Buddhist countries the lion dance is popular. One man is at the head of the lion's costume, another is at the tail. The lion is considered to be a protector of Buddhism. Loud cymbals are clashed and drums are beaten, to drive away demons.

Near Tozeur, Tunisia, a Berber woman danced with two jugs, one above the other, on her head, plus four sets, one above the other, with three Coke bottles on each set! In Asunción, Paraguay, a woman with three wine bottles on top of her head danced, lay down, rolled over, got up, and danced more, without touching the bottles with a hand! Three more wine bottles were added, one above the other, and she danced, again without touching the bottles!

During each trip to Ireland I have seen several dance programs. The girls usually wear expensive dresses with bright-colored designs drawn by monks 12 centuries ago in the *Book of Kells*. They danced fast reels with soft shoes, and stamped the floor with heavy shoes during hornpipes. Hands are kept stiffly at the sides in most dances, but the legs fly high and fast. Hands can be used in older *sean nos* dances and in some modern dances. Until recently Irish cottages had a floor made of packed dirt or stone. For a dance the doors were temporarily removed for a dance floor. Scots dance to the stirring music of bagpipes, often prancing with one arm held into the air, bent at the elbow. Bagpipes are still common in much of Central and Eastern Europe and in Ireland. For the *cueca*, popular in Chile and Argentina, men wear heavy boots and stamp the floor, as in Ireland's hornpipe. In the cueca, girls often twirl a handkerchief and flirt. In Chile and Argentina, dances may not begin until close to midnight, and parents bring small children with them rather than hire a baby sitter. It is cruel and unusual punishment for both the children and other guests. Finns say that the most graceful of all dances, the tango, originated in Finland. However, the Argentines have perfected it. We saw several sexy tango programs in Buenos Aires. In Islamic countries Gypsy men and women are hired to perform dances at weddings and feasts. I have watched belly dancers in Cairo, Morocco, and Istanbul. The gyrations of the hips can be almost as sexy as Spain's flamenco dance, popular with Gypsy women, or the hula dances in the South Pacific. In the more fundamental Islamic countries only men dance. In Yemen, men in long "gowns" dance forward and backward, hand in hand, often brandishing a jambiya knife with a curved blade. In Oman three young women in long dresses sang and made mild hip movements.

Missionaries fighting "sin" tamed many of the wild sexy dances of the Pacific but they are being revived on some islands. On some Vanuatu islands where missionaries are still strong women are not permitted to dance. In the U.S. some Christian groups prohibit all dancing, while other churches sponsor supervised dances. I was told in Vanuatu that some girls have their first menstrual period while watch-

ing some of the sexier dances by men. I have watched *tamure* dances
on Polynesian islands, where women dance suggestively around a man,
or men dance around a woman. Today each woman wears at least a
grass skirt. As the drums beat louder and faster the hips move fast,
faster, and faster. Grass skirts drop even lower on the hips, I keep waiting for one to fall off. In some Vanuatu men's dances they make a
noise like bees buzzing; it is said to be the spirit of their ancestors. It
reminded me of Bali's *Kecak* dance, where men chant *chuka, chuka,
chuka* while dancers enact one of the stories in the *Ramayana*. In the
Marquesas Islands the *haka* or pig dance is popular—men make a noise
like a grunting pig while dancing standing, then squatting. Women
usually dance in the background. Dancers are said to get the *mana* or
power of the pig. On some Melanesian islands only men can dance,
women cannot. On Vanuatu's Tanna Island in the *toka* dance men capture a woman and toss her high into the air many times, feeling for her
private parts. Some men believe they are entitled for the night to any
woman they catch. A husband must be alert to protect his wife. Any
woman present is likely to be pinched, a tactic also used by men in
Italy. At least one man in each village grows his hair long for the toka
dance. It often lasts four days and nights, and ends with the arrival of a
large totem on a pole—a sex symbol. Girls on Tanna Island do the
"hen and chick dance." In a dance in the traditional kastom village of
Yakel some 30 men dance in a circle, stamping their feet in unison so
the ground vibrates 20 steps away. Girls and women dance around the
outside edge, jumping up and down. Everyone claps hands, but only
the men sing. Men wear only a *namba*, a fiber penis shield that curves
upward, fastened to a waist belt. Women wear only a brief grass skirt.
In the Atlantic Ocean's Cape Verde Islands men and women dancers
like to dance alone in a circle, frequently meeting to bump abdomens
together. Shops sell pottery male and female dolls with their abdomens stuck together.

The moran of the Masai tribe in Kenya and Tanzania like to
dance. The young men wearing ocher-dyed robes jump high into the
air, often while carrying a spear. Girls wearing many brightly-colored
bead necklaces dance on the sidelines, swaying the upper part of the
body back and forth so the necklaces bounce into the air. Hottentots in
South Africa also dance a lot, the women are in the outside of the
circle. Sometimes the dances last all night, like dances of many North
American Indians. I enjoy watching the dances at meetings of various
tribes. Children also dance for hours, lifting one leg, then the other as
they move in a circle with the adults. North American Indian tribes
have great differences, some eat primarily salmon, some eat sheep,
some eat other foods. Members of the tribes have their own pecking
order. Once my wife and I went to dances with a Navajo friend, whom

I shall call Naomi. One of her friends from another tribe greeted Naomi, commenting that "you Yakimas have a strange way of dancing." When the friend left we asked Naomi why she didn't tell her friend that she, Naomi, was Navajo, not Yakima. Naomi answered "I didn't want to brag." The Sun Dance was popular with most Plains Indians of the U.S. but the U.S. military prohibited it because missionaries said it was a "pagan ceremony" and the Indians must become Christians. I never saw the dance but many books describe it. It was usually performed in the late spring or early summer. A virgin was selected to chop down the tree that would become the big Sun Dance pole. The dance lasted four days and nights, inside a big lodge with the big pole in the center. No one ate, or drank alcohol, during the four days. The songs, dances, and paintings represented the earth, sky, stars, the buffalo, war, and more. There were mock battles. One result was that the dance helped to unify the tribe. The U.S. military prohibited meetings of some warlike tribes, such as the Sioux, and the Sun Dance could be done only in a tribal meeting.

Sometimes acrobatic skills are amazing. In Burma, a girl of about 18 juggled a soccer ball, then a tennis ball also, while standing on a pedestal, jumping a rope! Several countries have a dance in which two men or two women bang together two long poles. Dancers step into and out of the poles. If they are out of step a broken foot or ankle may result. I have watched this dance with bamboo poles in Malaysia, Thailand, the Philippines, and in southern China. It is also a popular dance in the U.S. at meetings of tribes of Native Americans. Bamboo is scarce in the U.S., so ordinary poles are used. Did ancestors of the Native Americans bring this dance with them long ago from Asia?

Many peoples are accustomed to singing in groups, or even when walking or working alone. On Italian streets I have heard many potential Carusos. Zulus and several other African tribes, Pacific islanders, and many minority groups in southern China have, for many generations, enjoyed singing, alone or in groups. Christian missionaries took advantage of this natural talent by teaching them some of the beautiful Christian hymns. Song books in Fiji, Tonga, and Samoa often do not have musical scales, only a rough guide as to the pitch. However, it is a treat to hear them sing in church. Before radio and television was common, families in the U.S. and Europe entertained themselves by singing songs, usually with the accompaniment of a piano, guitar, or harmonica. Many of China's 55 minority groups, living mostly in southern or western China, entertain themselves by singing alone or in groups. The Mosuo live in and around Yunnan province's Lugu Lake, more than 8,600 feet (2,622 m.) high. Their hard work at high altitude helps them to develop great lung power. They have tremendous power to sing loud but beautiful traditional songs, even while dancing.

When I visited Tristan da Cunha, one of the world's most isolated islands, in the South Atlantic, I heard of their practice of singing and dancing. Both men and women sang folk songs, sailors' songs, and ballads, at family and other gatherings. They usually sang solo, without musical accompaniment. Dances, with stepping and swinging, are usually to the music of an accordion or fiddle. When the volcano erupted in 1961 all islanders left. When they returned from Britain two or three years later they brought back new songs, radios, and casette tape players, which have largely replaced the old tradition of singing, but dances are still popular. Many island girls now wear miniskirts. On St. Helena Island, girls at the Prince Andrew (High) School sang an old folk song, "Napoleon's Exile," about his life there, from 1815 until he died in 1821.

Estonia has a summer song festival every five years and smaller festivals more often. The open-air theater seats around 35,000 but far more sit or stand on the grass surrounding it. My guide said *one-third* of the country's population attend the big festival! When they were under Soviet occupation, Estonians opened the program with patriotic Soviet songs, then they were free to sing their favorite national and folk songs. Nearby Latvia, in Riga, also has a popular song festival every five years, and more frequent smaller song festivals. In Lithuania our main highway was closed for nearly a day because of a big local song festival.

Resting & Body Positions

Chinese children, men, and some women of all ages can sit comfortably for hour after hour on their heels, with feet flat, and hip in the air. Many other Asians in Indonesia to as far west as Syria choose this position. Some Africans, such as the cattle-herding Masai, stand comfortably for hours on one leg, often using a spear as a balance. Japanese and other Asians and North Africans sit cross-legged for hours. Some Japanese restaurants where the table is very low have a sort of well or compartment in which to put your feet. One of my most uncomfortable meals was with the Berbers in Tunisia, where the table was less than 12 inches above the floor and the banquet lasted for hours. Local people sat comfortably cross-legged or with both legs together, bent at the knee, the back straight. Twenty or thirty men and women often sit cross-legged on the roof of big buses in Nepal, Central America, and in the Andes Mountains of South America. Many carry goods for the market in a big sack. When they get to the bus station they carry everything on the head or on the back to their pre-assigned place, and spread their wares for sale on a cloth or mat. In public libraries in Thailand, people of all ages sit on the carpet cross-legged but comfortably for hours, reading. I visited many schools on Pacific islands. Some children sit on benches at rough desks made in the village, others sit cross-legged on the floor. In some of Mali's villages of the Dogon tribe the log ceiling of the men's meeting place is only about four feet high. If an angry man stands up to argue he gets a bump on the head. Perhaps Congress, the United Nations, and corporate conference rooms should have such a low ceiling.

It is important in most Pacific, Asian, and African countries, from Vietnam to Syria, and across North Africa, to not let anyone see the sole of the feet or shoes, and to never point your toes at anyone. Either is considered to be an insult. Men on Pacific islands often sit cross-legged, women sit with their legs to the side. If you can't do this, cover your legs with a mat or sweater. Pacific islanders are usually insulted if anyone points a foot, hand, or finger at them. Most Islamic men consider it abhorrent to see women in short skirts or short pants.

To say "yes" or "no" many cultures use a movement opposite of ours. They shake their head from side to side to say "yes," in Sri Lanka, West Bengal and some other parts of India, Albania, and Bulgaria. To say "no" they move the head up and down. Japanese believe it is awkward to refuse a request, so they don't say "no." However, that does not mean they agree with your request or suggestion.

Carrying Things

Women and girls carry things on the head in many countries. It results in good posture and graceful movements. They usually wrap a cloth around the head or use a Styrofoam circle about the diameter of the head to make the load more stable, and occasionally use a hand to balance the load. Australia's Aborigine women, like women in Indonesia, Papua New Guinea, the Solomons, and a few other western Pacific islands, carry things on the head. However, most people in the Pacific and Caribbean islands do not carry things on the head. Men and women in much of southern Asia do carry things on the head. In China's south I occasionally saw women carrying things on the head, but never in central and northern China. Bushmen of southern Africa usually do not carry their few possessions on the head, but the men have a skin bag carried by a strong stick over the shoulder, for their bow, arrows, spears, ax, and may have a net for game or fish. Women carry a baby, ostrich eggs with water, stones for grinding, a few cooking pots, wooden bowls or tortoise shell bowls, a stick for starting a fire, and more in a heavy net bag. They also carry a digging stick and wear necklaces, anklets, and bracelets. Bushmen women often have huge thighs and hips that protrude to the rear.

In Nepal, men and women carry things on top of the head, or with a shoulder pole, or in a basket on the back, or with a trump line at the forehead. In western Nepal near Anapurna I saw several haystacks moving along the shoulder of the road. When I looked closely I noticed a little woman under each haystack. In India, Pakistan, Bangladesh, and Burma, men and women carry things on the head. On the Arabian peninsula, women often carry things on the head, men and boys sometimes do. In Papua New Guinea men and women carry things in woven bilums (bags). Women have bigger bilums and carry heavier loads, so they carry theirs on the back, using the strap as a trump line at the forehead. Men wear theirs over a shoulder. Women carry things on the head in Mexico, most of Central America, and in many rural parts of northern South America. In some Latin American countries, such as Nicaragua and Guatemala, men, women, and children carry things on the head. Most men and women in Bolivia carry things on the back, with a trump line to the forehead. Tlingit Indians of Alaska also used the trump line but do not carry things on the head. Not much more than 100 years ago it was common for women in Italy, France, Spain, Portugal, and the British Isles to carry things on the head. Berber women of North Africa and most women in sub-Sahara Africa carry things on the head. In many countries, including China, Vietnam, Laos, Thailand, Burma, Bangladesh, Russia, the former Soviet Union, and most of Eastern Europe, men and women use a springy shoulder pole to carry two equal-weight loads in buckets, cans, or baskets. Sometimes the weight is carried on one shoulder, then the other. A flat bamboo pole may permit both shoulders to carry the weight.

Native women in North America carried a papoose in a back carrier, the baby could also sleep horizontally when the board was laid down. Moss, grass, or leaves was usually used for a diaper. In Papua New Guinea, women working in markets keep the small child in a big basket, giving it security. A baby is carried with a trump line in a bilum (bag), and it is sometimes hung up to sleep in the bag. Leaves are used as a diaper. Many young mothers in Europe and North America use a backpack or special front carrier for a baby. Chinese women have adapted many types of backpacks and headdresses to carry a baby on the back, the baby usually faces forward. In Africa and Indonesia a baby is carried, usually over the shoulder or on the back, in a big cloth sling. In Africa and Indonesia, women use a circular loop of black cloth draped across the shoulder. It is less than a foot wide, three or four feet long, used to carry anything from a baby to bundles of vegetables.

Greetings

If the place you are going to has a government tourist office, ask the staff any question that you have a doubt about. That is what they are there for—to help a foreigner or other traveler. Some are far more helpful than others. Two rules to follow in greetings: SMILE, and BE POLITE. When we speak English with those for whom it is not the mother tongue, we must be careful to avoid slang words and to speak clearly and slowly. It is difficult to understand the meaning of jokes in another language, or the words of a song. It is best to state numbers slowly or to write them. Chinese have a way of showing numbers six through 10 with the fingers and thumb of only one hand. For example, one finger up and another in a particular position represents "seven," a second finger in another position represents "eight." A telephone conversation is much more difficult than a person-to-person conversation. While living with a local family, I have learned four other languages, mostly by "total immersion courses" in 14 language schools in Quebec, France, Spain, Guatemala, Italy, West Germany, and East Germany. Even if we know another language it takes time to absorb what someone else has said. If you have learned another language you will understand.

It is common in many rural areas of Ireland, Africa, Asia, North America, New Zealand, and the Pacific, to give a friendly wave at everyone who passes in a motor vehicle. Drivers often give a friendly wave or "thumbs-up" greeting to other drivers. However, since the "thumbs-up" signal can be misinterpreted for the "up-yours" signal it should be used only after consulting local people.

In the U.S., we usually shake hands with someone and look the person in the eye. Some Americans now kiss someone of the same or opposite sex on one or both cheeks, European-style. In France, Quebec, Italy, and Germany it is common to kiss someone of the opposite or same sex on the cheek or both cheeks. In Albania, people usually only kiss someone of the same sex. Men then say "may you have a long life." In Yugoslavia it is common to kiss everyone on both cheeks on greeting, and to shake hands with everyone in the room upon leaving. In West Africa it is common to shake hands with men and to have a long conversation upon greeting people. They inquire about how we feel, how is everyone in our family, our health, and more. The men often want to shake the hand of Western women also, except in the more strict Islamic areas. In Tahiti it is common for men to kiss men, women, or children as a greeting. In the old days, Polynesians and Alaska's Inuits (Eskimos) rubbed noses and cheeks as a greeting. In the U.S. and part of Europe it is common for men and women to shake right hands upon meeting members of the same or opposite sex. However, men do not usually shake a woman's hand unless she first offers her hand. In Finland people often shake both hands at the same time. During a hike of four days through most of the Dogon villages in Mali we were usually greeted by all of the boys in each village, who were usually naked. We were each expected to shake the right hand of perhaps 100 boys in each village, and some of the men. We did so, not wanting to offend them. However, we scrubbed our hands well before eating. To fail to shake hands with all men in a room or group is considered to be bad manners in Africa.

Japanese and most other Asians shake hands weakly, if at all. In China I noticed recently, 1998, that many local men now expect to shake hands with a foreign man. Vietnamese believe that shaking hands is "barbaric," and it is impolite to look people in the eye. Looking people in the eye is considered to be impolite or even rude in much of Asia, Africa, the Pacific, and among Native Americans in the U.S. and most of the Americas. It is considered rude for Western men to look the local women in the eye, even if the women like to flirt. On crowded subways or on the metro everywhere, people do not look strangers in the eye. Koreans are perhaps the only East Asians who normally shake hands, and they often give a bear hug to someone of the same sex. Koreans also bow slightly. Bowing from the waist is the usual greeting in East Asia. In Japan the people bow low, hands at the side. Most Japanese do not like to be touched upon greeting a stranger. In China people bow slightly. In Thailand and Burma people bow lower upon meeting, and press the hands together. In Sri Lanka and Malaysia hands are at chest height. In the Thailand greeting or wai, palms are pressed together near the chest or head, with a bow. The higher the hands and the lower the bow, the more respect is offered. The honored or superior person in return does not place the hands so high nor bow so low. Men in India seem to prefer bowing rather than handshaking.

In India, Turkey, and most Islamic countries men do not touch a woman or a girl of any age upon greeting, men and woman do not look each other in the eye, and it is improper for a man other than the husband to be alone with a married woman. In many Arabic and Islamic countries it is common for men to kiss a man on both cheeks, and they sometimes shake hands, give each other a bear hug, and hold hands a long time. After shaking hands each man may touch himself on the chest. Customs vary slightly from country to country. I don't kiss men first, but if they kiss, I return the greeting. When my wife worked in Pakistan we learned to say *Inshallah* during a conversation when we were making plans—"Allah Willing." In China, men hug a friend and slap him on the back. In Greece, men kiss, shake hands with, or hug other men, but men do not normally touch women. In Latin America it is common to kiss persons of the same and the opposite sex on both cheeks upon greeting and leaving. Shaking hands with everyone in the room upon entering and leaving is also common. Polynesians usually shake hands with everyone upon meeting, and women kiss each other on both cheeks. In Guatemala and a few other countries men do not kiss other men, they hug each other. Germans and Swiss kiss people of the same sex on the cheek two times, but persons of the opposite sex three times, according to my unscientific poll. In Italy men and women kiss the same sex on both cheeks and hold hands a long time. Men should observe local customs before kissing an Italian woman. Latin Americans and Italians stand very close together when they talk. They also stare into the eyes. My wife and I at times rode buses and trains in which we were the only non-Italians; since we speak Italian, we were soon good friends. A statuesque young Sicilian, a stranger a few hours earlier, stood only inches away when we talked. The British, Scandinavians, and most other Europeans prefer a longer social distance when they talk. In France and Belgium men kiss men on both cheeks and hug, and women kiss women the same way but do not always hug. The Japanese do not like bodily contact except in private, among friends. In crowded Japan the waving of hands when Italians, Americans, and others talk is bad manners, as well as dangerous to anyone nearby.

Boys from China to Egypt, in other parts of North Africa, and in Latin America, often walk down the street holding the hand of another boy if he is a close friend. Men sometimes hold a man's hand. It is not a sign of homosexuality. Girls often walk hand in hand in China, Eastern Europe, and Latin America, again it is not a sign of homosexuality. In Indonesia boys walk arm in arm, and girls walk arm in arm. Many people do not like to see a male and a female of any age showing affection for each other in public. This is a *no-no* in most of Asia. However, on my last trip through China I saw local city boys and girls holding hands. In Latin America males and females often kiss and do more, but usually in dark corners of theaters, parks, or doorways. However, in Nicaragua I often saw boys and girls holding hands in public.

Certain subjects of conversation are taboo in other countries. We must always be careful not to discuss politics, the military, religion, or income unless we are sure it is acceptable in the host country. Criticism of the government, king or queen, or manners or customs of the host country is usually taboo. Any unfavorable comparison of the host country with the U.S. is usually taboo. Many people are embarrassed by compliments. Sports, music, and the family are usually safe subjects of conversation, but the French do not like to discuss personal subjects, including the family. If in doubt about "safe" subjects in the country, ask a friend or the tourist bureau.

Germans and people in Luxembourg often send greeting cards to friends on an anniversary or at Christmas. French and Italians do not send cards, they telephone their friends. Greeting cards are rare outside of the U.S., Canada, Australia, New Zealand, and a few European countries.

Many Africans, such as the Zulus, are taught not to stoop low or sneak behind the back of the speaker when entering a room where a group is meeting, it is "sneaky." When an important person enters a room they do not stand, because they may be taller, and they do not want to "look down upon" the important person. In Thailand, a local person passing by, or standing or sitting near a superior or older person, must be lower. The inferior or younger Thai may be required to stoop or bend his head low. Local women in much of the Pacific must be lower than a man.

Purchases & Gifts

In the former Soviet Union, many socialist countries, and in some stores and takeout restaurants in Europe, buying something can be complicated. The customer selects something, gets a bill from a clerk, goes to the cashier to pay for it, then returns to the first clerk to pick up the merchandise. Sometimes a customer must stand in a long line at each place. I have suggested several times that the customer take the merchandise to the cashier to pay, but I was told "We can't trust the customers." I have also suggested that one clerk collect money at the place where the merchandise is bought. I was told "We can't trust the clerks."

Koreans and Japanese give things to another person with both hands. In most of South Asia and West Asia only the right hand is used in giving or receiving a gift. The left hand is used as a substitute for toilet paper. Koreans, Japanese, and many other Asians have in the past been expected to give a gift each year to the boss or to anyone, government or private, that they want to do business with. After scandals in Korea and Japan, the giving of gifts may be frowned upon. When we visit friends in Latin America or China, it is customary to give the hostess a gift. Chinese and other Asians usually do not open the gift in front of the giver, and they don't express gratitude at the time. When we visit a village in lesser-developed countries we are usually expected to give the chief a small gift. Always check with a local expert before giving flowers to people of another culture. Some types of flowers or some colors mean good luck, others mean bad luck, some are given only on particular occasions, some have deep meanings.

Many men in the Highlands of Papua New Guinea wear a necklace with strips of little bamboo about three inches long. If there are six horizontal strips then six men owe him a debt. In other villages each horizontal strip represents a wife or a pig that the man owns. I saw one man with around 30 strips in his necklace, so he is considered a wealthy and important man. A stake in front of a village house indicates that the man who lives there is owed something. It is common on Pacific islands for wealthy men to throw a party and at the feast give away many pigs, mats, or other things of value. The more a man gives away, the wealthier and more important he is. Sometimes two wealthy men become great rivals, particularly if each also wants to be the chief, they give away food to attract supporters. Some islands in Vanuatu have an elaborate grading system, called *nimangki*, from 1 to 35, to determine the importance of a man who makes gifts. A young man slowly moves to a higher grade as he gives more feasts with roasted pigs. Wealthy Indians of Canada's West Coast and Washington's Puget Sound area formerly gave big parties, called *potlatches*. They gave away valuable gifts. Anyone receiving such a gift had an obligation to give a potlatch and give away even more valuable things. Everyone kept an unwritten score as to who gave what to whom. The government of British Columbia, Canada, in 1884 made potlatches illegal, but in 1951 that law was repealed. In New Caledonia it was common for Kanaks to plan the *pilou* dance and the exchange of valuable gifts far in advance. The French government banned the pilou because of the amount of time and effort it required, and the trance that the dance induced. It is common for Asian children to give a tourist a flower or other small gift. Unless it is quickly returned, the child expects *baksheesh*—money.

Names

People in most countries are less casual about names and titles than we are. With an adult in Spanish-speaking and French-speaking countries and in Italy never use the *tu* form of address, and in Germany never use the *du* form of address unless you are sure the familiar form will be welcomed. We must also often avoid the first name but use the last name with the formal terms of address, such as *señor* or *señora*, *madame* or *messieur*, *signore* or *signora*, *Herr* or *Frau*. If a person has a title, such as the local equivalent of *doctor* or *professor* we must use that term in Germany, Austria, Sweden, Italy, and many other countries. But in Iceland the telephone directory lists everyone by *first name* in alphabetical order, with the last name added. The address and occupation are also listed. Icelanders address each other and foreigners by the first name. In Tonga first names are used. Most Indonesians have only one name. In Italy and other European countries, a person was known by one name plus the village or town he came from. For example, *Leonardo*, the great artist and inventor, was from the village of *Vinci*, west of Florence. In Australia, telephone directories usually list only the last name and initials, so it is difficult to determine whether a name is male or female. It is common in Thailand to be called *Mister*, *Mrs.*, or *Miss*, and our first name.

In China and many other Asian countries it is common to write and to state the surname or family name before the given or first name. If in doubt, it is better to ask a person you have just met "What do you like to be called?" When a Japanese baby is born it is registered with the city under the name of the father. When a Japanese girl marries her name is transferred from her father's name to her husband's name. In Korea the clan, family, or surname name comes first, then the given name. Most surnames are Kim, Lee, Choe, or Kang. In Spain and Spanish-speaking Latin America, the father's surname is the important one, it is next-to-last in the long string of names. The mother's maiden surname is last. But in Portugal and Brazil the father's surname is the last. It is common in Asia to be asked our age, where we are from, and our name. It is not considered to be impolite. Anyone middle aged or older is respected more—the older, the more respect. But some Pacific islanders treat the elderly and infirm as badly as our Western culture treats them.

In some African tribes, such as the Anlo (Ewe) of Ghana and Togo, a wife does not call her husband by his personal name. She calls him "elder brother" or "children's father." In many African countries the first-born son has the name of the father's father, the second son has the name of the mother's father. Many Asian peoples use their names far less than Westerners. Babies are often given an ugly name so it won't attract evil spirits. In Thailand, people believe that the *phi* make a child, and after birth they will try to take the child away. A child is given a temporary name to mislead the phi. In Vietnam children are taught not to give their name to a stranger, it may expose them to evil. In Thailand even adults are reluctant to give their last name to strangers. They use only their first name. In many countries, such as Vietnam and Nepal, the first name is based upon the person's relation within the family, such as "Mister Two" or "Son Two" for the second son, or "Miss One" or "Daughter One" for the oldest daughter. In Bali, with a modified Hindu culture, the first name indicates both the relation within the family and the class to which the person belongs. My guide said that *Putu* means "First Son," and *Wawung* means "First Son of the Lower Class" of four classes. If a person tries to marry someone of another class "there is much trouble." In Nepal many people have a caste name: clerks are often *Newar*, farmers and trail porters are *Sherpas*, soldiers are *Gurkas*, others are *Rai*. In the Marquesas Islands when a couple are married, an elder in the village gives them a new name, replacing their original names. An elder also selects the name of their first child. A boy is often given the name of a god or hero. "Nicknames" are perhaps common everywhere, but in the Marquesas the nickname must also be used to fully identify an adult. Each of the "Saints," as natives of St. Helena in the South Atlantic are known, acquires a nickname. Many islanders don't even know the real name of a friend. Children in the Pacific islands are often casually adopted by someone else in the village, with the consent of everyone involved. The child may casually announce that he has a different surname— that of the adoptive parents. A girl only 11 or 12 years old may also announce to everyone in the village that she has adopted a neighbor girl or boy.

In many Southeast Asian, Pacific, and African countries and among all Indians of the Americas it is forbidden to speak the name of a dead person. They fear that the name will attract the ghost of the dead. Africa's Masai are careful to never say the name or nickname of anyone who is dead. In Fiji it was taboo to speak the name of a warrior who had gone to fight an enemy—he might be killed. Warriors could be talked about only by calling them birds. Many tribespeople in South America's jungles will not give their first names to a stranger. They believe that speaking the name shows disrespect for the named person and may attract the attention of evil spirits. On Malaita Island in the Solomons, a woman is isolated during childbirth. When the baby is 30 days old they return to the village and baby is given a name. On Vanuatu's Tanna Island a boy is given a girl's name until he is circumcised, at age four or five, indicating that he is then a male, therefore he is more important. In New Caledonia a tribe or clan has the exclusive right to use a particular name for a place or object, even though the name is not currently used. A name has an eternal copyright.

In China a name is very important. It must have an appropriate meaning, it must be pleasant to hear, and the written character for the name must not have negative connotations. Some names, when spoken in a slightly different tone of voice, may connote something highly undesirable. Anyone who spends much time in China should consult a Chinese person before choosing a Chinese name. If you use calling cards in China, Japan, or many other Asian countries, have them printed in English on one side and the local language on the other side. In Malaysia many names—such as a derogatory or insulting name, or for an animal, tree, fruit, vegetable, or professional title, is not legal. The government refuses to register an illegal name, that person will not be eligible for government benefits.

Names of places in China have descriptive, often beautiful, names. Bejing has the "Garden of Harmonious Interests" and the "Pavillion of the Fragrance of Buddha." Xi'an has the "Big Wild Goose Pagoda" and the "Small Wild Goose Pagoda." Hangzhou has "The Peak That Flew From Afar," and the "Watching the Goldfish In A Flowering Pond Park." Guilin has the "Piled Silk Hill," the "Two Cocks In Fighting Posture Hill," and the "Pretty Girl Looking At Herself In The Mirror Hill." Kunming has the "Reed Flute Cave." Yunnan Province has the "Tiger Leaping Gorge" on the Yangtze River.

CHAPTER 8:
BOOMERANGS, TOOLS, MANNERS, & NATURE

Boomerangs

Boomerangs are used by Australia's Aborigines. They learned how to steam wood to make boomerangs and spears. The returning boomerang is used mainly for birds. Other boomerangs are used for hunting kangaroos, wallabies, and other creatures. I learned how to throw one, almost vertically, and make it return. Kanaks in New Caledonia have traditionally used the boomerang for hunting flying foxes. Did they learn to use it from Australia's Aborigines, a thousand miles away? The Egyptian Museum shows returning boomerangs once used by ancient Egyptians. Weimar's Early History Museum shows that Germans hunted with the boomerang in 100 BCE. Ancient boomerangs carved from bone have been found in Poland and France. Oaxaca's Rufino Tamaya Museum displays ancient Mexican boomerangs.

Beggars

Beggars are a problem for travelers. I ask a local guide or local educated person whether I should give to someone obviously in need. They usually say "no." I am more likely to give food or my old clothes to a beggar than money. Beggars become pests for other tourists. In Bombay and Calcutta little children may walk with a tourist for several blocks, licking their own fingers and touching the tourist's shoes. Beggars often go into a busy street where vehicles are stalled in traffic, and they reach into an open car window, asking for handouts or grabbing whatever they can get. They are different from the vendors found on streets and sidewalks throughout lesser-developed countries. Beggars and vendors often congregate in busy tourist areas or near a church, temple, or mosque. Children often ask for pens, chewing gum, or candy. Sometimes they sell it. In many places when we give money to a beggar there are no thanks, the recipient often does not even look up. Begging and giving is merely a transaction between economic unequals. However, in poor countries of Africa and Latin America beggars often need help, there is probably no government plan to help them. If local people readily give money to beggars we should also.

Vendors

Vendors usually avoid starvation by buying a small quantity of something and selling it in smaller amounts for a higher price. They may buy a pack of cigarettes or a box of candy and sell them one-by-one. They stand in the middle of a busy street to sell newspapers, flowers, drinks, candy, automobile parts, or anything else to motorists caught in a traffic jam or stopped at a red light. They set up a folding stand or spread wares on a blanket on the busiest sidewalks, or in a busy plaza. A vendor may perform services, such as shining shoes, repairing bicycles, cutting hair, typing letters or documents, or weighing people or their purchases on bathroom scales. They entertain by singing, playing a musical instrument, dancing, or by being a silent mime. Vendors are often small children, even in the middle of the night, or a mother has a small child near the things she sells. I buy inexpensive things from vendors whenever it is practicable.

Baksheesh

In poor countries men and children are often quick to do what they consider to be a favor for a traveler. In airport terminals and railway stations they grab a suitcase to carry or steal and ask for baksheesh to get it back. In La Paz, Bolivia the train descends from the high altiplano into the city, only two and-one half miles (4 km.) high. Boys jump from the bank down onto the roof of passenger cars, and at the station they grab suitcases. In Calcutta and many other cities, anyone getting out of a taxi must hurry or boys grab suitcases from the trunk before the owner or driver can. In Kashmir's Lake Dal, children in a canoe throw a flower into a shikara with a tourist. The flower should be thrown back quickly, or they press their claim for baksheesh. In much of Asia and the Pacific the acceptance of a gift imposes upon the receiver a duty to give something of greater value in return. It is common in poor countries for men, women, or children to work in the toilet of an expensive hotel, restaurant, shop, or factory often visited by tourists. They keep it clean, offer toilet paper or a towel, or turn on the water in a sink only a step away—they perform any service that may result in a tip. Their pay is usually only the tips they get. It is better than begging as a way of making a living.

Photographs

In Islamic Pakistan I asked a guide for rules about taking photographs. He said never take a photograph of a woman unless she grants permission. If her husband is nearby, he must be asked. The guide said it is okay to take a photo of a girl age five without permission, but not of an older girl. However, I once took a photo of a girl about four at a water fountain. When she saw my camera she fled like a scared rabbit. Many primitive peoples, including Africa's Masai and Australia's Aborigines, believe that a photograph takes away a person's soul. Masai usually approve taking the photo of a man or a moran youth. Masai girls often want their picture taken, for a fee of about 25 cents U.S. Arab boys, youths, and men usually like for their photo to be taken. Many Asian and African men like to have their photo taken, and women do also, except in fundamental Islamic countries. In China, little girls and older men and women often do not like to have their photo taken, they believe it takes something away from them. When they see a camera they try to wave it away. However, Chinese parents will nearly always welcome a photo of their small child, especially a Polaroid photo. I take two photos, giving them the first.

Never take a photograph anyplace where a sign has a camera and a slashed line through it, meaning "no photos." In general, don't take a photo of a border area, military base, police, or people praying. Our small group left Albania and had entered "democratic" Greece. A woman in our group took a photo of our guide leaning against our bus. A Greek soldier saw it. He took her camera. She was queried for 45 minutes to determine if she were a spy. They finally let her go, confiscating only her roll of film. I have seen other countries confiscate the entire camera, and some innocent tourists are imprisoned. In nondemocratic countries it is wise not to take a photo at an airport or railway station unless a local guide or policeman okays it. Many museums prohibit cameras, others prohibit only a flash. A flash should not be used in any church, temple, or mosque where a religious service is in progress. Many East Asians do not like anyone to take a photograph of Buddha, especially a flash photo.

Droughts & Weather

A prolonged dry spell is unwelcome to farmers everywhere, and indirectly, to city people. Different cultures have various methods to end a drought. In Bulgaria a little girl is chosen and decorated with green boughs. In a ceremony, water is sprinkled over her, to make it rain like the sprinkling. In Thailand, farmers fasten a female cat to a stretcher and carry it throughout the village. Each farmer throws a little water on the cat, hoping for rain. Mayans in Mexico and Central America believed that tears of a child being sacrificed would bring rain to end a drought. In the Canary Islands, ancient Guanche people caused goats to bleat, to get the Supreme God to answer their prayers for rain. Goat kids were separated from their mothers without food for three days, to cause them to bleat continuously. Shaman for Australia's Aborigines used blue and white stones in a ceremony to bring rain; white represented clouds. Kenya's Kikiyu believe that a sacrifice must be made to *Ngai*, the god and creator, to end a drought. In a ceremony, a fire made of a sweet-smelling wood is built under a big fig tree, smoke attracts the attention of Ngai. A boy and a girl are selected to strangle a lamb. An older woman is selected to pour beer, milk, and honey on the ground to make Ngai and the ancestors happy. If it doesn't rain within a few days the ceremony is repeated until it rains.

Weather is of the greatest importance to farmers, fishermen, and others who work outside. When the radio first became common it was used to get the weather, as well as other news and entertainment. Man has learned to observe signals in nature to forecast the weather. On a clear day in the foothills of the Andes in northern Argentina our guide said it would soon rain—ants were moving fast, storing leaves. Less than 24 hours later it rained hard. The ants had detected a falling barometer. Rain fills the ant holes, requiring a day or more of work to dig them out. Polynesian sailors took ants with them on long voyages. If the ants moved slowly, good weather was ahead.

Volcanoes

Primitive people feared and sometimes worshipped volcanoes. They believed that gods, or ghosts of their ancestors, lived in volcanoes. Ancient Romans believed that the god Vulcan lived in volcanoes, where he made arms and armor for gods, and thunderbolts for Jupiter. Ancient Japanese believed that the gods lived on Mt. Fuji. Automobiles carry visitors up to Step 5, which has a Shinto shrine. Many hikers continue to Step 10 and the summit, 12,389 feet (3,778 m.) The Spanish erected a big cross on Nicaragua's Masaya Volcano to counter the native's belief that the volcano was a god. However, the cross did not prevent the big eruption of 1774, and its toxic gases continue to kill nearby coffee trees. The dust and smoke is killing coffee trees far away. Yasur ("Old Man") Volcano on Vanuatu's Tanna Island is a relatively easy volcano to climb. Local people believe that a person's spirit goes there when he dies. Many islanders say that John Frum, hero of the cargo cults that will some day bring all kinds of material possessions to them, lives in the volcano. Yasur makes a loud boom like waves, or a hissing noise, then red rocks of various sizes, plus lava dust rising much higher, shooting into the air. We arrived just before sunset, the red boulders are even more spectacular in the dark. Early Hawaiians believed that the god *Maui* lived on Maui's Haleakala Volcano. Maui is said to have ensnared the sun long ago, slowing it down, giving us longer days. Mauna Loa on the "Big Island" is said to be the world's tallest mountain, measured from the sea floor to its summit. The red boiling lava is always hot. New Zealand's Mt. Tarawera, on the North Island, erupted in 1886, burying four Maori villages and a big resort. One old hotel in Buried Village has been dug out of volcanic dirt eight feet deep. Mt. Lassen in northern California last erupted in 1921. A paved road, closed in winter, goes more than half-way to the top, a high rounded cinder cone. Martinique's Mt. Pelée killed all 30,000 people who then lived in the "Paris of the West Indies," St. Pierre, when it erupted in 1902. The only survivor was a prisoner in a deep underground cell, he got a job with Barnum and Bailey's Circus, where he told fantastic tales about his background. When I climbed Mt. Pelée, rising 4,583 feet (1,397 m.) above the nearby sea, lichens and mosses grew on its damp summit but we found no "hot spots." In October 1961 a volcano on Tristan da Cunha erupted. All of the several hundred people were forced to leave the island for about two years. They lived in Britain until their home was again somewhat safe. When we visited the lonely island in the South Atlantic in 1998 villagers had adjusted well to a hard life. The peak's summit, rising 2,061 meters (6,760 ft.) above the sea, was hidden in the clouds.

When Mt. St. Helen erupted on May 18, 1980, I lived in the first city downwind, Yakima, Washington. The dark cloud with lightning soon made the sky darker than on a cloudy night, for nearly 24 hours. My wife, pushing her bicycle home, ran into a parked car that she couldn't see. Our yard, everything, had about two inches of heavy gray ash. In 1968, we climbed Guatemala's Pacaya Volcano, getting as close as we dared. A boom like a cannon erupted every 25 seconds, then boulders the size of a house rolled down the hillsides. It has slowed down since then. In 1992 I lived for two months near two of Guatemala's many volcanoes—Volcan Fuego (Fire Volcano), which spits smoke most of the time, and Volcan Agua (Water Volcano), whose mud and water wiped out Spain's first capital of Central America, Ciudad Viejo, in 1542. Costa Rica's Poás Volcano has a huge crater, but Irazu Volcano, not far away, has five craters. One emits sulfurous gas continuously but the last major eruption was in 1863. My wife and I stayed a few days on a beach in Java, near Little Krakatau, which smoked continuously. In 1883, Krakatau erupted with the biggest bang ever recorded by man. The noise caused sheep to stampede 2,500 miles (4,025 km.) away in Australia. Big ships several thousand miles away were carried by the tsunami two miles inland and left there. My wife and I stayed a week in Catania, Sicily, while nearby Mt. Etna smoked continually. Its biggest recorded eruption was in 1669, when frame buildings were burned and brick buildings were half-buried. Newer buildings were built on top of the lava, awaiting the next big eruption. Jules Verne, the popular Nineteenth Century French author, had his hero begin his *Journey to the Center* of the Earth in Iceland's huge Snaefels Glacier. Several nearby volcanoes, steam, and bubbling hot water scared ancient settlers but produced a warmer climate so grass would grow for their sheep and little ponies. Today hot water is piped all over Iceland, for heating homes, commercial buildings, and greenhouses growing vegetables, oranges, and other tropical plants, near the Arctic Circle.

CHAPTER 9:
NATIONAL & OTHER TRAITS,
THE EXPLODING POPULATION, &
GOVERNMENT

Standing in Lines

In countries with shortages and incomplete rationing, people are quick to join a long line. On one of our trips in the Soviet Union our guide suddenly asked our bus driver to stop and let her out. She later said the line at a department store was unusually long, so some good product must have arrived. It was a shipment of good-quality shoes from Hungary, but they were all gone before she got to the head of the line. People in some countries form a queue at a bus stop, ticket counter, cashier's desk, or other busy place. Other peoples crowd ahead, and the young and strong get to the head of the line. Greeks are perhaps the rudest in Europe, Italians and French are not far behind, but men from India are probably the worst. Pakistanis are almost as bad. Chinese men also rush ahead and do not wait until a plane's seatbelt sign has been turned off before standing and removing luggage. Some Latin Americans squeeze ahead, but in Nicaragua and Buenos Aires people form a queue. The British always form a queue. I once told a British diplomat that they should have stayed in India another 50 years to teach them British manners. He said "We didn't have much choice in the matter."

National & Other Traits

On flights with many Indian passengers, when the plane's wheels touch the ground, they are on their feet, removing luggage. A flight attendant complained to my wife and me "We make the usual announcements to wait until the plane is at the gate and the seat belt sign is turned off. But they are impossible." In a conversation with a well-educated middle-age lady wearing a beautiful sari we mentioned a few things that we liked about her country, India. She said "But we have a problem. We can't control our people." In Singapore a flight attendant with long experience told me "Japanese have a difficult time making a decision, what to order or drink. People from India are the most independent. They do not follow instructions or rules, and they want the most services." One of my guides in China said "Thais (from Thailand) are the worse tourists, they don't respect property and they

steal things from hotels." One of the German families that my wife
and I lived with said:

"*Heaven* is where the police are British, the cooks are French,
the mechanics are German, the dancers Spanish gypsies, the lovers
Italian, and it is all organized by the Swiss. *Hell* is where the cooks are
British, the mechanics French, the plumbers Spanish, the lovers Swiss,
the police German, and it is all organized by the Italians."

I told one of the families that we lived with in Quebec, in
French, that they had several advantages—French cooking, British diplomacy, and nearby American technology. They replied "It doesn't
work out that way. We really have British cooking, French technology, and American diplomacy."

The experienced wildlife guide for our two weeks in the
Galapagos Islands told me her observations: she said Scandinavians
are nonexpressive, the French ask if each thing is edible, Italians like
animals and birds that put on the biggest show, and the Japanese like
scenery and landscapes. Many guides have told me that people from
the U.S. are the most curious, they ask many questions, but they are
also independent, do not follow instructions, and too many Americans
wander off on their own.

In Southeast Asia and on some Pacific Islands, hard-working
Chinese operate many of the retail and other businesses, often becoming rich. Local Cambodians, Vietnamese, Indonesians, Tahitians, and
others are more easy-going but are often envious. In Fiji, Indians, both
Hindu and Moslem, operate many businesses, while local Fijians, living on their bountiful land, again are much more easy-going. On Some
Pacific islands, such as Tonga, local people returning home after having learned to work abroad, own most of the businesses. In Sri Lanka,
Moslems usually live in their own villages and operate many businesses. Like the dour Tamils, the Moslems often work harder than the
local majority Sinhalese. In East Africa, "East Indians," both Hindu
and Moslem, operate many businesses and often quietly look down
upon local Black Africans. However, some Black tribes, such as the
Kikiyu in Kenya and Tanzania, are known for being successful in business. In South Africa, even under Apartheid, *Coloureds*, with a mixed
ancestry often including Indians or Javanese, tended to be more ambitious and had a higher status than the majority 10 Black tribes. In West
Africa and North Africa, Moslems tend to be more aggressive than
local Black tribes, but in Nigeria some tribes, such as the Ibos, are
better educated and more ambitious than Moslems. In the Middle East,
Berbers are often nomadic herders, lesser educated than the local majority. However, with their big flocks of sheep, goats, or camels they
may be richer than the Arab majority. In Europe, Jews were often hard-
working skilled jewelers or money lenders, but many popes, kings,
and others discriminated against them. When the Spanish Inquisition

chased Jews out of Spain, the Islamic Turks invited them and their skills to live in North Africa, Eastern Europe, and the Middle East, all then mostly controlled by Turkey. Russia, under the tsars, discriminated against Jews, particularly in the Nineteenth Century. In the former Soviet Union, Russians were encouraged to live in all 15 republics. Russians were often leaders in the government of the republic, and were military leaders, their children went to separate schools where Russian was the main language, and the local language was secondary. Naturally, the Russians were resented. When the Soviet Union split apart at the end of 1991 the newly independent countries began to pass laws discriminating against Russians. The three Baltic countries decided not to join the other 12 republics in a loose confederation, and their laws encourage Russians to leave. Latvia, where more than one-third of the people are Russian, does not permit Russians to become citizens unless they learn the Latvian language. Local people in Latvia, Estonia, and Lithuania have told me that the Russians "don't know how to work."

In South and Central America Whites ("Europeans") tend to be better educated and richer than dark-skinned people who descended from local Native Peoples or Africans. Lebanese operate many restaurants and other small businesses. Whites with German, Italian, or Spanish ancestors tend to be richer than dark-skinned people. In the three former Guianas of northern South America and on nearby islands such as Trinidad there are at least three competing groups: (1) Native Americans often lived in the Bush, when they fled from White colonialists (2) Black Africans were brought in as slaves for plantations. When slavery ended they refused to work on plantations. (3) "East Indians" from India or Java, Moslems or Hindus, were brought in to work on plantations. Some are now small farmers. Blacks often control politics and work for the government.

I have found that discrimination is worse against the poorest group that has habits, language skills, or appearances different from the majority of the people. The poorest try to survive somehow; they may have to adopt antisocial behavior, such as theft, drug peddling, or prostitution to survive. The poorest usually have the least education, but they may not be less intelligent. In Eastern Europe the gypsies or *Roms* are perhaps the group most discriminated against. India's government has been trying to abolish the caste system since Mahatma Gandhi became the leader, but the *Harijans* or *Children of God* (once called *Untouchables*) are still discriminated against. In Southeast Asia the Akha are considered to be the poorest minority group.

In Arab countries the ruler is often a fair representative of a majority of the people. If an emir or sultan is mean, there are likely to be many beggars in the country. If the ruler has a sour disposition there are likely to be public executions or the chopping off of hands of thieves.

If the ruler is always smiling and jovial, the people are likely to be comfortable. When billboards, windows in homes and businesses, and the rear windows in taxis usually have big photographs of the king or president, it is not a democratic country. However, many Arabs do not want democracy, they like to have strong ruler. Opposition parties may be tolerated but they are kept weak. Some strong benevolent rulers are perhaps better than pure democracy in Arab countries. Newspaper articles critical of the ruling group are seldom tolerated in Arab or Latin American countries, nor in much of Africa or Asia. There is little understanding of any right of free speech.

When we look at a map of the world we see lines drawn around the edge of each country, indicating the national boundary. But many countries are a nation in name only. The average person owes loyalty to his village or tribe. National boundaries in Africa were drawn by Europeans, mostly in the Nineteenth Century. The boundaries of a tribe may extend into the next country, and the tribe is more important than the nation. In the Arabian Peninsula, in South America, and other parts of the world the national boundary is in dispute. Any change in the boundary as it is typically drawn is likely to result in war, so we let sleeping dogs lie. In countries such as Yemen the tribes control the mountainous north, the south is much different. In North Africa, the northern part of several countries is Islamic, in the southern part, people follow animistic religions or Christianity. There is no national feeling.

In New Zealand, stacks of newspapers are left outside of stores. A buyer takes one, makes change using money left on top, and leaves the correct amount of money. In New Caledonia, many villages on the east-central coast have an unattended booth near the road to sell little statues carved from soapstone. A buyer examines them, looks at the price marked on the bottom, and leaves the proper change. At least once a day a villager collects the money and brings out more statues. Stealing is also rare in fundamental Islamic countries, but we must use common sense to be secure. In Morocco, one man straggled behind the rest of us, eating fresh fruit. A youth grabbed the wallet from his hip pocket and ran away. The straggler called to our elderly local guide, who then shouted in Arabic. Local men ran from all directions, finally catching the youth. When we arrived they were beating and kicking him. Our guide retrieved the wallet and asked the 18-year-old where he lived, where he came from, and who was his father. He then let the youth go free. I asked our guide why he didn't call the police. "Our way is better," he said. "I know his village and his father. That boy won't steal again."

Latin America. There are great contrasts in much of South America and Central America between the very poor Indians, Blacks, and Mestizos, and a small percent of the very rich, mostly Whites or Mestizos. Unemployment sometimes approaches 50 percent, under-employment is much higher. I have traveled in all countries of South America and Central America. Our fluent Spanish helps my wife and me to talk with local people. Five factors have kept the poor from starving and/or somewhat tranquilized:

(1) many are street vendors of anything that people buy, making a small profit, and keeping them occupied in a "productive" activity,

(2) most of the poor are Roman Catholic, and the Church has told them that they are blessed, that though they suffer much, when they will die they will live in paradise,

(3) they scrape and save Pesos, Bolivars, Sucres, or other currency to enter the national lottery— some day they will "win the big prize,"

(4) they look forward to the big annual carnival or fiesta, often just before Lent, and

(5) many of the poorest Indians, especially in the high altiplano, chew coca leaves to numb the pain from cold, heavy physical labor, or hunger. The growing, processing, and distribution of coca and marijuana provides a living for many and riches for some.

Noise & Privacy

In much of Asia, Latin America, and in lesser-developed countries there is little awareness of the harmful or disagreeable effects of noise. Motor vehicles have no muffler or a defective muffler, they use horns instead of brakes; radios and TVs are turned up to maximum volume even at night; sound trucks are used by politicians, preachers, and advertisers; firecrackers are used during, before, and after holidays; dogs run wild and frequently bark all night, waking up the roosters to crow, and street or building construction machinery is as loud as in the U.S. The barking of dogs at appropriate times provides good security, but many old churches, nunneries, and monasteries prefer to use geese. When a stranger approaches they make an awful fuss. In Argentina, farmers like a tame *tero tero* bird—the loud noise it makes when a stranger arrives sounds like *tero tero*. Chinese often talk loud and turn up the volume of a radio or TV. Parades in China, Southeast Asia, and Africa include noisy drums, gongs, and firecrackers to drive away the devils—evil spirits that bring disease or bad luck. When I arrive in Japan or Germany after travels in much of Asia I notice how quiet it is. In Malaysia we met several times with a German professor who had been advising officials in Southeast Asian countries on how to reduce noise levels. He was disillusioned, he said there was little awareness of the harmful effects of noise, and little interest in having a quieter country.

In crowded Asian and African countries there is little privacy. Local people grow up and live surrounded by millions of others wherever they go. They work, play, sleep, eat, urinate, and defecate with many other people nearby. In India I became fully aware that Earth is approaching the time when there will be standing room only. In a typical "small" city, Agra, on a pleasant evening, my little three-wheel taxi passed hundreds of thousands of people on the crowded streets, out shopping or to see and be seen. When my wife worked in a hospital in Agra, a house boy was assigned to clean the room. He never knocked before entering and he always left the door open upon leaving. He was difficult to train in Western ways. We visited a village. Little boys wanted to introduce us to the grandfather of one. He was the headman. We spent most of the day talking with him. He proudly led us to the nice homes he had built or remodeled for his three daughters and two sons. In each house he led us, without knocking or announcing our presence, into each house and each of its rooms, including the bathroom. We tried to talk loudly so the family would know that strangers were present. Chinese grow up in a crowded room or apartment, and they live in a crowded city or village. Anyone, including a foreigner, who wants privacy is considered to be strange. Little kids and even adults come close to look at the strangers with big round eyes and big noses, often pointing at us. On an expedition in a truck through West Africa we camped out every night, usually out of sight of any village. Within minutes after our beginning to pitch tents some 10 or 15 men, women, and children arrived, quietly staring at us. When we buried aluminum cans and other trash they quickly dug it up. We learned not to smash them before burying. People who live in Pacific and African villages also have little privacy, except for menstruating females. Some villages have a place of retreat for older men, such as the *dare* in Shona villages of Zimbabwe.

It is common in Asia, Africa, and the Pacific islands to be asked questions that many Americans and Europeans consider to be an invasion of privacy. However, no harm or insult is intended. A common question is "How old are you?" In those cultures, where age is respected, the older person is respected and honored more. Other common questions, asked in friendly curiosity, are: Are you married? Do you have any children? How old are they? Boys or girls? Are they married? Who is your prophet? What is your sign? When is your birthday?

The Exploding Population

Governments such as China realize that if population grows much the standard of living for everyone will drop. There is considerable pressure for a family to limit the number of babies. There are many signs reading in Chinese "Control Population Growth, Raise Population Quality." In Egypt I asked our elderly guide what are the greatest problems of his country. He said "Too many babies. Too many children who never go to school." Jamaica has a slogan "Two is better than too many." There are almost four times as many people on Earth as there was at the beginning of this century! The U.S. has only twice as many people as it had 60 years ago. However, in our affluent society each baby born in the U.S. uses in its lifetime as much of the planet's resources as 30 babies born in a poor country!

It was common in some societies, such as the Polynesians, to kill up to two-thirds of the babies at birth. Perhaps this should have been done on Easter Island, where overcrowding, the depletion of forests, and starvation caused battles until nearly everyone died. One reason for the shortage of food was that it was taboo to fish near an *ahu* (platform for *moai* statues), and most of the 245 or so ahus are near the sea. After the trees were gone people could not build a boat to fish or to escape. On our visit we were shown some of the caves where the few remaining survivors hid. Our planet Earth is now a big Easter Island. Many primitive peoples killed any baby who was not born under a favorable sign. South Africa's Zulus killed defective babies, and all but one in the case of multiple births, by suffocating it with a clod of earth. They were thought to be evil spirits. Many minority groups in southern China, including the Yi, believed that a second baby, a twin, was a demon. Until some 50 years ago that twin and the mother were sometimes killed, as demons. However, the Dogon of Mali hope to have twins. They make offerings of koala nuts to little figures of a deity to get twins. In Tahiti if the father was of a lower social class than the mother, the fetus was aborted or the baby was usually killed.

When Europeans first arrived the Arioi Society on several islands of Tahiti worshipped the fertility god *Oro*. The followers believed in absolute free love between any man and any woman, but the babies were often killed. In the Marquesas Islands girl babies were often killed. This led to a shortage of women. A girl married at age 12 or the early teens. An older man soon moved into the hut, becoming the second husband. Some women had 30 "husbands." Early visitors reported that family strife was rare. Some large Pacific islands are still underpopulated. The large populations of the past were killed by alcohol, firearms, "Blackbird" ships capturing people to become slaves, smallpox, venereal diseases, and other diseases brought by the White Man. Now the population is increasing fast on many islands. Highlanders in Papua New Guinea told me that 40 years ago one or two babies was the standard number. The husband, wife, and children had to be ready to flee from "the enemy" at any time. They did not want to be encumbered with babies or possessions. Now that there are fewer tribal battles, the average family has five children.

Overcrowding causes many problems: a lowered standard of living, starvation, more diseases of all kinds, traffic jams, short tempers, tribal and racial fighting, wars, unemployment, juvenile delinquency and other crime; cutting down most trees for fuel and lumber, a shortage of water, pollution of the air, water, and the soil, growing crops on land that should be left in its natural state, resulting in erosion and the disappearance of irreplaceable topsoil, and using irreplaceable petroleum and other minerals at an alarming rate. In a good year many countries, even China and India, can grow or buy enough food. But a change in the weather pattern or a war causes mass suffering and starvation. This will become much more common, with overcrowding and more people living in inhospitable areas of the planet. No country with a fast-growing population has yet provided "full employment." The unemployed are often youths. They become restless and are a threat to the stability of any government.

Overcrowding is caused by (1) more births, (2) more immigration than emigration, and (3) by reducing the death rate. No one advocates increasing the death rate, which only increases suffering. Immigration can be reduced by increasing the standard of living of poor people so they will stay in their home country, by making short-term legal employment possible in a rich country, and by making other employment difficult in a rich country. The U.S. had a successful *bracero* program, the Migrant Labor Act, until it was unwisely repealed in 1962. In Mexico I met men who had legally worked several summers on farms in the U.S., they saved their money, returned home and bought a farm. Making illegal employment more difficult can be done by requiring that everyone in the U.S. have a "foolproof" identification card, with a number (such as the Social Security number), photograph, fingerprints, or other positive identification. Most countries, rich and poor, require that all citizens and legal residents carry ID, often called a carnet. Only the U.S. and a few lesser-developed countries do not have a carnet for everyone. Tightening the borders does not stop illegal immigration, it only slows down the rate of immigration.

The best way to slow the birth rate is better education of girls and women. They need attractive opportunities to work, so they can accomplish something in life without producing a house full of children. Many families want sons to give financial help to parents when they are too old to work. The best way to reduce the need for many sons and daughters is a good government Social Security retirement system, controlling inflation, and encouraging a family to save for the future. Each child should be a child wanted by the parents. Since females of child-bearing age will continue to have sex, they must be able to control whether or not they have a child. Information about morals and abstinence from sex, as well as physiology should be taught to all boys and girls, no later than age 12. The prevention of pregnancies is far better than abortion. Contraceptives of all kinds must be readily available to everyone, as well as information as to how they should be used. The U.S. is far behind many other countries in making contraceptives readily available. If a female is pregnant and she does not want to deliver a baby, abortion must be readily available, free if she is unable to pay. The woman may have good reason to believe that the fetus will result in a defective baby, mentally or physically handicapped, because she had a deficient diet, used alcohol or drugs, has AIDS or another serious disease, or other reasons. The cost of a medically safe abortion is less than one percent of the cost of raising a healthy baby, but a premature, handicapped, or deformed baby may cost taxpayers many millions of dollars. I have seen too many babies and children suffering from diarrhea, malaria, and other chronic diseases, but their main concern when they wake up every morning is "Am I going to get anything to eat today?" Each year more than half a million women die in the world during or because of childbirth. Most Europeans and European churches believe that government health plans should pay for abortion at will. They cannot understand the fuss made by a few people in the U.S. over abortions.

China's socialist government has for 20 years used the carrot-and-stick approach to reduce the birth rate. A first child is given free schooling, an allowance, and sometimes health care, but parents must usually pay for school for a second child, and much more for a third child. The cost of childbirth in clinics increases greatly after the first child. People in minority groups can "legally" have a second child (or even a third or fourth in remote areas) in villages, but not if they move to a city. A couple wanting a child apply to the boss where each works. If the child is approved the couple have a year to have a child, then the permission is withdrawn. Campaigns to persuade men to be sterilized have not been successful. Some wives dragged the husband away from the clinic, wrongfully believing that a sterilized man would be weaker. While some countries discourage parents from having more than one child, other countries reward them. In the U.S. a family can deduct part of the cost of raising a child from income taxes, and families on welfare often get an allowance for each child. Many European countries pay a large monthly subsidy for each child and the mother, if she does not work outside of the home.

If a nation has the same gross domestic product (*GDP*, or total income) but its population doubles, then the standard of living is cut in half. Likewise, if two nations have the same GDP but one has twice as many people, the standard of living will be much less. A good example of this is Yemen and Oman in the Arabian Peninsula. Yemen is larger but much of it is desert or mountains, they have about the same oil reserves, and Yemen's GDP is only one-third larger. Yemen has six times as many people, so the average income is less than one-fifth as much as in Oman. This is readily noticed when we travel through both countries. Oman has modern homes, cities, streets, roads, and water supply. Yemen is less affluent, it is more traditional, with older cities and roads, and more trash.

During my travels in much of the world I study the history of each country. Many countries that are today called "Lesser Developed" have a glorious past when the people lived well. Long ago people often had a much higher standard of living, more security, enjoyed better health, and had more leisure time than they have today. Most of those countries had a moderate climate, adequate rainfall or water for irrigation, rich soil, and a government that was not too harmful to most people. Today those countries have almost the same climate, the soil usually has not eroded greatly, the government is often no worse than in the past, but the people now suffer greatly. Why? There are now far more people to share the limited food production and other assets of the country, so the share that each gets is much less than in the past. Also, some nations, such as the U.S. and Western Europe, have a very high standard of living, in terms of material possessions and technological development. In contrast, the Lesser Developed Countries seem to be poor. The best way to improve the standard of living everywhere is to reduce the population, by peaceful means.

Battles & the Military

Nations and tribes who develop and use a new military weapon have an advantage, at least temporarily, over the enemy. When the Magyars invaded what became Hungary they brought the use of the stirrup, so they could stand up and shoot an arrow from a running horse. For nearly a hundred years they defeated neighboring armies. They learned how to use the stirrup from their former neighbors in central Asia. Some powerful weapons, such as poison gas and dangerous chemicals, are by international law or mutual understanding not used in war. In the former battles between tribes in New Caledonia it was taboo to use bows and arrows for battles. They were used only for shooting fish.

South Africa's Hottentots were primarily herders of cattle. They trained their cattle to run at an enemy, like a stampede. Kenya's Masai warriors wore steel bracelets. When the leather edge band was removed the sharp outside edge was used like a knife, to slash the enemy. The spear thrower or *atlatl* is used like an extension of the arm to throw the spear with more force. It was used long ago in much of Africa and Europe, and by North American Indians, but was little used in the Pacific, except by Australia's Aborigines. In the last century several tribes in Samoa were defeated by a tribe led by a ferocious warrior. He was dark and hard to find at night. The prettiest girl in a village was selected to seduce him one night. She tied white tapa cloth on his arms. Warriors then found and killed him. Carvings on the great stone temples of Cambodia's Angkor Wat area show Cambodian soldiers celebrating a Thirteenth Century victory. They sacrificed a buffalo and drank its blood, mixed with its urine, for strength.

In the Highlands of Papua New Guinea, several villages may meet for a *sing* that lasts a month. More than a thousand pigs and many cassowarys may be ceremonially butchered, to impress men in other villages with the wealth of the party givers. Men also sing and dance to whip up their courage before a battle. They chew a native plant to become brave. Men shoot arrows with bows, and throw spears. Each warrior carries a big heavy wooden shield, hardened in the fire. I watched one of their battles, they are fierce. When someone from a tribe steals a pig or a woman from another tribe, the culprit has two choices: negotiate compensation by paying far more than the value of the thing taken, or to be killed, or have a relative killed, in a "payback." Several times a year there is a battle with up to a thousand warriors on each side. The long heavy hardwood shields protect most of a warrior's body, they are usually wounded on the lower leg or feet. In Fiji the warriors were among the most fierce in the Pacific until missionaries tamed them little more than 100 years ago. Sailors hated to be shipwrecked near Fiji, they would be eaten. A *lalidrum* called warriors together. Fijians danced to whet their bravery. They used slings, clubs, and spears, and protected themselves with shields and padding from plants.

In North America through the Nineteenth Century Indians of the plains were often at war with at least one neighboring tribe. A warrior cut off the scalp of each enemy warrior he had killed, proudly displaying it on his horse or teepee. There was a constant cycle of the killing of a warrior, then one or more revenge killings. In other parts of the world, headhunters proudly displayed the skull or the shrunken human head with hair, eyes, and the skin of the enemy.

South Africa's Zulus became fighters who nearly always won their battles after Shaka became the chief in 1816. He made the warriors strong by dancing for hours and by calisthenics. They had to walk in bare feet on thorns to show toughness. He armed them with a short stabbing spear and told warriors they must keep it and not throw it at the enemy—if they lost the spear or ran from the enemy, Shaka killed the warrior. However, Zulus each had a heavy club to throw at the enemy. Shaka used spies and smoke signals. He had a harem of 1200 women whom he called "sisters," but he was afraid to sleep with any of them, because he might have a son who would later depose him. Others say he was afraid of women. When his mother, Nandi, died Shaka changed; he killed 7,000 warriors because they failed to cry over the death of his mother. Ten girls were buried, alive, but with arms and legs broken, with her. He was no longer an effective leader, and he was killed by his brother.

For centuries, tribes and nations have found it helpful to have a neutral place and procedure to trade peacefully with each other, or to discuss peace and the settlement of disputes, as an alternative to fighting. They learned how to approach the enemy and strangers in a manner signifying a peaceful intent. The enemy or strangers were approached in the daytime in open view, making noise to indicate they wanted to be seen. Weapons were not carried or they were carried in a manner indicating that they would not be used. In modern times a white flag may be carried. In Vanuatu peace negotiators carried a big *carma* palm leaf. Organizations such as the League of Nations or United Nations, and dozens of regional groups, have been established to discuss problems. Native peoples, such as Indians in North America, have long met in neutral areas to get something, such as flint or obsidian, in trade for something they had, such as dried fish or berries. Certain areas, such as a small island near Nuku'alofa, Tonga, were long used as a peaceful meeting place for tribes that were often at war with each other. Traditional peoples believed that a host owed a duty to protect an invited guest, even though they were traditional enemies. In Albania, guests checked their weapons as they entered the host's home. The host gave his *besa* or word that he would protect the guests, even one who had killed the host's brother. "Civilized" peoples sometimes did not have such high moral standards. In 1692, soldier's of England's King William III stayed in the homes of Scotland's MacDonald clan. During the night soldiers carried out orders to murder 38 members of their host families. Similar treachery was used by Piluge, chief of the Nanzhao tribe, one of the "Six Kingdoms" near Dali, Yunnan, in the Seventh Century. He invited the other five kings to a banquet, then killed them all, and took their wives. One beautiful wife committed suicide rather than become Piluge's mistress. China's annual Torch Festival honors her.

To settle a minor traffic accident dispute in Yemen the Bedouin victim asked for an outrageous amount. A friend of the guilty driver finally settled it by offering a fair amount, then his rifle "to become weak in your hands, like a woman." The subdued Bedouin rejected the rifle. Some early people, such as the Cherokees in the U.S., had a peace chief, who had equal status with the war chief. The Navajos had a war council and a peace council. After many years of a devastating war, Guatemala has a secretary of peace. After a civil war, Costa Rica in 1948 abolished its military, it has only a militia. It now has more money for health and education. The U.S. needs a peace department. Peace is far from the main objective of a typical foreign ministry.

Land mines planted during wars continue to kill or to blow off the legs of men, women, and children, for 100 years after the war has ended. A military strategist knows that badly wounding the enemy is more harmful than killing him, for people and money are needed to care for the wounded. Bulgarians are still angry at Greeks because a Byzantine army put out the eyes of 15,000 Bulgarian soldiers in 1014 and sent them home blind; one in 100 kept one eye. I have watched the wounded in Cambodia hobbling on one leg toward any tourist, to ask for money to keep from starving. The other leg was lost to a land mine. When a leg of the husband or the family buffalo is blown off in a land mine a formerly prosperous peasant family quickly starve. When the Argentines were chased out of the Falkland Islands in 1982 they left behind 120 mine fields They removed the metal tag from the plastic mines, making them hard to detect. The mine fields are now fenced off, and in some of them penguin colonies grow. Sheep can graze there but they can be herded only by dogs—a man's weight would detonate a mine. In Cambodia, Vietnam, Kashmir, Libya, Sudan, Chad, Somalia, Angola, Mozambique, and elsewhere, much good agricultural land is unusable because of land mines. Land mines, like poisonous gas, chemical weapons, and nuclear bombs, should be made unlawful everywhere. In my three-volume set of books, *Countries & Cultures of the World, Then & Now*, I computed the number of people per square kilometer of *arable* land for most of the countries of the world. But many of those countries are infested with land mines, the land is not arable, it is unusable, it cannot be cultivated. An already-crowded country shrinks and becomes more crowded because of the land mines. Civilized countries should not use them.

The U.S. exports far more military weapons than any other country. Many of those weapons are used by an unpopular ruler to stifle dissent, and to maintain his power by force. Military supplies sold on credit by the U.S. and other countries drive up their national debts. Consequently, the future of the country is mortgaged. More and more land must be used to grow crops that can be exported, to get dollars to pay interest on the debt. There is little land left to grow food for the people. They suffer from malnutrition. The list of poor countries that spend more on their military than on education and health combined, is very long. A typical view is that of a schoolteacher in Honduras, who told me "Of course we need an army. But we lost control of it long ago." One of our guides in Argentina said their problems are "the Catholic Church, the military, big landowners, and the big foreign corporations that pay money under the table so they don't have to pay taxes."

The U.S. has chosen to spend a large portion of its tax income on the military. It spends more for the military each year than any other six countries combined. Any member of Congress who fails to vote for money for the military is said to be "soft on defense." Contracts and subcontracts for suppliers for the military are spread around in the districts of those members of Congress who vote favorably. President Eisenhower, our commanding general in the ETO, Europe, during World War II, warned us in 1959 that the military and military suppliers were about to control the U.S. With 4.5 percent of the world's people, the U.S. spends 35 percent of the world's military expenditures. Other countries, such as Japan, have chosen to keep taxes lower and to spend much of the government's income on helping businesses, by low-interest loans, creating appropriate monopolies, discouraging imports, and nonmilitary research centers so the nation will have a prosperous future. European countries have chosen to spend more of their income as a social cushion for citizens, helping the needy to avoid the worse hardships of capitalism.

Business & Time

Educated Asians, Africans, and others always carry a business card, which they are quick to present to a stranger. We should also always carry business cards. Japanese are quick to determine the pecking order when they meet a stranger, whether another Japanese or a foreigner. However, Japanese are taught to be polite and modest. I chatted for several hours with a man in his sixties seated next to me in the crowded coach class on a trans-Pacific flight. He told about how he started with his company as a boy of 12 during World War II and he had slowly been promoted. Near the end of the flight he gave me his business card. He was the operating vice-president of a company larger than General Motors! I have never met the president of a large U.S. corporation flying coach class across the Pacific. They usually fly first class or in private jets, eat in private dining rooms, stay in expensive hotels and resorts, and try to avoid mixing with the *hoi polloi*. With a salary and stock bonuses their annual income is several hundred times as much as a beginning hard-working employee. In 1950, a chief executive in the U.S. received an income only 40 times as much as a beginning employee.

A higher percentage of children in the U.S. live in poverty than in any other industrial nation, and millions more will live in extreme poverty as new laws limiting welfare benefits become effective. More children will drop out of school to try to find work. Those who cannot find work will have little alternative but starvation or crime. All recent studies show that in the past 20 years income adjusted for inflation of the U.S. middle class has dropped, while income of the richest one percent has shot up like the space shuttle. Recent studies also show that the U.S. has by far the most lopsided distribution of income and wealth of any industrial country in the world. The U.S. now meets a frequent definition of a "Third-World Country"—the rich are getting richer, the middle class is worse off than 30 years ago, and the poor are now much poorer.

Businessmen and women soon learn that other people treat business matters differently than we do. Japanese, Chinese, and other Asians like to get well-acquainted before talking business. In southern China business deals have traditionally been concocted in a tea house. To indicate that an offer was accepted the offeree put his hand into the shirt sleeve or coat sleeve of the offeror. Today suspicion might arise that a bribe was offered. Chinese businessmen often consider a business deal to be an occasion to try to outwit their customer, supplier, opponent or partner. During negotiations with Asians we learn not to back an opponent into a corner. We always let him save face. Saving face is important in Asia. In much of Asia, Africa, and the Pacific, a signed contract is considered to be only a rough guide. Few countries have the great mass of written laws and the thousands of judges that enforce them, as we have. Europe and Japan are becoming much more legalistic, but far less than the U.S. Japan graduates many students from law schools but most of them never go to court, they only advise executives of the company they work for. Travel guides say Japanese are very slow in making a decision. Japanese are used to presenting a problem to a group and letting the decision gradually develop or evolve. A Japanese manager does not like to "stick his neck out" and make a decision alone that could be controversial. Japanese say "The nail that sticks up gets hammered down." Chinese government officials believe it is safer to do nothing than to do something and possibly make an error. It is frustrating for Western business people, who typically want to do something, to move ahead, even though it may be a mistake or bad judgment. Many French treat a contract as only a guide, but it may not be followed closely. Laws are important, but since the Revolution in 1789 individual rights are more important. A law may require that a motorist stop at a red light, use yellow or amber headlights, that a dog owner clean up his dog's mess on the sidewalk, or that there be no smoking in a train car or movie theater: but those are only guidelines, which are sometimes ignored. France, Italy, and Greece have many labor strikes, more than half of them are illegal.

A traveler or business person should be punctual for a meeting or appointment in the U.S., Canada, nearly all of Asia, Australia, New Zealand, and Europe. However, punctuality is not so important in the southern countries of Greece, Italy, Spain, or Portugal. In Latin America, *mañana* may be okay. Pacific islands vary, people in some are more "laid back" than in others. The length of the noontime siesta is often three hours long near the Mediterranean and in tropical or rural Latin

America. It is often two hours in France, northern Spain, tropical Asia and the Pacific, and large Latin American cities. However, some department stores and businesses in Santiago and Buenos Aires now don't even close at noontime.

There is no concept of *time* as we understand it in much of the world. Many Africans, Asians, Latin Americans, and others wait patiently for hours, even days, for an office to open or for a bus or train. There is little need for a watch or clock. Only "sun time"—daylight or darkness—is used. People who live in a rural village and grow or make most of what they consume, do not work outside of the home, and do not travel farther than the next village, have little need for "Western time." In many areas with a mild climate, good soil, and no overcrowding of people, an adult can get enough to eat and have a place to live with work averaging only two hours a day. Play and ceremonies fill up most of the rest of the time. Scheduling and planning are unknown. There is little or no thought about tomorrow, next week, or next year. Farmers must plant seed in the proper season in order to harvest in the right season, but that is easy to remember. Women must care for the children, but older siblings or anyone else in the village will also care for them. Children grow up quickly, to become independent of the parents. The "world" of many people is their village, nearby villages, and their tribe or clan. There is little understanding of national borders. The concept of saving money or food is unknown by many people. There will be food tomorrow, as there is today. Why worry?

Labor

As a labor negotiator representing corporations for 20 years, I learned to think quickly about total labor costs—wages plus all fringe benefits. Typical total labor costs for a factory worker at the end of 1995 were $31.88 an hour in Germany, $29.28 in Switzerland, $26.88 in Belgium, $25.38 in Austria, $24.78 in Finland, $23.66 in Japan, and $17.20 in the U.S. Among the 15 countries in the European Union ("EU") only the U.K., Ireland, Portugal, Spain, and Greece have lower labor costs than the U.S. Unemployment rates early in 1996 averaged 11% in the EU. Unemployment was 23% in Spain, 17% in Finland, 15% in Ireland, 12% in France and Italy, 10% in Belgium and Sweden, 9% in Germany, 8% in the U.K. (two years later it was down to around 5%), 5% in Portugal, 7% in the Netherlands, 6% in Denmark, 4% in Austria, and 3% in Luxembourg. In the U.S. it was 5.6%, in Japan 3.5%. The EU had a net increase of only 800,000 private jobs, 1974-1994, while the U.S. added 31 million private jobs then. Unemployment has recently been slightly reduced in several countries in the EU.

It is time for rich countries such as the U.S. to reduce the standard work week. Employers usually oppose any cut in the regular work week because it results in an increase in hourly pay and labor costs, unless weekly earnings are reduced. Workers and their unions object to a reduction in weekly pay. Assuming that the productivity rate remains the same, weekly pay will be reduced. Employers call this "sharing the work," some unions call it "sharing the misery." The average number of hours worked in a year in the U.S. is 1,951 hours, in France it is 1,645 hours, and in Germany it is only 1,560 hours. The recent study, reported by the Organization for Economic Cooperation, found that hours worked in the U.S. was more in 1996 than 23 years earlier, but hours worked in France decreased 13% and in Germany they decreased 16% during the same period. The new French government plans to cut the standard workweek from 39 hours to 35 hours. Another possibility in the U.S. is to increase vacation time. It has long been standard in Western Europe to provide 22 to 32 days of paid vacation per year. In the U.S. 11 days is the average. Australia averages 22 days, Canada 15 days, and Japan averages 22 days. Adding another week of paid vacation in the U.S. will help to create more jobs. Since labor costs in the U.S. are currently below costs in much of Europe and Japan, now is a good time to cut the work week and to increase vacation time.

Metric System

Nearly every country in the world has changed to the metric system of measurements. Exceptions are a few lesser-developed countries, and the U.S. The metric system is much easier to work with, once we get used to the basic values. Since almost anything shipped for export must be based upon the metric system, and the U.S. hopes to export more, now is the time to start getting used to metric measurements. For those who don't remember, 1 centimeter = about 0.4 inches, 1 meter = about 3.3 feet, 1 kilometer = about 0.6 miles, 1 kilogram = 2.2 pounds, 1 hectare = about 2.5 acres, and 1 liter = slightly more than a quart. Also, to change temperature Fahrenheit (F) to Celsius (C) we subtract 32 and divide the result by 1.8. To change Celsius to Fahrenheit we multiply by 1.8 and add 32.

Firearms

Most countries strictly regulate all firearms. Some countries permit the ownership of a hunting rifle or shotgun if it is registered. Few countries permit anyone except the military or law enforcement personnel to own a pistol, or an automatic rifle or powerful rifle. In Canada, the United Kingdom, and most of the world anyone wanting a powerful weapon is considered to be a "gun nut." Australians are very independent, but private ownership of most weapons other than hunting rifles or shotguns, was made unlawful in 1996. Australia's Medicare fund was used for a year to buy powerful weapons now illegal; the amnesty period ended late in 1997. In the U.S. there are some 221 million firearms—almost one for every man, woman, and child. The U.S. has far more firearms than any other country. More than 40,000 people are killed in the U.S. by firearms each year. Firearms may soon surpass automobiles as the leading cause of accidental deaths in the U.S. Far more people are wounded by firearms. Anyone who lives in a home with a firearm is at risk of being shot, accidentally or in anger. Each firearm wound costs an average of more than 50,000 dollars. Nearly all of that cost is paid by others who pay premiums for health insurance, or by taxpayers for the thousands who must use welfare for treatment of the wound. Some men in the U.S. believe they are more *macho* with a gun. Perhaps guns are a phallic symbol for some men who were shortchanged by nature. Many countries ex-ray incoming luggage, checking mainly for firearms. Customs forms nearly everywhere warn travelers that to attempt to import a firearm results in a long prison sentence.

Election Campaign Reform

It is unlikely that laws favorable to the general public will be passed in the U.S. unless politicians can vote their conscience rather than their pocketbook. Election campaigns in the U.S. begin more than a year before balloting and are very expensive, with TV and newspaper ads. Only the very wealthy or those who receive fortunes from special interest groups can hope to be elected. Some of our politicians are perhaps "the best that money can buy," or "the best that money has bought." France, Italy, and other countries prohibit election campaigning within 15 or 30 days before balloting. They also prohibit the publicizing of poll results during that period. This helps to create a period of calm before the actual balloting. Most of the peoples of the world vote on the weekend, and a far higher percentage vote than in the U.S. The long campaigns with much mud-slinging seems to turn off many voters, who look upon all politicians as "dirty" or "all the same."

It requires initiative to register to vote in the U.S. Registration to vote is automatic when a person reaches age 18 in Australia, Belgium, Costa Rica, and many lesser-developed countries. Failure of a registered voter to vote is usually unlawful, punishable by a fine. Perhaps the U.S. should follow the practice of Australia, Argentina, Ecuador, and others in fining any eligible voter who does not vote, unless he/she has an acceptable reason.

Many countries prohibit campaign contributions greater than just a small amount, and the government provides a campaign fund for each candidate or political party able to show a minimum of support. Campaign contributions should be limited to a registered voter who lives in that electoral district. Since the U.S. Supreme Court's unwise decision in 1976 holding that campaign contributions are "free speech," a constitutional amendment would be needed. All contributions by political action committees, corporations, organizations, and associations should be prohibited. Gifts of more than the value of the cost of a typical restaurant meal should also be prohibited, to a member of Congress, the Senate, to any member of their staff, and to any political party. The government should pay a stated amount for the election campaign of an individual or a political party who/that demonstrates support of a particular number of people, such as an incumbent, or for a challenger by a petition with signatures. Candidates who have received a minimum number of votes in a primary election should receive a limited amount of free time on TV. Germany and several other countries provide government financial support for political parties or candidates who receive at least five percent or so of the votes. Candidates for re-election, as well as competitors who show support by five percent of the voters, would get a credit, not money, from a government agency. All election expenses would be paid by the agency.

Even without a constitutional amendment in the U.S., all "soft money" to political parties should be prohibited, and any party or anyone receiving federal money would have to agree to receive no private contributions. Election reforms are badly needed to return America to democracy, rather than to continue the control by the rich and special interest groups.

Calendars

Our calendars usually have the day of the week at the top. Calendars in many countries, such as Hungary, have the names of the day at the left end, in horizontal rows. In some languages, including Arabic, we read from right-to-left. In Tunis, a statue seemed to say that the young man was born in 1948 but he died in 1925. I finally realized that I should read from right to left, he was born in 1925. In many East Asia languages we read down, in columns.

The Gregorian Calendar was adopted in Europe in 1582 during the reign of Pope Gregory XIII. It is based upon the length of the solar year. It corrected errors that had accumulated since the Julian Calendar had been adopted in 46 BCE during the reign of Julius Caesar. The U.S. and much of the world use the Gregorian Calendar. China adopted it in 1912 but still uses the Chinese Lunar Calendar for festivals and holidays. Ancient Mayans used a more accurate calendar, their year was 365.2422 days, the Gregorian year is 365.25 days. Mayans began their calendar in 3114 BCE. Their astronomers and priests developed a civil calendar of 18 months of 20 days each, with a 5-day holiday period each year. They also had a religious calendar with 13 months of 20 days each. The Jewish Calendar began "with Creation" in 3761 BCE. A year has 353 to 355 days, while a leap year has 383, 384, or 385 days. The Buddhist calendar began in 544 BCE when he had the "awakening." The Islamic Calendar began in 622 AD, when Mohammed left Mecca for Medina—the *Hegira*. It is a lunar calendar of 354 or 355 days, divided into 12 months.

Birthdays and Holidays

The New Year is celebrated nearly everywhere, but the New Year begins on different dates in various countries. Chinese celebrate their birthday on the Chinese New Year—everyone is considered to be a year older that day. In most countries, each person has a private holiday—his/her day of birth. In Latin American countries each person also has a personal saint, to be used as a holiday. Many Africans do not know the day on which they were born, or even the year, but they probably know the season or the moon and season.

Travelers are often surprised to learn that banks and most businesses are closed on the day they arrive or had planned to do things. It is a holiday. Most countries celebrate Labor Day. In the U.S. it is the first Monday in September, but most countries honor Labor Day on May 1—May Day. Nearly all countries have a holiday celebrating the day of independence, or the forming of a republic, or other national day. Most countries honor the winning of a major battle, the dead killed in wars, and the birth of one or more national heroes. A day to give thanks for a good harvest is common, like Thanksgiving in the U.S. I attended a school in Germany one fall. We had a holiday on November 11—not to celebrate Armistice Day (the end of World War I, celebrated in most of Europe) but to celebrate San Martin's Day. German children go to the park then for music and goodies, something like Halloween in the U.S. A planting holiday in the spring is fairly common. In Switzerland people, dressed in costumes welcome spring by blowing up a "snowman" representing winter.

Each religion also has its own holidays. Christianity has Easter, honoring the rise of Jesus after three days in a tomb. In 325 AD at the Council of Nicaea, churches decided to celebrate it on a Sunday, but the Orthodox and Roman Catholic churches now choose different Sundays. In Central and Eastern Europe people boil hens eggs and decorate them with colors. Sometimes an onion skin is wrapped around the shell and boiled, for color. In some countries the eggs are not hidden. Boys sometimes hit each others' eggs, the boy with an unbroken shell was the strongest. One Easter my wife and I were in Armenia. Our hotel served colored eggs for breakfast. They were artistic but not so beautiful as Easter eggs in Ukraine, which we visited a few days later. Designs are written in wax—triangles represent the Holy Trinity, fish represent Christianity, curls represent water. Many colors are then used. Black represents night, when evil spirits came out. When people went out at night they would carry a rooster to scare away evil spirits. Now some eggs have a rooster design. Good Friday, the last Friday before Easter, is sometimes a holiday. Christmas honors the birth of Jesus. Lent is the 40-day period of toned-down eating, drinking, and frivolity before Easter. Some churches also honor particular saints as a "holy day." Many churches honor All-Saints Day on November 1, just after Halloween in the U.S. Most Christians recognize Sunday as the holy day, the Seventh Day Adventists recognize Saturday. In the "Bible Belt" of the U.S. South, Samoa, Fiji, and Tonga, fundamentalists try to force stores and other businesses to close on Sunday. Judaism recognizes Saturday. Islam's holy day is Friday, but that is the busiest market day in many Islamic countries, even those near Mecca on the Arabian Peninsula.

Christians adopted an ancient Roman holiday to celebrate the birth of Jesus, now called Christmas. Romans celebrated the Saturnalia in late December to celebrate the winter solstice. Feasting, fun, and frivolity reigned, and gifts were exchanged, like Christmas. The statue of Saturn was unwrapped. Mithraism was the main religion in the Roman Empire when Jesus was born. The birthday of Mithras, their main god, was celebrated on December 25 by the giving of presents. Most experts say that Jesus was not born in December, but early Christians had to keep a low profile. They chose the date of the Romans' main holiday for their main holiday. Many experts also believe Jesus was born four years before the time we recognize as the beginning of the Christian era. Boxing Day is the first weekday after Christmas. Until recently presents were given on Boxing Day in Great Britain. Christmas ends on Epiphany, January 6, honoring the visit of the three wise men, and the baptism of Jesus, with a feast. *Yule* is another name for the celebration of Christmas. In Europe it was common to burn a Yule log at Christmas. In Albania before the Hoxha government, ashes of the Yule log were spread in the fields, to make the land fertile. In Serbia, Yugoslavia, some people carried a little of the ashes with them, to protect against lightning. The English kept a little of last year's Yule log to light this year's Yule log. The French kept a little of the Yule log under the parent's bed to protect the house and farm from all kinds of catastrophes in the coming year. The French traditionally eat goose on December 25 because geese are said to have witnessed the birth of Jesus. One family that I lived with in France said they always eat oysters on Christmas.

In the U.S. and some European countries, during the Christmas season, if you hold mistletoe above the head of someone of the opposite sex, you are supposed to kiss that person. Mistletoe has long had special meaning for people, since it grows on a tree in the air, without touching the ground. Many Europeans believed that mistletoe would cure ailments such as epilepsy. They thought it protected anyone against witchcraft, sorcery, and nightmares. People put a sprig of mistletoe at the door threshold to protect the people who lived inside, and also fed a little to their animals to protect them.

Mexico has nine days of *posadas* before December 25, when children carry candles and go to a different house each evening. It represents Mary and Joseph searching for an inn. In each house they have refreshments and dancing. Blindfolded children break a *piñata* to get the candy inside. Presents are opened on December 24. On January 6, the Day of the Kings, a *rosco* pastry is baked with two ceramic dolls inside. Each child cuts the pastry. The child who cuts a doll must give the party the next year. In Cuba, Epiphany, January 6, was once the children's favorite holiday, they received toys then. The Castro government moved the holiday to July 26 and called it "Children's Day" or "Revolutionary Day." Each child then received only a number, which determined what toy the child would get. Christmas and Epiphany were no longer celebrated. Late in 1997 Castro changed the celebration back to the traditional date, before the pope's visit to Cuba in January 1998. When I was in Amsterdam, St. Nicholas arrived by barge on November 17, with the mayor. Good children get a present each week for three weeks. Bad children get a tree limb in the shoe. Gifts are given on December 5 or 6, as in several nearby countries. In France, presents are usually removed from under the tree and opened on December 24. One year I was in Vietnam and Cambodia in December. Stores, tourist hotels, and other businesses in Southeast Asia sometimes put up a decorated Christmas tree in December and play Christmas carols on the loudspeakers. Local people always like a holiday, but only a few celebrate Christmas as a holiday.

Mexico celebrates the Day of the Dead, something like Halloween in the U.S. People make fun of death, and eat a special kind of bread, *pan de muerto*— "bread of death." After a feast, some families leave delicious food decorated with flowers out overnight, for the souls of little children and other relatives to eat. Church bells are rung to attract the souls. A day or two later the family eats the food that the souls, mice, and the insects did not eat.

When our two sons were young we put them into a school in Guatemala. On Bruce's birthday we bought two large piñatas and filled them with wrapped caramel candy. Each child in the school was blindfolded and took turns hitting the piñata with a bat to knock out some candy. When little was left a teacher gave the signal and they rushed to grab as much candy as they could.

Jewish holidays include New Year or *Rosh Hashanah*, usually in September or October. The Feast of the Tabernacles or *Succoth* is a week-long harvest festival celebrating the 40 days of Moses in the wilderness. *Hanukkah*, usually in December, is celebrated with a candelabrum with eight candles. Gifts are often exchanged. The Day of Atonement or *Yom Kippur* is the 10th day of the seventh month. Passover or *Pesach* is a week-long festival in the spring celebrating the exodus from Egypt. The holy day is Saturday. Some businesses are closed Friday and Saturday, and conservative and orthodox fundamentalists are trying to get all Jewish businesses to close on Saturday.

Buddhists celebrate the birth of Buddha, usually on the eighth day of the fourth month. A procession follows a statue of Buddha. It is bathed with tea or water, following the belief that Buddha was bathed by heavenly beings when he was born. Incense is burned and paper flowers are spread. The Feast of the Dead is often on 15th day of the Seventh Month. The spirits of the dead leave their tombs for a few days. The Chinese New Year is the second New Moon after the winter solstice, which is on or near December 21. Thus, Chinese New Year is as early as January 21, or as late as February 19. Families get together, visit shrines and tombs of ancestors, and eat special foods. Parades and fireworks are common. Children receive toys, Buddhist monks are given robes and alms, others are given presents symbolizing wealth and prosperity. The Lantern Festival is usually 15 days after the Chinese New Year. We were in China one year during the festival. Shops sold colorful paper lanterns. There were parades with them, and street dances by people dressed as dragons or lions.

Islam has a holiday on the birthday of the Prophet Mohammed. Shiites also honor the suffering of his grandson Husayn. During Ramadan they fast from dawn until sunset. Naturally, men may be a little cranky then, so Ramadan is not a good time to visit an Islamic country. Local men usually take the afternoon off from work. The time of Ramadan is based upon the lunar cycle, so it changes. Friday is the holy day, many people do not work on Thursday or Friday.

PART II:

BELIEFS

CHAPTER 10:
DEATHS & FUNERALS; SACRIFICES

Deaths & Funerals

On Pacific islands the dead are often buried in concrete tombs or vaults in the front yard. It is considered to be barbaric to shovel dirt on a woman's body. The home is not sold, it must be kept in the family for generations. When no one remembers the deceased the burial vault becomes overgrown and may be removed. In Tonga, tombs are often buried in a cemetery near the sea, occupying the best real estate. In traditional villages of the Pacific, a death not from an apparent cause was considered to be caused by a religious fault or the breaking of a taboo. A priest is often asked to determine the cause. In Papua New Guinea some burials are in simple tombs, little marked. Sometimes bits of a yam are sprinkled on top of the grave, for the soul to eat. However, each person killed by "the enemy" in a "payback killing" in Papua New Guinea is buried in a brightly painted tomb like a dog-house, usually made of concrete, along the road, where everyone in the tribe will continue to see it. The death must be avenged. On a 25-mile stretch of rough dirt road out of Tara there are at least 30 recent payback graves. Late in 1996 a battle arising from a payback killing involved around 1,000 warriors on each side, armed with spears or bows and arrows. Hundreds of years ago deep ditches were dug in the Highlands of Papua New Guinea to hide the movement of warriors from the enemy. The ditches are still used by warriors and to mark property boundaries. It is common in Papua New Guinea and much of the Pacific to keep a fresh body in a storage shed and not to bury it for a year or more after death. The bones are usually then buried, but the skull is saved. On Easter Island a dead body was usually cremated in a pit near an ahu. After washing, the bones were then buried elsewhere.

It has been common in many countries to bury a body in a large pottery jar. A hole is often made in the bottom of the jar for the soul to escape. China's Panpo Museum near Xi'an displays jars with such a hole dated as early as 6,000 BCE. China's government encourages cremation of a body. With 1.2 billion people and little arable land—only 10 percent of the total—tombs would soon use up all of the land. The bodies of Zhou (Chou) Enlai and the recent president, Deng Xiaoping, were cremated, to set examples for the people. But the body of Chairman Mao was preserved, like that of Russia's Lenin and

Vietnam's Ho Chi Minh. However, I have seen many cemeteries with tombs, sometimes decorated with paper flowers, in more isolated villages. I have watched Hindu cremation ceremonies in Nepal and India. After burning the ashes are swept into a "holy" river. Tibetans traditionally threw, and still throw, entire bodies into a river. Today many Tibetans do not eat fish. Lamas (priests) are often cremated but the bodies of higher lamas are left exposed on a mountain, to be eaten by eagles. Some Tibetans first chop a body into small pieces. The Mosuo near Lugu Lake and Tibet, like many Asians, believe that death is a natural event, leading to reincarnation, therefore a happy time. The corpse is washed, dressed in new clothes, and silver is put into the mouth. The body is put into the fetal position, in a dry room for a few days, and lamas read sutras from the Buddhist "Bible" to guide the soul. After a few days the body, in a coffin painted with the stars, sun, and moon, is put on top of the kitchen stove. Offerings are made, then lamas read more of the sutras and everyone prays that the spirit will arise. The coffin and body are cremated, then the bones are gathered and buried in a graveyard. The Bai, in and near Dali, Yunnan, prefer to bury a body intact, with the head to the west, so it can look east at the rising sun. Chinese, until recently, believed the location of a burial site was even more important than the location of a house. If the site is good, the clan is strengthened, if bad the Earth is displeased and the clan is weakened.

Peoples over the centuries in many cultures have buried with the body or the bones things believed to be useful in the afterlife. Tombs in Ancient Egypt and China are well known for containing the things that would be helpful to the living. Many American Indians, such as the *Anasazi* ("Old Ones"), also buried pottery and tools with a body. Peru's National Archeology Museum in Lima and Bolivia's National Archeology Museum in La Paz have mummies, usually sitting in a fetal position, wrapped in a blanket, with food and other objects they would need in the afterlife. Some were buried in a basket. The mummies were well-preserved in the cold dry Andes Mountains.

Survivors have many ways to mourn the death of a loved one. Wailing or crying is common, sometimes for several days. In Papua New Guinea widows are expected to cut off a finger or an ear. A visitor reported that he saw a recent widow scratch her face with long fingernails until the scratches bled profusely. Until recently Tahitians expressed their deep sorrow, as well as great pleasure, by scratching the face with a shark's tooth until each scratch bled. In Papua New Guinea, all female relatives of the deceased are expected to wear a necklace made of "Jobs Tears," the seed of a local plant, usually for two years. One tribe mourns for only two weeks. A new widow in Papua New Guinea sometimes puts clay all over her body. It is not washed off but gradually falls off. Men and women in many countries put wood ashes on the face or the entire body when mourning the death of as loved one. On Tanna Island, Vanuatu, widows blacken their faces. In Vanuatu a man growing a beard is in mourning. A woman cannot remarry if her son is still growing a beard. If a husband or wife dies the surviving spouse is expected to stay in seclusion for 100 days. In Tonga and most of the Pacific black is the color of mourning. Women wear black much of the time, because they have so many relatives in the extended family, and several may die each year. In Uzbekistan men in mourning wear blue or black, with a green hat. Women in mourning wear a blue dress and white shawl.

On many Pacific islands, when a person dies the family gives a feast for five days or so, and villagers bring gifts of mats, pigs, and other valuables to the family. This helps to spread and diffuse the grief. Funeral ceremonies were also intended to appease the soul of the deceased, so it would not return to torment the living. After a death in Vanuatu and Fiji a village has 100 days or more of mourning. In Fiji some 700 guests or more come to a feast, bringing gifts of fine tapa mats for the survivors. When the chief dies, fishing by any member of his tribe is prohibited for a period of four months, some tribes prohibit fishing for a year.

In Ghana we returned late in the afternoon in the expedition truck to our campsite near a village. However, since that weekend had been chosen to honor the deaths of all villagers in the past year, we brought the truck in later. They had strung a low electric line with lights over the road, to provide light for the festivities of dancing, drinking, and eating. Each man wore a black sash, and women wore red and black dresses. Ghana's Ashanti tribe shave their head six days after the death of a family member and hold ceremonies to say goodbye to the departing spirit. Hottentots in South Africa mark a grave with a pile of stones. Any passing Hottentot is likely to add a stone or a stick and make a short prayer for the soul of the dead. In China and Southeast Asia, stores sell realistically shaped briefcases, cars, airplanes, toys, refrigerators, and more, all made of paper pulp. Most of them are natural color. They are for burning at the funeral of those who follow Taoism (Daoism), so the real thing can be enjoyed in the next world. When someone dies among the Naxi in Yunnan province, an old man of the family puts into his mouth tea, bits of silver, and grains of rice—seven for a female and nine for a male—wrapped in red paper. After three days of mourning the coffin with the body is carried to the pit, where the son is first to put dirt on top. Many people worry that the soul of those who committed suicide wanders forever, lonely and forlorn. The Naxi priests in China's Yunnan province long ago devised for their Dongba religion a ceremony to put at ease those souls.

Monuments are often erected to represent ancestors. On Easter Island each of the big moai represents an ancestor or many ancestors of a particular clan. Many of the moai erected on an ahu (stone platform) are believed to have had a topknot made of red *scoria* stone found on the island. Red is a sacred color in many countries. The moai nearly always faced inland, toward the village. Many moai have petroglyphs carved on the back. Nearly 900 moai were carved, but almost 400 of them are still in or near Rano Raraku, the hillside with the stone quarry where they were cut out with stone chisels. Some moai are up to 33 feet long. The red topknot alone sometimes weighs more than 10 tons.

In Christian countries tombstones were rare, except for the famous, until 250 years ago. In Islamic countries only a simple stone headstone is often used. Religious professionals and soldiers, such as the *mujahideen*, usually have a flag of a particular color at the grave. Only wealthy or famous deceased people, or rulers, have an elaborate tomb everywhere. I visited the big cemetery on a hill above Zagreb, Croatia. Separate sections are for Roman Catholics, Orthodox Christians, Jews, and Muslims. They are separated in death, as they were in life. In Argentina a cemetery usually buries Indians separate from "Europeans." In the U.S. until recently Blacks were buried in a separate cemetery or in a distinct part of a cemetery. They are separated after death, as they were when they lived. On many Pacific Islands, Asia, and Africa a cemetery is the home of ancestors. It is often taboo to wander in a cemetery unless you have permission from the village chief or an elder.

In Papua New Guinea and islands of Melanesia every death has a cause, and it must be discovered. After a death for unknown reasons the brothers of the deceased must go to a special "dreaming house." where they take herbs to make them dream. If they decide that a particular person caused the death, that person must be killed within a reasonable time. The name of a dead person is never spoken. Sometimes the skull of the deceased is taken to the medicine man and left there, usually in a wooden shed, for four years. A family wanting to know the cause of death gives a pig to the medicine man. He usually determines during the night who caused the death. That person will have a short life. Don't make an enemy of the medicine man! A windstorm tells everyone in the tribe that the medicine man has sent a spirit to kill someone. Who? The Achuar Indians of Ecuador had almost identical beliefs and practices, according to an article by Mary Roach in *Discover* magazine, December, 1998. She reported that a shaman comes out of a hallucinogenic trance with the source of a curse that caused a death. The person named may be assassinated. The Achuar believe that the spirit of the deceased will not rest until the death is avenged. Many Achuar, like the Papua New Guinea Highlanders, die from violent acts.

Among the Aborigines of Australia any person who dreamed of a person who had recently died had to bathe thoroughly to wash away the soul of the deceased, which could make the dreamer sick. In the Marquesas Islands relatives of the deceased burned the home and the hair and all personal belongings of the deceased, partly to erase memories and partly to prevent a sorcerer to cause harm to the soul of the deceased.

Death is treated as a natural event, like birth, eating, sleeping, and parenthood, in many traditional societies. In a crowded village or city where the life expectancy is low, death is common, not a big event. Few if any tears are shed when a family member or other relative dies. After a ritual death or funeral ceremony the survivors try to carry on their life as before. Children learn quickly that death is normal, and it is not hidden from them. Children and adults are not afraid of death. In Islamic countries death is considered to be natural and innocent. Mohammed the Prophet said "You must not weep or cry over your dead." There was no original sin, and man is innocent, not a fallen creature. Since man and the world are innocent, there is no need for a savior. In Islamic countries tombs are usually simple. However, in Egypt many people seem to be obsessed with death, and tombs in Cairo are sometimes elaborate and expensive.

Sacrifices

Upon the death of a king or other important man it was common to kill at least some of his wives and servants, perhaps to serve him in the afterlife. China was not unified until Emperor Ch'in united several provinces in 221 BCE. Prior to his rule it was customary that when an emperor died his wives, servants, and large numbers of his bodyguards were killed and buried with him. Emperor Ch'in had each of his bodyguards make an exact likeness of himself, to be buried to protect the Emperor's body. I saw them at the ancient capital of *Chang'an*, near Xi'an. Each is armed with a brass spear or a crossbow. The bodyguards were then permitted to continue to live. The practice of burying wives and servants with a dead king existed in many parts of the world until fairly recently. In Egypt there is a pit near each of the early pyramids where slaves of the deceased were buried alive. Later, little figures, *Ushabtis*, were buried to do work for the mummy. In Bulgaria the Thracian king at Kazanluk limited the ritual killing of wives to only his favorite wife. Each wife then wanted to be killed when he died around 2,300 years ago, but only one was selected. The king's favorite horse was also sacrificed. Missionaries ended the practice of strangling wives of a chief when he died, in Fiji, Vanuatu, and other Pacific islands. In Fiji and Vanuatu, like many countries, when a chief died his wives were buried with him. If the chief had 100 wives, all had to die. Later only the finger was cut off and put into his grave. Still later only her hair was cut, but today a chief's wife can remain intact when he dies.

Incas of South America sacrificed a young woman each year, so crops would be more fertile. When a new Inca was inaugurated as many as 200 children were sacrificed. The well- preserved mummies of teenage girls and youths have been found in several parts of the Andes Mountains. They were left on a high cold mountain to freeze to death as a sacrifice. Mayans of Mexico and Central America sacrificed young women and men by throwing them into a *cenote* or natural deep well. A night club in a cenote in Merida, Yucatan, re-enacts the ceremony of sacrificing a maiden. Lights are turned off and the show ends just before the knife enters her body. When Mayans adopted some of the culture of the Toltecs in the Tenth Century AD they cut out the heart of a living person to be sacrificed. In many cultures animals were sacrificed more than humans. The Chinese emperor in the recent Ming Dynasty, on the winter solstice, December 21, sacrificed animals at Beijing's Temple For A Good Harvest. Africa's Zulus made an animal sacrifice for ancestors when anyone died. If no sacrifice is made the ancestors may return, often in the form of a poisonous mamba snake. If the snake has appeared it is believed to go away after the sacrifice. Many of the ceremonies and offerings throughout Africa are to honor ancestors, so they won't return and harm the family or the tribe.

Early altars had a deep well nearby to catch the blood of sacrificed animals. A typical example is Lebanon's Balbak, a temple dedicated to the god Baal, in a wide valley. The altar of early Christian churches, like St. Siliyus Convent in Maaula, Syria, had a ridge all around the outside to prevent sacrificial blood from flowing out except at one corner, where it flowed into a deep well. Christians in the Council of Nicaea, 325 AD, prohibited any further use of new altars with ledges. In the Middle East the blood from sacrificed animals usually flowed from ancient stone altars through a trough with the carved head of a bull or an ibex. The blood went into a deep hole, where it was said to enrich the soil.

A female virgin has status in many cultures. In Samoa and other Pacific islands during the many ceremonies the *taupou* or village virgin sits with the talking chief, who carries the symbols of his office—a long carved pole or staff, a whisk, and a special necklace. Some villages have a difficult time finding a teenage girl who meets the qualifications to be a virgin. She is often the daughter of the chief or talking chief, and must be chaperoned all of the time to protect her chastity. On Easter Island, when the trees had been cut so big moai could no longer be transported from the quarry to the ahus, the people changed to the Birdman Cult, around the Fourteenth Century. Each year men competed in climbing down a steep cliff, swimming a mile or so in shark-infested waters to a small island where sea birds (the sooty tern) nested, and returning, climbing the steep cliff, with an unbroken egg. The first to do so became Birdman of the Year. During the ceremony priests chanted the *rongorongo* tablets. Chanting unintelligible words or in a language unintelligible to most people (such as Latin) by priests is common in many religious ceremonies around the world, today and in the past. That enhances the professional status of the priests. On Easter Island the athlete himself did not become Birdman, but the man who hired the winning athlete was the lucky man. He practically ruled the island for a year and was given the "virgins" who had been hidden in a cave during the contest. He stayed in the cave with them in seclusion for a week. Any child fathered by the Birdman also had special privileges.

In ancient Carthage a boy was given by his parents to be sacrificed by burning. The ashes were proudly stored in big pottery urns. It was common in Europe, to make a city wall or fortress stronger, to sacrifice someone and bury the body under the wall. In Vilnius, Lithuania, a mother volunteered to have her son killed and buried under a wall of the Upper Gedimanas Castle. The reluctant son said "the lightest thing is a baby, the sweetest thing is mother's milk, but the heaviest thing is my mother's heart." Later, only the shadow of a military officers was buried. How can we bury a shadow? In Fiji it was common, before building an important temple dedicated to the gods, to kill at least 10 warriors and bury their bodies under it to protect the temple. A family, building a house, killed one warrior and buried him under it so his spirit protected the house. Until recently, in Papua New Guinea, bones of pigs or of an enemy were buried below posts for a new men's spirit house (Haus Tamboran). Carvings on the great stone temples of Cambodia's Angkor Wat area show Cambodian soldiers celebrating a Thirteenth Century victory. To become stronger they sacrificed a buffalo and drank its blood, mixed with its urine.

In the Marquesas Islands, the strongest man in a tribe or the oldest son of an important family, when killed in battle, was eaten by men in his tribe, to get his strength. It was important to save the corpse from the enemy, for they might eat him and get his strength. Huron Indians in the U.S. and Canada ate the flesh and drank the blood of an enemy warrior to get his strength. Sometimes the important or strong man was sacrificed and killed, to be eaten by "friendly" tribesmen. The priest or chief was given the best parts of a victim—usually the eyes, brain, intestines, and liver. Many other Pacific islanders, including Melanesian Fiji, Papua New Guinea, the Solomons, and Vanuatu, and Polynesian Tonga, Samoa, and New Zealand, and the Micronesian Gilbert Islands practiced cannibalism. Other cannibals were in tropical South America, the Carib Indians of the West Indies, the Aztecs in Mexico, some Indians in today's U.S., Sumatra, the Amazon basin, and the Congo basin. Many peoples throughout much of the world ate a deceased relative to conserve his spirit or soul in a friendly place. Most of the 18 tribes in Paraguay sacrificed victims or relatives, eating the entrails and drinking the blood to get the strength of the deceased. They preserved the head. Some Indians of Paraguay, Amazon Indians, and Pacific Islanders learned how to preserve the skin, eyes, and hair of the deceased, friendly or an enemy. They drained the blood, soaked the head in strong herbal mixtures to weaken bones and shrink everything, then dried the head and added preservatives like salt. Occasionally a shrunken human head with features well preserved could be bought in Amazon or Pacific markets as recently as 1946.

A male or female selected to be sacrificed within a few months or years had a high status and privileges in many cultures, in North America, South America, Africa, and elsewhere. It was considered to be an honor. They were usually sacrificed to the Earth Goddess near the time for planting so the crops would grow well. Blood of the victims helped the crops to grow. In the Solomon Islands a child captured from an enemy tribe was sometimes designated as a *vela*. It was well fed, then sacrificed in a big ceremony. Warriors tossed the child back and forth, it was drowned and cooked over a fire, but only the priests ate the vela. Those to be sacrificed were often considered to be divine, a representative of a god. Toltecs and some other tribes in Mexico, including the later Mayans, after adopting some of the practices of the Toltecs, ate the heart of the sacrificed victim. The Pawnees of the U.S. Midwest were said to eat the victim's body. Sir James Frazier in *The Golden Bough* tells us that by eating the flesh of a divine creature men thought they were partaking of the body of their god. Is the partaking of communion in Christian churches somewhat similar?

CHAPTER 11:
LEGENDS, TROLLS, & ELVES

Legends

Legends help to show the right way to be by examples from the deeds of heroes. Legends in Estonia, Latvia, Lithuania, Poland, the Czech Republic, and Slovakia are nearly always sad. They are often about a pretty girl or a likable young man who are forced to choose between ill treatment by the powerful, or death. They choose death. The people have been surrounded by stronger countries that have invaded many times in history. Portuguese like sad *fado* songs. A woman singer often cries before the end of the song. In the U.S. popular "country" songs are often the story of a man or woman who lost in the game of love.

A story about the gray and pink dolphin is told the length of the Amazon. Young men at a dance held in a town on the river were jealous of a handsome stranger. He had his choice of the prettiest partners, and he led several into the bushes. Just before sunrise several of the jealous young men had enough. They followed him with an intent to stop his dancing forever. The stranger headed quickly to the river, then disappeared. The young men trailing him heard a splash, saw a pink dolphin swim away, but could not find the youth. Local people believe dolphins can become human beings. If an unmarried village girl becomes pregnant, she says "The dolphin is the father." They do not eat dolphin, it may be an ancestor. Environmentalists encourage the legend, to protect the dolphin. Tahitians believed that the soul of a person who drowned entered a dolphin or a shark. Some Lowland tribes in Papua New Guinea believed that an eel could put its head into the vagina, causing a woman fishing to become pregnant.

My wife, two sons, and I took the little ferry to Chile's Chiloé Island in 1970. The Pan American Highway ended at the ferry terminal. Ancestors of the island people, living in their isolated little world, brought some of their legends from Europe. Others developed locally. Unmarried island girls who become pregnant often say that *Trauco*, a legendary little man only a meter tall, is the father. He apparently has more success with women than Cassonova.

My wife and I hiked part of two summers on the Forbidden Plateau, Vancouver Island, in British Columbia, Canada. One August more than 100 years ago all of the women and girls of a Native Peoples village were out picking the tasty berries. At nightfall they had not returned. Strange. The men slept little during the night. With sunrise they searched for the women and girls—the route to the berry patches, and all around. They were gone, without a trace! They were never found. It is said that a woman alone should never enter the area. However, my wife and I did not meet any ghosts or other problems. In the Solomon Islands we heard a similar legend. The *Kakamoras* are said to be like humans, only smaller, faster, and stronger. Many young village women are said to have been carried off by the Kakamoras.

During studies at one of my schools in Germany, a visiting lecturer analyzed popular *Märchen* or children's stories, including *Hansel and Gretel* and *Little Red Riding Hood*. Many other stories feature a giant and a dwarf. He said that the stories warn little girls that men are dangerous, whether in the form of a man, a wolf, or an evil witch. The Brothers Grimm compiled a collection of stories nearly 200 years ago, they are still popular with children of all ages. Many of the stories are about magic, communication between man and animals or birds, or the successful marriage of a poor but moral person.

Parents in many countries attempt to persuade unruly children to behave themselves by telling children that a bogeyman or evil person or thing will get them if they don't behave. In central and Eastern Europe, long occupied or threatened by Turks, parents still warn children that "the Turks are going to get you." Sometimes they warn that "the Gypsies will get you, and sell you for a slave." South Africa's Zulus warn their children "if you are not good I will give you to the White man to be eaten." In the past, in Polynesia, children were warned that the *Popaa*, or European, would get them. Children there are still warned that the *tupapau* ghost will get them at night. Adults often keep a lamp burning all night and if they walk around at night they carry a light, to keep away the tupapau. In northern Alaska, Iñupiaq (Inuit) parents tell their children to beware of *Tutu*, who has a caribou's head and a man's body. He is said to live in places that are dangerous for children.

In Tonga and many other Pacific islands fishermen carve and paint a lure to look like a mouse. They say that a mouse once persuaded an octopus to give it a ride across a stretch of water to the next island. As they neared the shore the mouse defecated on the octopus. Since then every octopus is said to hate mice, and they try to catch them. Local fishermen kill an octopus by biting it between the eyes. In New Caledonia our small bus arrived at the wide Quaïème River in the dark evening. Sometime later the little ferry chugged over and took us across the river. Roads in New Caledonia are usually good but no bridge has been built across the river. A giant shark-like creature is said to live in the river, and a bridge would block its way to the sea. The creature would then bring bad luck to nearby villages. Villagers swim in the sea and other rivers, but never swim in the Quaïème.

The dung beetle often works hour after hour pushing a small ball of dung across the desert. In Yemen, with much camel dung, I was told that an ancestor of the beetle wanted to marry a princess. He was told that he first had to clean the desert of all dung. He is still busy, burying the balls of dung in sand.

Trolls

Trolls in Norway are considered to be ugly little people who live underground. They are said to be stupid. Tourist shops in Norway sell troll dolls. In Iceland trolls were giants, they are said to capture people at night to eat or to take as slaves. In the daytime trolls change to rocks. Iceland has many rocks "which proves that there are trolls." Icelanders point out places where the highway that goes around the big island was moved slightly to avoid disturbing a rock, said to be a home for trolls. *Sagas* are popular short or long stories about giants or battles. More than 700 years ago Iceland's Snorri Sturlson wrote many sagas that are still popular.

Elves

Elves are usually bad or mischievous. They are said to be able to change themselves into any form and to vanish. They do bad things, like blowing out a candle, leaving a gate open, or causing the chimney to smoke. Some are helpful and good, they live close to man in fields and woods. The *hidden people* are usually good, especially to those who help them. In Ireland they are really fairies. Many great Irish stories have been told about them. They include little green *leprechauns*, who make shoes with silver buckles. Sometimes they fight giants and win. The Celts, who wandered over most of Europe but ended up in Ireland, were great story tellers. Some tales are about fairies, hobgoblins, or others, some tales tell of mythical heroes, some have supernatural characters such as animals that speak, and others tell of amazing cunning or stupidity. Scots are also great story tellers, especially their tales of folk heroes.

CHAPTER 12:
SPIRITS, THE SOUL, EVIL EYE,
SUPERSTITIONS, SHAMANISM, PROPHETS,
DRAGONS, & WITCHES

Spirits & the Soul

Primitive societies and some modern societies believe that each animal, bird, human, and tree has a soul. Pacific islanders believe that there is great power, a supernatural force, *mana*, in many persons and objects. People on Easter Island believed that a big moai was the home of the spirit of their ancestors. When warfare began on the island around the Fifteenth Century the white coral eyes of the moai were destroyed to destroy its *mana* and all of the standing moai were pushed over. A round stone three feet in diameter is near the sea on Easter Island. It is said to have come from Hiva, the mythical home of the Polynesians. Called the "navel of the earth," it is said that a person hugging it tightly can feel the stone's power, its mana. I hugged it tightly and felt nothing but a cold rock. Polynesians, from Tonga to the Marquesas, Tahiti, and Easter Island believed that each marae or ahu and the stone tikis or moai on it, had mana. A stone with carved petroglyphs of sacred symbols had more mana, more power. A stone tiki or moai was believed to have inside a life force, as some people believe a statue of Jesus or Mary is far more than merely an inert representation of Jesus or Mary. Other Pacific islanders had beliefs similar to the Easter Islanders. Many Polynesians believed that the first thing evident after creation was stone, so anything made of stone has mana. Our small group asked students in the high school in Hanga Roa, Easter Island, "what is the most important thing about your island?" They answered "the mana."

Europeans from Scandinavia to Rome had sacred trees and sacred forests until as recently as the Fourteenth Century. In Togo, West Africa, some large kapok trees are sacred; a ring of palm leaves is sometimes tied around their trunks. Before cutting a tree or killing an animal, a ceremony had to be held to appease its soul. Hunters had to be sure to honor the soul of any animal or bird they killed. Indians of the U.S. Northwest prayed when they caught a deer or salmon. They said "I pray when I use you." Before they set fires to clear the land they prayed to the souls of the trees, bushes, and land that would be harmed. Our driver in New Caledonia said he "talks with the land" and asks its permission to go hunting on the land. When the "barbarians" of northern Europe adopted Christianity after the Fifth Century they no longer had to pay respect to the soul of a tree before cutting it. With new metal axes they soon cleared the forests and planted crops, permitting a big expansion of the population. New Zealand's Maori had different names for female and male trees. Koreans believed that the soul of women who die in childbirth lives in particular trees. A heap of stones is placed under these trees. Until recently offerings of food and wine were made to the spirits. In Europe the oak was often considered to be sacred. Druids, the priests of the Celts, often had religious ceremonies in an oak grove. When a million chickens were killed in Hong Kong in 1997 to stop a virus, Buddhists prayed to their souls to speed up their reincarnation.

The Masai in East Africa believe that to dig or till the soil makes the earth angry. They would not plant a garden, dig a well, or even dig a hole to bury the dead. They are cattle herders. Recently, with the population explosion and scarcity of land to graze cattle, some Masai have become farmers to avoid starvation. Vultures sometimes eat their dead, left on top of the ground. The Kalash in Pakistan also leave bodies of the dead on top of the ground. Kalash are believed to be descendants of Alexander the Great, who controlled the area 2,300 years ago. In Bombay, India, Parsis likewise do not believe in contaminating the earth. They leave their dead in towers, where the vultures tear away bits and pieces and sometimes drop them onto city streets. Their beliefs began as Zoroastrianism. They keep a fire burning in their fire temples. Ancient Chinese, like the general who completed the Great Wall for Emperor Ch'in more than 2,200 years ago, believed the Earth was pulsating with vital energy, qi, like the human body. When he built the Wall he thought he had cut the veins of the Earth. Hindus have some 33,000 gods, including animals, snakes, birds, and insects. Some Hindu sects do not believe in killing any living creature.

A scary mask is often worn by men and youths in West African dances. The wearer often claims that he can communicate with and even drive away evil spirits. They claim to represent the dead—the ancestors—and often carry a stick to hit anyone who does not give them money. It is not a good time for travelers to visit the village.

In many cultures, each person is believed to have a spirit or soul. The soul is believed to enter a baby when it is born, and to reside in the body, except when a person is sleeping. The soul then wanders during a dream, but returns upon awakening. The soul may also leave, at least temporarily, a sick person. When a person dies the soul may become a ghost. Funeral rites are usually designed to free the soul of the deceased, as among the Ewe tribe of West Africa. Funeral rites also attempt to satisfy the soul so it will not harass the living. In ancient Egypt, the body was preserved to provide a home for the soul.

When a rich person died the inside organs were removed, the body was covered in salt and wrapped in cloth, to be preserved. The early Egyptians, up until the Fifth Dynasty, did not know whether the mummy would stay preserved for a long time, so they also had a statue made of the deceased as a home for the soul. Egypt's pharaohs, queens, nobles, and other rich people built pyramids, or elaborate tombs in the cliffs of West Thebes, for homes for the souls. Food and rich offerings were left for the afterlife. The soul was often given a boat to cross the Styx ("River of Death") to go to the other world. In the Marquesas Islands, priests and chiefs were once buried in caves in a tomb shaped like a canoe, so the soul could go to the "other world." In China, emperors of the Ming Dynasty, 1368 to 1644 AD, have big tombs with rich offerings for the afterlife. They were sometimes robbed, but Egypt's tombs were usually robbed soon after burial. In Laos, the rich have a small plywood shed built on the grounds of a Buddhist temple as a home for their spirit when they die. When anyone in Laos dies banners are strung on a cord from the ground to a tree on the temple grounds. When the banners flap in the wind they send the spirit to the heavens. Until recently, Chinese believed that every person has three spirits. When a person dies the first spirit goes into the spirit world. For a month each year a table with food was set up before the entrance of a home to feed these spirits to bring prosperity to the family. The second spirit lives in the bones of the dead, a body was not buried for several months. A chicken was carried to the grave to bring with it the spirit of the dead. When a man was near death an ancestral tablet was prepared for the home and his family paid devotions to it. The spirits of people who did not have friends to bury and honor their spirits wandered everywhere, living in rocks and trees, flying low through the air in a straight line.

In Laos, Vietnam, and Burma each village has a post near the center of the village. Each day rice is put on a small platform on the post to feed the spirits. Many homes in rural Vietnam have a small spirit house in front. In the home's main room a corner has an altar for Buddha. Another altar honors grandparents and other ancestors, with their photos. In Ghana, homes of the Ashanti tribe often have a brass pole six feet or so long leaning in the corner of a room. It holds a brass tray with eggs for the great god. The great god also protects the "servant of the stool,"—the current king of the tribe. In Thailand nearly every home has a small spirit house, like a bird house, usually on a post in front of the house. Each day rice, water, flowers, and sometimes a candle are given to the spirits. If they aren't fed the spirits may bring misfortune to the family. The spirits are believed to live at the threshold of the entrance door, so we never step on the threshold.

In Poland many homes have a religious shrine in the front yard. Poland, like Ireland, was long occupied by another country that discouraged Roman Catholicism, so the people became very devout Catholics when they were freed of foreign oppression. In another strongly Catholic country, Malta, many older homes have a statue of Jesus or Mary near the entrance door, and a small shrine in the front yard. In an ancient Jewish cemetery in Prague, in the Czech Republic, some head-stones have small rocks on top, to keep the soul from wandering. The practice apparently began during the 40 years of wandering in the desert—the followers of Moses put rocks on tombs to keep the soul from leaving. Jews still leave notes asking for help on the headstones of popular rabbis. Little rocks keep the notes in place. Amazon tribes near Manaus, Brazil grind the bones of a deceased relative and eat it with mashed banana. They believe that it preserves their memory of the deceased. In Korea, wealthier families have a shrine, usually in the back yard, to worship ancestors. A Korean diviner asks for the name, address, date, and year of birth of a client.

In Java a group of university students and graduates told us "Everyone in Java believes in magic. Magic and the spirits control our lives." Ancestor worship and spirits seem to be much stronger than the official Islamic religion. Magic is important in all African animistic religions. Medicine men, or *juju priests*, found in public markets, sell various fetishes to keep away evil spirits. The skull of particular birds, and shells—especially cowry shells—are common fetishes. Some, *grigris*, are worn around the neck. Local people say they must be blessed by the medicine man to be effective. He charges a fee for the blessing. In Togo a man "gave" me a good-luck charm, then asked for many dollars for it. I gave it back, it seemed to be only a few cowry shells on a cord. When Highlanders in Papua New Guinea first met white men from Australia in the 1930s they believed they were spirits of their ancestors. The Highlanders were amazed at a phonograph, they thought the singing came from their ancestors. Today, men in one village put light gray mud all over their bodies and wear large grayish-tan face masks. When a nearby village tried to take some of the land the "Mudmen" claimed, they advanced silently toward warriors of the tak-ing village. The culprits thought they were spirits of their ancestors. They withdrew and abandoned their claim to the land. We watched a performance by the Mudmen. They were scary. Also in Papua New Guinea, the medicine man of the large Huli tribe of Highlanders led us to a holy place, a small cave on a cliff. A woman's body had been painted on it in red. On a ledge there were seven shiny round black stones each perhaps five inches in diameter, painted with red and white stripes. He called them "meteorites," but all of the meteorites I have seen were rough, not smooth and shiny. He said "the sun is our god, and the meteorite is its son." The medicine man said nearby small red stones were weapons used by the spirits. The shaman keeps several stones for healing, more to insure that the crops will be good, and other stones for other purposes. During ceremonies men are painted with red and white stripes, they sacrifice a pig in a fire, and look up to the sun god. The shaman talks to the sun and tells the tribe when it is time to kill a pig. Roman Catholic missionaries have made inroads in the Highlands. The Catholic priest said it is okay to erect many crosses to keep out evil spirits. However, the priest persuaded them to stop the dances in honor of the sun, "except on special occasions." They build a fire for the dances, and dance to the sun and the spirits. They believe that the smoke carries the spirit to heaven.

Polynesians on Tonga, Tahiti, and elsewhere built a stone wall around a big earth-filled marae or platform, some are several hundred feet square. Sometimes a statue of their fierce god of fertility and war, *Oro*, was erected on the marae. Animals, and occasionally people, were sacrificed on the marae. Today, some people go to a marae on the night of a full moon when the spirits are most active, write down their evil or negative thoughts on a piece of paper, which they burn on the marae. They are then said to be free of evil or negative thoughts. The chief usually sat in a nearby courtyard, with a huge stone backrest, to discourage anyone from assassinating him from the rear. Tikis, carved from stone or wood, large or small, have different meanings in different parts of Polynesia. They were often erected on the edge of a marae or near it, to protect it. In New Zealand, Maori women wore a tiki around the neck as a fertility symbol. In Hawaii they were fastened to the mast of a sailing vessel for good luck. In Tahiti stone tikis were erected and worshipped on a marae, men prayed to their ancestors there. Many marae have a big flat stone where a solo dancer performed, a chief gave a talk, or anyone with unusual tattoos displayed them. There were both public and private marae—the public ones were the most important. However, it was usually taboo for anyone except the priest or a chief to be on a public marae. In the Marquesas Islands a thatch building was often built on the *meae* or marae, as a home for the priests. The meae is always above a village, so the priest could see any enemy approaching. A priest also liked to live in a high place to make it easier for the gods above to give him instructions. It was taboo for anyone but a priest or a chief to visit a meae. When a chief died his body was placed on the meae until it dried, then the skull was carefully preserved and the other bones were buried elsewhere. Some meae had many stone tikis, the Ipona site at Pamau on Hiva Oa Island has a big collection. Most are made of sacred red scoria stone. One tiki, kneeling, represents a woman priest. Many tiki have six fingers on each hand. Some fingers meet in front of the body to retain the mana or power of the tiki in the belly, so the mana cannot escape. Nuku Hiva Island has perhaps the largest collection of marae or meae in Polynesia. One meae has a carving of a couple making love, and of a turtle. Turtles were sacred because they can live in two worlds, land and sea, and were thought to live in the present and future worlds. On Easter Island it was taboo for anyone but a priest to eat a turtle.

The construction of a marae in Polynesia was a sacred event, women and children usually had to leave the village for many weeks during its construction. Polynesians who settled on Easter Island probably came from the Marquesas Islands in the Fourth Century AD. Their moai were much larger than tikis, and they were erected on an ahu, not a marae. However, an ahu was also usually taboo except for a priest or chief, or perhaps important members of the clan that erected the ahu. A taboo area on Easter Island was often marked with white coral. In most of the Pacific it was taboo for anyone except the select few to see the carved image of a god. Local people tried to prevent White sailors and explorers from seeing an image of their god. In Tonga, when the king converted to Christianity he ordered everyone in the kingdom to become Christian. At the request of missionaries, he ordered everyone to burn or destroy all images of their traditional gods. The people blindly followed his orders, like sheep. Today no one knows what the traditional Tonga gods looked like.

Lowland tribes of Papua New Guinea believe that the water spirit uses the crocodile as transportation to move around. Local people set fires in the tall *pitpit* grass, like sugar cane, to drive the "crocs" out. They eat the smaller crocs and use the hide. However, big crocs are considered to be sacred, they are not bothered. One village caught a croc about 16 feet long, tying it up in the village with several ropes. They wanted to ship it by boat down-river, then to a foreign zoo. They said they would never kill the sacred croc. The stone spirit inhabits stones, mostly large stones. Some Pacific Islanders believe that a perfectly round stone is the home of a spirit. In Vanuatu the spirit of a person who dies is believed to live in the banyan tree. In Papua New Guinea the tree spirit lives in the strangler fig—the same family as the banyan. It starts as a sprig, but in a man's lifetime it grows to a huge size, strangling and killing a tree with a trunk seven or eight feet in diameter and more than 100 feet tall. Therefore, it is considered powerful. I noticed local men stopping awhile, then quietly passing larger strangler figs. They said they were honoring the tree spirit. Many tribes honor the strangler fig tree and big crocodiles because of their power. Some tribes in Papua New Guinea believe their ancestors live on branches of big trees, they hang red and white strips of cloth on the limbs and make offerings of food in a basket to the spirits. In southern China, the Bai minority group plants a banyan tree when they build the first houses. If the tree dies it is a bad sign, the village must be moved to a new site. Some tribes in Papua New Guinea and other Pacific islands plant a tree when a baby is born. It is always that person's tree, they protect each other. Several minority groups in China's Guangzhi province plant a gingko tree when a girl baby is born. When each is about 20 years old it is capable of bearing fruit.

The shark is feared as a man killer in much of the Pacific. Some tribes in Vanuatu believe that some men can turn themselves into sharks. If a village man has an enemy he may turn himself into a shark and eat the man. Most Pacific islanders believe that sharks (except "harmless" reef sharks) will not cross a coral reef around an island, so it is safe to swim inside the reef. People on Laulasi, one of the Solomon Islands, worship sharks and give pigs to them. They believe that spirits of the dead live in sharks, the sharks won't bother them, and to kill a shark there is taboo. Local people don't wear black because it is the color of pigs fed to sharks. They don't wear red because it is the color of blood, which attracts sharks.

Many of the men's spirit houses in Papua New Guinea's villages have a small entrance door. That is to be used only by the crocodile spirit. A large mask on the gable end of a spirit house is to keep out evil spirits, especially those spirits that bring illness. Some spirit houses have two large eyes near the eaves, for protection. We visited many large spirit houses. Local women and uninitiated youths cannot enter them. Each has many carvings, usually masks representing spirits of ancestors. Tourist women can now enter those spirit houses where carved masks, crocodiles, story boards about fish and cormorants, slit drums, woven masks with long noses, and other things are sold. The story boards often show a woman in a canoe with a cormorant on top of her head. Women do most of the fishing, and a legend says that cormorants taught them how to catch fish. However, it is taboo on many Pacific islands for a pregnant or menstruating woman to fish. Some villages have an enclosure, a high fence made of pitpit, near the spirit house. We watched some of the dances. The bamboo flutes are sacred, the sound they make "is the spirits of our ancestors." Some villages have several oval-shape stones five or six feet long stuck into the ground in front of the spirit house. They are bloodstones. Until the late 1960s they received the blood of defeated enemies. Spirits of the enemies then go into the spirit house, and become friendly. Older men said some of the bloodstones were captured and brought from an enemy village. Until the late 1960s men in many villages were headhunters. Each man tried to have a collection of the skulls of enemies he had killed. They believed the skull was the source of an enemy's power. One older man said he had five skulls. I asked him if he would show them to me. After hesitating he did so. They were normal skulls, cracked at the back, half-hidden behind his house. Missionaries had told the village men to get rid of the skulls. Until recently the large curved *kina* shell that many men wear around the neck had one hole drilled for each man they had killed. In West Africa some local men ask White men for a lock of their hair. They believe that if they carry it they will acquire the White man's knowledge and skills.

Many skulls that I saw in the Pacific islands were cracked at the rear, indicating a fatal blow by a headhunter. A type of club used by some Fijian warriors has a long spike to kill without damaging the skull bone. After the body of an enemy was eaten the skull bone was used as a ceremonial bowl. In the Solomon Islands, skulls of enemies were put on the roof of each warrior's home to show the chief and others what a great fighter he was. Many warriors were said to have 30 or 40 skulls. Some skulls on Pacific islands are of friendly village people. Survivors want the power of the friendly spirit of the deceased. On many Pacific islands a skull of an ancestor was put on a post in the village for a year or more, then placed in a shrine. Skulls are often not buried because the place of burial would then be taboo, it could not be used for other purposes. Missionaries made enemies when they asked villagers to bury or destroy skulls of their ancestors. Some villages complied, others refused to. Villagers on New Georgia Island in the Solomons showed me three skulls buried in rocks at the edge of the village. They told me they had hidden and preserved the skulls of their ancestors in a cave on the hill behind the village. Throughout the Pacific skulls were often placed among the many roots of the sacred banyan tree.

On some Pacific islands, including many in Vanuatu, a mask used in a ceremonial dance is destroyed after its use, for fear that the dancer's spirit may live in the mask. In Vanuatu and many other islands, the ghosts of people who recently died are believed to be powerful, often harmful, even to members of the family. In Tahiti many people leave a light on all night to keep out ghosts. In New Caledonia and many other Pacific islands, spirits live where people are buried and in the site of an abandoned village. The sites are taboo. South Africa's Zulus believe that spirits of their ancestors live in the pits used to store grain. Some grain is reserved for them. In times of drought sacrifices must be made to the spirits. Many of Europe's old castles are said to be haunted by the ghost of someone who had lived there but died, usually in a tragic manner. I have visited and have slept in several places that are reputed to have ghosts. I was warned in Siem Reap, Cambodia, that my old hotel had ghosts of the many people that the Khymer Rouge killed there when they used it as a prison. I never noticed anything unusual, except that my gecko seemed to be busier than most, eating mosquitoes.

Today in Papua New Guinea, local people do not arise immediately upon awakening, they give the soul time to return to the body. On many Pacific Islands people are warned not to change the position of a sleeping person, for the soul may not recognize the body and won't return to it. Some North American Indian shamans used a carved "soul catcher," like a big spoon, to catch and return the soul of a sick person. Some tribes had objects to protect a baby from bad dreams. Wisconsin's Chippewa (Ojibwa) Indians fastened a woven "dream catcher" to a papoose carrier to catch anything evil so it could not get to the baby. On the Arabian peninsula, evil spirits, *djinns*, are believed to attempt to entice away the soul of a sick person at night. Native American shamans in what is now Ohio used a bone carved like a duck's bill to attract evil spirits away from a sick person. The Inuit (Eskimos) of Alaska and Canada believed that if a person was sick the soul had left the body. A shaman was hired. He went into a trance and sent his own soul to find the sick person's soul. When it was found the shaman tried to bring the sick person's soul back to the body. South Africa's Zulus believe that if a person is sick the gall of a sacrificed animal should be poured onto the body. An invisible *iThongo* spirit will be attracted to lick the body, and it will cure the patient. Bats are eaten in Southeast Asia and many Pacific islands. Men build a smoky fire at the base of a tree, the bats fall and are killed. However, many men in West Africa believe that bats are sons of the Devil. If bats are disturbed they steal the souls of young villagers, causing their death.

Many primitive people believe that taking a photograph of a person takes away the soul. Always get the permission of the East African Masai and of the Australian Aborigines before taking their photograph. Many people believed that each person has a soul so long as the body is preserved. Followers of some animistic beliefs in the Pacific preserve only the skull, they believe it is the home of the soul. Eskimos in Greenland believed that the soul had a *Ba* and a *Ka*. The Ka looked like the deceased person, the Ba looked like a bird.

In Laos the Hmong tribe put a necklace on a boy to keep the three spirits of his soul from leaving his body. In Thailand each person, animal, tree, and even a rice field is believed to have a khwan or soul. A big tree has a *khwan*, either male or female. If a person's khwan is frightened it may leave the body. That person will become ill. The khwan must be attracted back. A sick child may be taken to a Buddhist monk to tie a particular kind of knot to keep the khwan. It is said to enter or leave at a tender spot on the head. Boys have a topknot to protect the tender spot. The topknot is shaved off when the boy reaches puberty, around age 14. In much of southeast Asia the topknot is also said to trick evil spirits into believing that it is a girl, therefore of little importance, not worth bothering. In southern China boys are sometimes given a girl's name and dressed in girls' clothes. A Thai boy does not want anyone, especially a woman or a woman's clothes, to touch his head. If his head is touched he is susceptible to magical powers. The first post to support a new house in Thailand is called the *khwan post*, it must be protected. The taboo against touching a boy on the head is strong in Southeast Asia, at least from Cambodia to Malaysia. People on Pacific islands do not like to be touched on the hair or head, nor to have hands or feet pointed at them.

Many peoples believe in evil spirits. In northern Thailand I visited the homes of the Akha, Yao, Hmong, and other tribes. The Yao tribe often hires a shaman to make a writing on paper, something like a picture of a tree. It is then hung on a wall of a room to keep away evil spirits. In Japan the *Tori* entrance gates to Shinto shrines separate the divine area of the shrine from the outside world. Inner shrines have strips of paper in particular shapes, representing lightning, to purify. They reminded me of the writing of the Yao shaman. Homes of the Akha, and Shinto shrines, are protected by a gate post with a top bar, and a nearby post or drawings to keep out evil spirits. The Akha tear down the gate posts and all homes each year, and rebuild them. Rebirth apparently cleans and purifies them of evil spirits. At Japan's sacred Ise Shrine, a building has been torn down every 20 years for nearly 13 centuries. The building is rebuilt, and so purified. Religious sites around the world are thought to be protected by evil spirits. There are many tales about the death, illness, or other bad luck that befell someone who did not treat a religious site properly. A common belief is that anyone who opens the tomb of an ancient Egyptian pharaoh will be cursed. However, my elderly guide was present with archaeologist Howard Carter when King Tut's tomb was discovered in West Thebes and opened in 1922. My guide was never cursed, nor did he have bad luck.

In New Caledonia, the local Kanaks plant a reddish ti bush near the front door to protect the home against evil spirits. The ti plant is used throughout the Pacific for its sacred red color to protect homes from evil spirits, as fuel for earth ovens, to provide fiber to make the "grass" skirts for dancers, and sugar is made from its roots. Kanaks traditionally put a carved pole in the ground to represent a dead person. It is covered with a cloth to protect the body from evil spirits. Particular plants are connected with death, they are planted at grave sites. They believe that the spirit escapes, it goes through a hole in a big sacred rock, then into the sea. There it is reborn, usually as a small child. We were reluctantly shown an ancient bone of a flying fox, wrapped in a container made from the fur of the flying fox. It is used in *coutume* (custom) religious ceremonies. In the Marquesas Islands a family kept at least one dog, to chase away evil spirits.

Little children in Southeast Asia often wear a hat that looks like a bird or an animal, so evil spirits will not know it is a child. Many peoples give a new baby a temporary obnoxious name, to keep away and not attract evil spirits. When the baby is a year old it gets its regular name. Mothers of the Siua, a matrilineal tribe in Papua New Guinea, hid a new baby and kept its name secret. They believed that if a sorcerer knew the name, the baby could be attacked by evil spirits. When the baby was six weeks old a feast was given, along with announcement of the baby's name. In many parts of Papua New Guinea's Lowlands a new baby is hidden for six months, so evil spirits can't find it. The feast celebrating the giving of a name to a baby was held when it was a year old in many parts of Southeast Asia. Many people there do not leave a window open at night, because the evil spirits may enter. In China and Taiwan, buildings have a barrier at the entrance door, requiring anyone to go to the left or the right. They keep out ghosts, "who can go only in a straight line." Mirrors may be put over doors to repel demons. A large older traditional home of the Bai minority group in Dali, Yunnan, has a plain white wall on the inner court, used as a mirror wall to drive out evil spirits. The Bai were (and are now) ambitious, often rich; the rear wall has no window "so money cannot go out of the home." Bridges in China are curved to keep ghosts from crossing them. In China and Taiwan, women and girls wear a jade bracelet to keep away evil spirits. In Malaysia the Sunday newspapers regularly have articles telling the reader how to avoid or defeat evil spirits. One article warned to be especially wary at "T junctions." In Bali, with a modified Hindu culture, evil spirits are believed to live in the sea. Women and girls don't swim. In recent years some brave youths, copying foreign tourists, have learned to swim, risking attacks by evil spirits. In Bali the gods live in the mountains. Boys and girls in Bali dance in a trance to drive away evil spirits. They are revived by holy water sprinkled by a priest. In Thailand anyone bathing in a river must face the current. If they turn their back to it they may become the victim of black magic. Thais should also pay homage to the water goddess. In Latvia, Christmas decorations were left up in the living room all year to keep away evil spirits. Vikings in Norway believed that the bad little people were kept away by dragons heads on the roof of a church and home. Village homes in Asia, from Japan to Indonesia, have dragons heads on the roof to keep away evil spirits.

Europeans, until recently, believed that animals had a spirit or demon. A bad dog or bull, in Germany, for example, had a trial. If it were found to have a demon inside, the animal had to be punished to get rid of the demon, sometimes by killing. When a person was sick some South American Indians used pain to drive out the demon that had taken possession of the sick person. Sometimes they spanked the patient with nettles, other times they covered the patient's body with ants whose bite was painful. Spain's Canary Islands celebrate San Andreas Day on November 30, by making a lot of noise, to drive away evil spirits.

Agricultural people have always had ceremonies or practices to make the crops do better and to protect farm animals. Some Southeast Asians, including Indonesians, still bury a few betel nuts, as an offering to the rice spirits when planting rice. The sacrifice of people or animals was common in North and South America and Africa, at both planting time and harvest time. Blood of people or animals was believed to make crops grow better. When rice is growing in Indonesia and Burma, local people do not use firecrackers or make a lot of noise near a field of growing rice. The noise might scare the soul of the rice so it will not produce grain. Zulus in South Africa believe that if someone points a finger at growing crops the plants will shrivel up and die. In Europe it was common until this century at harvest time to honor the spirit of the crop being harvested. For example, when the last grain was harvested the farm workers made it into a female figure called "the Old Woman" or "the Grain Maiden." Other crops also had an old woman or maiden. In Papua New Guinea, when land is cleared for crops at least one big tree is left, to provide shelter for friendly garden spirits. Until recently, before the rice harvest, the Wan minority group in China's Yunnan province chose a man with long hair and beard. They then cut off his head, mounted it on a pole, and danced around it, so the rice would grow fast, as did his hair and beard. Now they substitute the head of a buffalo for the man's head. To predict how good the harvest will be next season, on the first day of the Lunar New Year, Yunnan's Naxi offer rice or meat to dogs, to see which they eat first. Yunnan's Yi minority group have a Torch Festival around the 24th day of the sixth Lunar Month. In the evening they carry torches and stick them into the ground to drive away insect pests that might harm their crop. Villagers then make music, dance, drink wine, have fun, and pray for a good harvest.

Incense is believed to have special meaning in many cultures. Guatemala's Indians have combined their ancient religion with Catholicism. On the steps of the Roman Catholic cathedral in Chichicastenango, Guatemala, local Mayans swung buckets of burning incense. Later that evening I saw them swinging buckets of incense before statues of their ancient Mayan gods, *Pocojil* and *Pascuala Abaj*—probably the same buckets of incense. That is like buying two insurance policies. In Korea's Full Moon Festival, youths swing buckets of live coals, like incense. Buddhist temples always have a place to get *joss* (incense) *sticks*, and to make a donation. Some temples, like the Heavenly Lady Temple in Ho Chi Minh City (Saigon), have dozens of large coils of incense hanging near the ceiling. They burn for a month, giving merit to the rich donor. Hundreds of red slips with the name of each donor are also hung on the wall of the temple for a month, giving merit for that period.

Yemen and Oman have many trees that provide frankincense. The first cutting of the bark has a white resin that is burned to provide a pleasant odor. It was burned in temples and was an important trade item. Myrrh is also a gum resin that oozes from cuts in bushes in Yemen, Oman, and nearby areas. It is used in perfume and Chinese joss sticks, burned before statues of Buddha. The Nabataeans in southern Jordan controlled main trade routes for frankincense and myrrh for centuries, beginning before 500 BCE. They built a great city in a *wadi* (a valley, usually dry), using Greek slaves to carve the *Treasury* and other buildings in the red rock cliffs. In Yemen and Oman I examined the trees that produce the sap that makes frankincense and myrrh. I also studied ruins of ancient cities that prospered long ago. One claims to have the throne of the Queen of Sheba (Saba), who took incense to Israel's King Solomon nearly 3,000 years ago. Incense is still important in the ceremonies of several religions, but it was even more important in the ceremonies of ancient religions in Greece, Rome, and elsewhere. When Christianity became the main religion, trade in frankincense and myrrh almost ended.

Many peoples built monuments or tombs that follow the sun through the seasons, the rays shining on particular places at the spring and fall equinoxes, first day of summer, first day of winter, and other important days. These were especially important to agricultural people. Farmers need to know when to plant a crop and when to expect seasonal rains. Ancient astronomers include the Egyptians, Chinese, Arabs, Mayans of Mexico and Central America, Incas of South America, plus Celts and pre-Celtic people of France, the United Kingdom, and Ireland. For example, on the equinox, the sun's rays shine in deep dark passage tombs some 5,000 years old at Newgrange in Ireland, signifying rebirth. One expert found that rocks have been arranged long ago in New Mexico, U.S., so that the sun's rays makes a shadow on circular rings of Fajado Butte at the winter solstice, and on the summer solstice the sun shines in the exact center. On the summer solstice the sun rises through a particular hole in the stones at England's Stonehenge. Visitors are no longer permitted to walk among the stones, as I did in 1982. Stonehenge is the best known of more than 100 ancient stone circles in Britain. I saw several stone circles on the Coast-to-Coast Walk.

Ancient man, and men and women today in lesser-developed countries, often have great artistic ability. Their art usually has a religious purpose, dedicated to one of the gods or to ancestors. Other art has fertility symbols, for a better crop, for good hunting or fishing, or for many sons. Their wood carvings, stone carvings, etchings on pottery, and petroglyphs are often fascinating, done with great skill. Simple things, like stone axes and adzes, house roof beams, and poles supporting the hut, are often beautifully carved. Christians have also produced beautiful carvings, paintings, and stained glass windows, as well as wonderful hymns. Hindu temples, with carved figures of gods in bright colors, are often the most beautiful structure in a city. Buddhist temples, with gold and carved statues of Buddha and his followers, often represent many years of work by artists. Islamic mosques, with colorful ceramic tiles, and no ornaments, show how a simple design is often the most beautiful. Christian missionaries, Islamic fundamentalists, and others have made great mistakes by destroying art because it was made by people—"heathen," "pagans," or "infidels"— who followed another belief.

The Evil Eye

Many people worry about the evil eye. In Nepal the entrance gate to nice homes have a big painted protective eye. In Albania, restaurants often have a big painted eye outside for good luck. In West Bengal, southern India, and some other parts of India women put a black circle made of *kohl* around their eyes and children's' eyes to keep evil spirits away. In southern India if someone has had bad luck, he or she goes to an old woman who knows how to exorcise the evil eye. She often wraps sugar, salt, pepper, rice, and sometimes other things in an old cloth, carries it around the unlucky person five times, then burns it. Many Afghans and Pakistanis in Pakistan's Northwest Territories also wear black kohl around the eyes to keep out evil spirits. In Yemen, men put the long straight horns of an ibex on the corner of a home to keep away evil spirits. Older village homes and *tavernas* (inns) in Italy have a cow's skull and horns on the roof to keep away evil spirits.

The powerful crocodile is feared and worshipped in many cultures. In Vietnam boats on the Mekong have a painted eye on each side of the bow to frighten away crocodiles. In Singapore our Chinese junk had eyes painted on the bow so it could see better. Near Africa's Niger River in Mali several tribes display crocodiles carved from wood to protect their buildings. Dugout canoes in Papua New Guinea, such as those on the Sepik River, Korasameri River, and Blackwater Lakes, have a carved crocodile at the bow. This is to inform crocs that it is only another croc, so it won't try to eat the people in the canoe. In Togo and Benin, many people wear a ring carved in the shape of a snake. They believe snakes don't bite other snakes.

In much of Asia, Africa, and the Pacific, it is considered bad manners to stare at anyone, especially someone of the opposite sex. Africa's Masai believe that some people who stare at them can see through them, doing harm to the person stared at. The starer must spit to stop the harm. Spitting represents the pleasant falling rain. Children run from strangers to avoid being stared at.

Superstitions

Wooden dhows in Oman often have a string of cowry shells near the bow, to keep away the evil eye. All of the dhows used by smugglers who go to Iran are said to have a string of cowry shells. Men on Georgia Island in the Solomons fasten a string of cowry shells to the prow of their big sailing canoes to serve as eyes so they can find the best way across the ocean. In West Africa, many people wear a necklace with one or more cowry shells for good luck. Cowry shells have been used as money in many cultures, beginning in China before 1,000 BCE. In the Americas and Europe some people carry a rabbit's foot for good luck. Others wear a Christian cross around the neck for blessings and to show their devotion. Some people in the Americas and Europe fasten a metal horseshoe above the entrance door to a home to have good luck. In the Appalachian Mountains, three nails in the shape of a triangle were driven into the door for good luck. In Japan a twisted straw rope is put over the doorway for good luck. In the U.S. some people cross their fingers when they make an untruthful statement, or they knock fingers on wood when they make a doubtful statement. The girl who takes the last goodie, who steps over a broom, or who cuts her fingernails on a Sunday, may be an old maid. If a butterfly flies around the head of a young woman she will marry soon. It is bad luck to change the marriage date, once it has been definitely set and publicized. Don't tell anyone your bad dream before breakfast, for it may come true. If your ears burn, someone is saying bad things about you. Cross your ears with a wet finger to stop it. If you break a mirror you will have seven years of bad luck. Opening an umbrella inside a house will bring bad luck. Don't walk under a ladder, it will also bring bad luck. If you leave a horsehair in water a week it will turn into a snake. In Germany, if you treat a cat badly storms will pound your grave.

A woman brings bad luck if she is working on a ship or in a coal mine. Zola's great novel *Germinal*, written in 1885, tells of the horrible conditions of women a century ago when they worked in French coal mines and were expected to have sexual relations with the male miners. Nearly every state in the U.S. between 1900 and 1960 passed laws and regulations prohibiting women from working in coal mines or other places hazardous to their health. The "women's protective laws" also limited their hours of work, how much weight they could lift, and how many months they could work when pregnant. When laws prohibiting discrimination against women were passed in the 1970s, they repealed the women's protective laws, or the laws were found to be invalid. Practices that favor females are now usually unlawful. Customs sometimes change. What was required by law in one era may be prohibited in another era.

My wife and I trekked a few days through the Dogon country in Mali. They have many fetishes along trails. We were warned not to touch them. The ancient Tellem people who lived along the same cliffs left many fetishes on big rocks, the cliff sides, or on walls of ancient grain storage towers. Monkey skulls were used for healing. Various other animal bones are arranged in a particular order. Geometric designs were also painted on the cliffs. The Tellem escaped from the Islamic horsemen long ago by moving into the isolated rocky valley. The Dogon followed, for the same reason, in the 16th Century, after the Tellem were gone. Ghana's Ashanti tribe escaped from Islamic horsemen by moving into a forested area where the tsetse fly is too bad for horses. The Ashanti must till their gardens by hand but they became rich, by mining and trading in gold. All three tribes wanted to continue their animistic religions.

Shamanism & Sorcerers

A *shaman* acts as a medium between the visible world and the invisible spirit world. Many people in Asia and Africa consult a *diviner* (shaman) when they have problems or want to make a tough decision. Some diviners claim to be able to reconstruct a past event, and to foretell the future, using messages from the spirits. On Pacific islands, as in many traditional societies, war was never begun without first consulting a diviner. In Zimbabwe the Shona tribe's diviner tossed carved bones or shells and studied the way they landed after several throws. He then told us his conclusions. In Mali, deep in the isolated area where the Dogon tribe lives, I watched a diviner work. He shook rocks in his hand, then made thumb and finger marks on a board covered with reddish sand. Cowry shells and the skull of particular birds surrounded the board. He then studied the marks to forecast what will happen or what has happened. He said he cannot forecast the future. Diviners often use elaborately carved rocks, shells, or bones. Many villages in Oman have a *soothsayer* who claims to be able to predict, for a price, which boy or man a village girl will marry. A shaman on Pacific Islands is often considered to be superior to other local people. A shaman will usually refuse to shake hands even if other villagers do so.

In Togo I studied the voodoo market of the Ewé tribe. Voodoo is believed to have originated there. Black slaves took it to Haiti, Brazil, the U.S., and elsewhere. Supernatural forces, including spirits of ancestors, may cause trouble. The supernatural forces are said to be created by *Mahou*, the Supreme Being. Mahou is said to have created some 600 deities, the spirits. A shaman said he can communicate with the great spirits. He explained how a stick held by a man is used for virility, and a rock held by both a man and a woman is used for fertility. Two flat round stones rubbed on the head help make a child more intelligent and results in better memory for adults. Two small cowry shells on a stick are used to kill an enemy. *Obi* or *Obeah* is the Ewé goddess of evil. An *Obeahman* may use particular fetishes to get rid of an evil spell. They include a kind of blood, an alligator's tooth, a parrot's beak, dirt taken from a cemetery, balls of clay with feathers and a cord, and eggshells. Some people believe that zombies have existed, that a powerful drug given to an enemy takes away his memory but he may continue to live, like an automaton, for many years. When an Ewe baby is born it is believed to be the reincarnation of someone in the area who died. The shaman is asked to tell who the baby was in its prior life. Earlier people who believed in a rebirth include the Cherokees, who believed in a "Seventh Heaven" somewhere in the clouds.

Brazil's huge Ver-O-Peso market in Belem sells voodoo charms and dried snakes, plus dried alligator and animals skulls for shamans and others. A *macumba* voodoo ceremony is held every few nights in Belem. In Papua New Guinea, a medicine man had a collection of human skulls, some of which were inherited from his headhunting ancestors. If any member of his tribe died without apparent cause, the relatives bring a pig and ask the medicine man to determine what caused the death. The next day the medicine man usually gives the name or location of a particular person whom he believes caused the death. That person will, sooner or later, be killed, in a "payback." It is important not to be an enemy of the medicine man! The voodoo priests and priestesses have an elaborate hierarchy or pecking order. Those with greater status or experience wear feathers of a particular color.

A *sorcerer* or *wizard* is believed to have supernatural powers over others, by using evil spirits or witchcraft. An older or eccentric man or woman is sometimes charged with being a sorcerer, they are blamed for causing bad luck. One man in Vanuatu was charged with sorcery for throwing "poisoned leaves" at a girl a few days before she died with mysterious symptoms. He was found guilty in a tribal court. Some people believe that a sorcerer can bring evil upon anyone if the sorcerer has a lock of the person's hair, fingernail clippings, some personal possession, or even the full name of the victim. Food scraps not eaten by high-ranking ancient Hawaiians were destroyed or hidden, so a sorcerer could not use them to bring evil against that person. In much of the world, the body of a dead warrior is quickly hidden, to prevent the enemy from getting it. The enemy might eat the body, or save the skull to use as a bowl, or a sorcerer could use the body to torment the soul of the deceased. In Papua New Guinea, a particular kind of wild apple, put into the garden of an enemy, is believed to cause him much bad luck. Several men in Vanuatu told me that if a witch doctor or *clever* puts a "spell" on a local man, using his hair, fingernails, or anything personal, the victim will die. If anyone suspects that he is a victim of sorcery he goes to a village elder, who advises that he drink a particular potion to defeat the spell. In the Marquesas Islands, any body part or excrement of a chief or a priest was buried in a deep pit to prevent a sorcerer or an enemy from getting it. In the Marquesas the afterbirth was usually buried at night in a secret place, often in the garden, to prevent sorcerers from harming the family. On other Pacific islands the afterbirth was fed to fish in the sea. The more affluent people on Vanuatu's Tanna Island hire a clever to put a curse on anyone who steals from their house. A man wanting to seduce a girl may also hire a clever. He draws a big circle around her home, then throws a stone over the house. The people inside are said to be under the control of the person who hired the clever.

In Martinique we heard about the "magic men," the *quimboiseurs*. They say they can, for a price, make a girl fall in love with the man who hires them. They can also bring bad luck to someone who jilts a lover. Some magic men or women sell dolls, *bois-bois*, that represent an enemy. The buyer sticks pins in the effigy or burns it to bring pain to the victim.

A shaman must be able to go into or out of a trance when he wishes. They sometimes used drugs. In Alaska's southeast coast a child with unusual hair or other qualities, or some post-menopausal women, were selected to train to become a shaman. A good imagination or a near-death experience helps to become a shaman. Myths are used by story tellers to explain the origin of man and the meaning of religion and the universe. Shaman used masks and puppets whose chin, arms, and legs moved. Some masks open two times to transform a person into different characters. They dug tunnels under longhouses, and used long hollow kelp from the sea, up to 50 feet long, to make speaking tubes, to act out myths. Rattles and whistles were believed to make sounds of the spirits. Protruding eyes or horns indicate the supernatural. On Malakula Island, Vanuatu, a shaman buried hollow bamboo pipes in the ground and spoke through them to produce "voices of ancestors" magically.

Some people, including Plains Indians of the U.S., took drugs or designed conditions so they would have visions or dreams, even without a medicine man. Sometimes a man went alone to a lonely place and stayed there for several days, without food or water. He asked the spirits to have pity on him and he sought to have a revelation. Sometimes a man cut himself to get pity. A dream or revelation sometimes explained the meaning of things that had recently happened to the man or the tribe.

Military leaders in some African countries are reported to tell their youthful fighters that they are invincible if they fight naked, if they dress as a girl or woman, or if they smoke cigarettes rolled in pages torn from the Bible. They are also told that wearing the skin of particular animals, or a juju necklace of cowrie shells, will give them protection.

Prophets

When we were in Martinique, the worldwide meeting of French-speaking *voyons* or fortune tellers was held in Fort de France. They use astrology, paintings, drawings, crystal balls, the reading of palms, and a variety of methods. We were not permitted to attend the meetings. The ancient world had several famous *sibyls* or prophets. The one in Delphi, Greece, was the best known. Others were in Tivoli, Italy, plus Cimmeria on the Bosporous, Cumae in southern Italy, Erythrae in Lydia (Asia Minor), Persia, Phrygia on the Hellespont in the Dardanelle Islands (Turkey), and Samia. The oracle at Delphi was a middle-age woman. In the beautiful temples and other buildings on a high hill overlooking a pretty valley she was the main money-earner. Rich men and rulers came from afar to ask her questions. She sat on a tripod, breathed sulfur fumes coming from the earth, and chewed laurel leaves believed to be narcotic. While somewhat under the influence she muttered answers to questions. The priests sagaciously interpreted her responses, getting huge tributes in return. A large building might be begun, or a war started or ended, based upon her mutterings.

Some prophets are ignored and discouraged by the authorities. A prophet may object to the beliefs or practices of the existing religion and lead a sect to reform it. A prophet sometimes attracts a large following and establishes a new religion, such as Moses and Judaism, Jesus and Christianity, Mohammed and Islam. However, once a religion is well established its professionals discourage new prophets.

On many of the islands of Melanesia in the Southwest Pacific local people believe in *cargo cults*—that much material wealth will come to them. During World War II the U.S., Japanese, and other military, brought steel axes and knives, gasoline stoves, rifles, ships, planes, jeeps, and more. The Melanesian culture did not teach them how the products were made, therefore many local people thought they came from the spiritual world. Some local men attracted a big following by telling people that if the people followed them and carved wooden objects like those they wanted, and used them, material goods would be brought to them by magic. They built airstrips so planes could deliver the wanted cargo. People on Tanna Island, Vanuatu, believe that a mythical or spiritual John Frum will bring them the things they want. On Tanna Island men who belong to the cult sometimes wear white chalk marks on their faces. The belief began when Captain John Cook brought trinkets and steel axes and knives in 1774, and was reinforced when other Europeans, Americans, or Japanese brought material goods.

The son of the chief of the main village on Sulphur Bay said they are Christians, and that Jesus was a Black Man. The flag of the U.S., the Navy flag, plus the provincial flag, are displayed in the village's open area, where youths play football and do military marches. The chief's son said John the Baptist visited the island long ago. He showed us the rectangular simple building where religious ceremonies are held two evenings a week. On Friday nights they sing songs inviting John Frum to appear. The building has a red cross, a "blackboard," flowers, and a bottle of holy water from the nearby sea, used to wash the head of a sick child.

Dragons

Dragons are believed to have supernatural power in many cultures. Priests of Babylon and ancestors of today's Jews believed that a dragon was slain to bring order out of chaos, thereby creating the universe. In southern China, plus Thailand, Indonesia, and some other parts of southeastern Asia, dragons are good. In China the dragon represents authority, including the emperor. The empress was represented by the phoenix bird. Longevity is represented in Chinese art by pine trees, turtles, and cranes. The dragon symbol began to be used in the Shang Dynasty, around 1100 BCE. Early drawings or paintings show dragons to be like snakes. Around 800 AD the emperor adopted the dragon as his symbol. The dragon was then shown to include parts of the body of many animals, birds, and fish. The number of claws shown on the paws is either four or five. Dragons are believed to protect against evil spirits, floods, and droughts. Dragons are shown on top of the wall surrounding important gardens, such as Wu Gardens in Shanghai and many gardens in Suzhou. The dragon's head faces the entrance gate to keep out undesirable things. Chinese patent medicines often include "dragon bones," perhaps from a pig, goat, or other animal. Rain and thunder are often shown as a dragon, in temples like Beijing's Temple for a Good Harvest.

In East Asia Temples have "dragons tails" on the roof, especially at gable ends, to keep away evil spirits. The Dragonboat Festival was believed to keep away evil insects, snakes, lizards, and toads. In Indonesia, village homes have carved figures on the roof to keep away evil spirits. Many traditional homes in China have carved fish on the roof, a symbol of "plenty to eat" and good luck. In Norway, old wooden stave churches have carved dragons on outside walls to keep away evil spirits. Vikings from Norway and Denmark carved a dragon's head on the prow of their ships and boats to keep away evil spirits. Vikings traded with the Orient then—Denmark's National Museum has local coins that prove it.

In other areas dragons were evil. In Japan, village people occasionally throw rice into Lake Hakone to appease the dragon who lives there, so it won't cause trouble. In Sweden, Stockholm's cathedral has a bronze statue outside and a wooden statue inside of St. George killing the dragon, around 330 AD, after weakening it with a Christian cross.

Witches

Witches have been part of folklore and religion in many parts of the world. They are usually evil older women. When Christianity arrived in Europe the old religions did not die, they were absorbed into Christian beliefs and practices. Missionaries erroneously taught that all pagan beliefs and practices honored the Devil. Witches are believed to have magical powers, and to use herbs and drugs as magical potions. They are usually active at night. Some people believe that the early witches became Satan or the Devil in Christianity. Joan of Arc was burned as a witch by the British in 1431, but some French helped in her capture. Today she is a heroine in France, and a group meets at her statue in Paris to honor her each year. In the Carpathian Mountains of southern Poland many people still believe in witches and the supernatural. In China, a guide of the Naxi minority group told me that his friend had a son who went out often at night, spending too much money, coming back late, half-drunk. He consulted a witch, taking one of the son's shirts. The witch advised him how to sacrifice a pig and "bring your son back." My guide said the son stays home now. In Lithuania's Witches Hill many woodcarvings show mostly good witches. Young, pretty witches liked to entrap fishermen in fog. In recent years witches have become good in Germany. In East Germany a few years ago I bought a book of delightful short stories about good *Kleinen Hexen und Gespenstern*, or *Little Witches and Ghosts*. Barns and other buildings of Amish in Pennsylvania sometimes have a hex symbol to keep away evil.

In 1484, soon after the pope iissued a *bull* (a document with instructions) against witches, older or eccentric women throughout Western Europe were burned as witches. In Salem, Massachusetts, a Protestant clergyman started the witchcraft hysteria in 1692. Male ministers are said to have insisted upon thoroughly inspecting women's bodies, looking for signs of any mark that the devil might have made. Judge William Stoughton sentenced many innocent women to death as witches. Mass hysteria, usually coupled together with race, religion, sex, or patriotism, sometimes envelopes a country. In the U.S. after the Japanese attack on Pearl Harbor on December 7, 1941, Japanese Americans were rounded up and sent to camps like refugee camps. In the late 1940s and early 1950s, McCarthyism charged liberals with being "communist stooges." In the 1980s and 1990s many innocent adults were charged with operating sex groups with little children, who were brainwashed by adults interviewing them.

CHAPTER 13:
LUCK, COLORS, & NUMBERS

Luck

For good luck in Albania, a bull's head with horns is buried in the foundation of a new home. In Bolivia the fetus of a llama is buried under the threshold. In the U.S. a horseshoe is sometimes fastened above the entrance door. The Dai minority group in southern China put holy water onto the skin with a particular kind of leaf, to bring good luck to the anointed person. Fortune tellers are often found in shopping areas in East Asia. They are consulted before an important decision affecting the family or business is made. A bank official is likely to consult a fortune teller (soothsayer) before making a big loan. In Japan and Hong Kong they often sit at a small table where many people pass nearby. Gypsies tell the fortune of a customer in Europe and the Americas. They often walk slowly in places where many people are on holiday, such as a beach, carefully observing potential customers. In some places they rent a room and wait for customers.

East Asians like games of Chance. *Yut* is popular in Buddhist temples and busy shopping areas. The game varies from place to place, but it usually consists of tossing four wooden sticks about 10 inches long, flat on three sides, curved on the other side. A customer watches carefully how they land, usually on a straw mat, to determine the future. In Taiwan two sticks are usually tossed. Some landings mean good luck, others mean bad luck, and some landings do not indicate anything. Customers often toss the sticks several times, until they are satisfied. In Pak Ou Caves, Laos, with statues of many Buddhas, customers toss numbered sticks. They land on a number. A printed sheet with that number describes the fortune. A customer may try many times until he gets a particular number. Vietnamese like several kinds of games of chance. Slot machines are found in hotels. They take only coins from the U.S., but were popular even during the many years of hostility between the two countries. In Chinese restaurants in the U.S. and some in Europe, a fortune cookie is given to each guest at the end of the meal. I never found fortune cookies in China, Hong Kong, or Taiwan. Cock fighting is or recently has been a favorite sport in much of the world. Ecuador has many palenques or pits where men watch cockfighting. It is a favorite sport in Thailand. England has several pits for the fights, but they are no longer used.

Colors

Colors have important meanings in many cultures. Brides usually wear white in the U.S., most of Europe, and some brides in Southeast Asia wear white. Some brides, particularly those who were married before, wear another pretty color. In Germany some brides wear black. In some countries local people do not wear the two or three colors of the national flag. People who wear those colors are marked as foreigners.

For Buddhists and Hindus, in much of southern Asia, white and blue are colors of mourning. In Nepal our Hindu guide was expected to wear white for a year after his father had died. In Papua New Guinea women in mourning wear a black robe, men wear a black band around the wrist and let their beard grow. In most of the rest of the world black is the color of mourning. In the U.S. and part of Western Europe black means bad luck. If a black cat walks in front of you, expect to have bad luck. In Latin America black and purple are colors of mourning. In ancient Rome the emperors wore royal purple. On many Pacific islands red is a sacred color, it helps to protect one against evil spirits. In China and Taiwan, and among other Chinese in Southeast Asia, red represents happiness. A bride usually wears red. In China a white cat or a drawing of one represents tranquillity. In old China only the emperor could use the color yellow. Now important government buildings have a yellow roof. However, buildings at Beijing's Temple for a Good Harvest have blue roofs, the color of the sky. Many ancient Chinese believed that the original five colors on earth were red for fire, yellow for the ground or soil, black for minerals, green for water and trees, and white for heaven. In old Korea, common men wore white, nobles wore a blue jacket. Buddhist nuns everywhere wear white or pink. Most Roman Catholic nuns wore black or gray until recently. In much of Latin America nuns wear white. In North America and part of Europe nuns now wear ordinary clothes but in much of Europe they still wear black or gray.

In the St. Simone Church, in San Andreas, Itzapa, Guatemala, believers buy a candle of a particular color and light it. Red is to be successful in love, green indicates success in business, blue is for success at work and general good luck, black is to defeat enemies, brown is to protect yourself against the vicious, light blue is to get better grades and more money, and yellow is for protection against evil. Among Africa's Masai, black beads represent night, white is day, and green is for peace after a rain. South Africa's Zulus believe that opaque red beads represent blood and tears, transparent ruby-red beads represent unbounded love. Another shade of red represents anger. White is for love, purity, and vision. Green represents jealousy. Dark green for a bride represents happiness and fertility. Yellow represents wealth, but several successive gifts of yellow beads means "its all over between us." Dark blue represents faithfulness, light blue represents "don't gossip about me." Black represents unhappiness, but it also means re-assurance. Black and red beads indicate grief due to the absence of the recipient. If a Zulu girl gives a man white and pink beads it means she loves him but can't marry yet because he doesn't have enough cattle for her bride price.

When a girl on isolated Tristan da Cunha gives a youth wool socks with blue stripes it means "I love you." On Turkish rugs red once represented blood and war, but now represents love. Yellow signifies happiness, blue is for destiny, and bronze signifies abundance.

An old U.S. and British superstition is:

> Marry in white, you'll marry all right,
> Marry in blue, your love is true,
> Marry in brown, you'll live in town,
> Marry in green, you'll be ashamed to be seen,
> Marry in black, you'd better turn back,
> Marry in yellow, you got the wrong fellow,
> Marry in gray, you'll be sad someday,
> Marry in red, you'd better be dead.

Egyptian tombs show men in reddish brown and women in dull yellow. Drawings 3,800 years old at Crete's Palace of Knossos show women with white skin, men with red skin. Indonesians are fond of puppets of all kinds, either shadow puppets or three-dimensional operated by the hands. A puppet with a red face is a bad person, like a man wearing a black hat in old U.S. Western movies. An Indonesian puppet with a white face is good. Primitive people like bright-colored feathers to decorate the body. Amazon Indians use several colors. They capture little birds and feed them particular foods to cause their feathers to be a particular color, or to brighten the color. Yellow bird feathers are the most rare, so it is prized the most. In Papua New Guinea's Highlands men wear elaborate wigs and feather arrangements. The country has more than 600 varieties of birds, including 38 types of bird of paradise. Many headdresses have two bright tail feathers more than two feet long from a bird of paradise. As they fly, they wave up and down. The tail feathers often stick high above a man's headdress. Papua New Guinea also has the world's largest butterflies and the largest moth. One morning our waitress Maria caught a black Hercules moth 45 cm. (18 inches) across, and pinned it to the front of her dress, still alive.

In the U.S. a superstition is:

> White denotes all that is pure and desirable,
> Red indicates love, lust, and anger,

Bright red signifies fire, power, confidence, and
courage,
Yellow signifies infidelity and shame,
Orange indicates simplicity and freshness,
Brown signifies worldly knowledge and
distinction,
Green signifies youth and hope,
Blue denotes tranquillity, and
Black is the color of sadness, gloom, and death.

Numbers

In China and elsewhere nearly all Buddhist pagodas have an
uneven number of roofs—five, seven, or nine, etc. However, in Tibet
and near Tibet, pagodas may have an even number of roofs, since yin
and yang, together, are an even number. The tall Chin Pagoda in Dali,
Yunnan has 16 roofs and is 69 meters high. Nearby are two smaller
pagodas, each 43 meters high with 10 roofs. In Hong Kong the number
3 is lucky, indicating a person of action. An 8 shows prosperity, and a
2 indicates that the owner will have an easy life. The Chinese 4 is like
the Chinese character for death, so 4 means bad luck. In the U.S. you
may have good luck if you find a clover plant with four leaves, rather
than the usual three leaves. Four and nine are unlucky for Japanese. In
Japan's Buddhist temples the bell is rung 108 times at midnight on
December 31, to drive out the "108 evil desires" that man is subject to.
In Taiwan 100 is considered to be "perfect." Six is considered to be a
lucky number in much of China. A youth of the Bai minority group in
the area near Dali, Yunnan gives the parents of his bride 666 yuan,
6,666 yuan, or some other multiple of six. In the U.S., Latin America,
and part of Europe the number 13 is considered to be unlucky, but in
most countries it is treated like any other number. I have stayed in
room 13 or on the 13th floor of European hotels, in Germany and Eastern Europe, and I had no bad luck. Among Africa's Masai 9 is a magic
number, because there are 9 orifices on the human body. In European
fairy tales the number 3 is predominant—the protagonist has three
wishes or three chances. Ancient Babylonians, like many others, believed that diseases were caused by evil spirits or by curses of witches
or wizards. To get rid of the evil spirits or the curse an incantation had
to be repeated three times.

During the cremation of the body of a Hindu, survivors typically carry the body clockwise two times around a funeral pyre with
firewood. A man with a burning stick walks two times around the pyre
before lighting the wood. Chinese like lists of five: there are five phases
or elements (wood, fire, earth, metal, and water), five regions or areas
for Chinese cooking, and five common grains.

In the Middle East the number *7* is popular. Ancient worshippers walked around a Temple of Baal, honoring a Babylonian god, seven times. Middle East Islamic worshippers now walk around the Kaaba at Mecca, Saudi Arabia, seven times. When I visited the airport at Jeddah, nearest to Mecca, in March, the big annual onslaught of pilgrims were beginning to arrive. The ancient Sumerian queen of heaven, Inanna, is said to have passed through seven gates on a visit to the underworld. At each gate a piece of her clothing was stripped off. When I visited the museums at Ugarit and other cities in Syria, I was unable to learn whether she had worn only seven pieces of clothing. Inanna is said to have stolen the "tablets of destiny" from her father, and his messenger unsuccessfully tried seven times to get them back. Babylonians believed that their goddess Ishtar also had to pass through seven gates to visit the underworld, and at each gate she also lost a piece of clothing. In his great epics Gilgamesh had to cross seven mountains. Babylonians believed that creation required seven days. The later Jewish priests also believed that Earth was created in seven days, including a day of rest. Most of the Jewish people were captives of the Babylonians for several centuries, and acquired many of their beliefs. Ancient Jewish people believed that seven priests each bearing trumpets marched around Jericho for six days, and on the seventh day they marched around Jericho seven times. When the priests blew on their trumpets the walls of Jericho are said to have fallen. When I first visited Jericho I could see in big holes the 23 levels of cities that archeologists had dug out, each city on top of the other. However, no trumpets were found.

The number *40* is a common symbolic number in the Middle East and in Central and Eastern Europe. In much of Eastern Europe a mother is expected to stay isolated with a new baby for 40 days. In the Jewish and Christian Old Testament Noah's Great Flood is said to have lasted for 40 days. Other Middle Eastern myths say the flood was for only 7 days. Moses and his followers are said to have wandered in the desert on their return from Egypt for 40 years. Moses stayed on Mt. Sinai for 40 days, where he was instructed on the Ten Commandments, but he had no food or water! When I visited the Jebel Musa Mountains, including Mt. Sinai, I found them to be very dry—I doubt that a camel could survive 40 days without water. On another trip to Mt. Sinai Moses is also said to have stayed there for 40 days, when he received tablets with the Ten Commandments. Elijah required 40 days for his trip to Horeb (Sinai). The Christian Lent was originally 40 hours, to commemorate the 40 hours that Jesus spent in his tomb. It was gradually increased in length, and within a few centuries it became 40 days. This period is now said to represent the 40 days that Jesus spent fasting in the wilderness.

PART III:

RELIGIONS

CHAPTER 14:
RELIGIONS

Creation

There are many religious beliefs of creation and a virgin birth. Some Indians in Canada's Yukon Territory believe that Crow made the sun, moon, and the stars. Crow then created man by causing a girl to drink water with a spruce needle in it. She became pregnant, with the first man. The Haida Indians of Canada's West Coast believe that after the great flood Raven found the first humans in a giant clam shell. Many Pacific Islanders also believe that earth was created from a giant clam shell. The top was lifted to become the sky. Plains Indians in the U.S. believed that coyote created earth, but that the sun was also important. Anasazi Indians of the U.S. Southwest had a small hole, a *sipapu*, near the fire pit in their *kivas*, used for ceremonies. The hole represents the hole that man emerged from onto the face of the earth. It is also called the "spirit hole" and represents the entrance to the underworld. Australia's Aborigines believe that the god *Baime* created earth. A big rainbow was broken into 1,000 pieces, they became birds. Some fell into the sea, grew scales, and became fish. Some Shinto followers in Japan believe that long ago a rooster crowed, it woke up the sun god, bringing light to the world. Chinese believed that *Pan Gu* was born of the egg *chaos*. As he grew he separated heaven and earth. The mountains and water came from his body, his eyes became the sun and the moon, his beard became the stars, his hair became vegetables, and fleas on his body became humans! Chinese believed in an afterlife in the "Yellow Springs," not far below ground level. Ancient Hawaiians believed that man came from the leaf of a taro plant, which grew above the buried body of the child of a god. Kanaks in New Caledonia believed that the moon lost a tooth, which gave birth to humans. A big rock in the Jean Marie Tijabou Cultural Center in Noumea symbolizes the tooth. People living near Yasur Volcano on Vanuatu's Tanna Island believe that the universe originated at the volcano. They also believe that it has the spirits of their ancestors, in both heaven and hell. Tanna islanders believe that human life began there. As the island became more crowded men and women left in boats to populate the rest of the world. Some boats were shipwrecked and the people spent a long time in the sea. They were bleached, becoming White Man. Villagers on Papua New Guinea's Sepik River believed that a big croco-dile carried the entire world on its back and delivered it to the present location. The "croc" opened its mouth to create wind.

The Mayan Indians' great book, the *Popol Vuh*, has stories that tell how the earth was created, with plants and animals, and how a creature like man was created, from mud, wood, then flesh. They were destroyed in a great flood. Finally modern man was created from dough made of maize or corn. The Dogon of Mali believe Fox created the Earth from its placenta. Amma, the Great God, created two pairs of hermaphrodite twins. One pair was called *Nummo*. The other pair are called *Ogo* and *Nommo*. Ogo creates a dry, arid Earth. Nommo is sac-rificed to create humidity and water, so there can be life on Earth. The Dogon culture has constant opposing factors—wet and dry, old and young, male and female (like the yin and yang of Eastern religions, and the heaven and hell of many religions). Other tribes in West Af-rica, including the Anlo (Ewe) of Ghana and Togo, believe that a su-preme being, *Mahou*, created the world and men. He is a personal god, there are no priests or shrines. He is said to have disappeared because people made frequent demands upon him. He also created lesser gods to do some of the work. South Africa's Zulus believe the Great Spirit *Unkulunkulu* created everything, including the Earth, sun, moon, and stars. His daughter *Nomkhubulwana* tells the Zulus many things—when there will be feast or famine, when to wean a baby, when to brew beer, and when to make a sacrifice. If her orders are not followed it will result in death. Ancient Babylonians believed that the god *Marduk* made man out of clay mixed with the blood of the god Kingu. Ancient Egyptians believed that man was made of clay by the god *Khnum*.

It was common in early Eastern religions for a god to have a virgin birth, a symbol of human sanctity and purity. In addition to Jesus other gods who had a virgin birth were Buddha, Mithras, and the Hindu Surya. Hercules, the mythical son of the Greek god Zeus and the wife of a king, was often said to have had a virgin birth. Myths that Alexander the Great had a virgin birth were widespread before Jesus was born. Ancient Egyptians in Memphis believed that the sacred bull *Apis* was born of a virgin cow, impregnated by a god. Lao Tzu, founder of Taosim (Daoism) is said to have been fathered by a shooting star. The great Hindu book, *The Mahabharata*, also tells of a great flood, and how the child *Karna* was saved while floating away in the bulrushes, like Moses, many years later.

Many religions have a place where the soul is expected to go when someone dies. The concept of paradise or heaven is somewhat different from the Christian concept of heaven. Ancient Sumerians, predecessors of the Jewish people in the Middle East, thought that *Dilmun* or paradise was a place full of vegetarians—animals did not eat others, and the sick and lame were made well. Muslims, living mostly in dry areas, picture paradise as green, with pretty streams and black-eyed maidens. The Vikings of Norway, Denmark, and Sweden believed that a Viking who died in combat would go to *Valhal*, where he would feast and fight forever. Religions also have different concepts of where bad people go when they die, but most agree that it is a hot place.

Gilgamesh Epic

The Gilgamesh Epic is a literary work widely read in the Middle East since 1800 BCE. It was written about a powerful tyrant in Erech, Mesopotamia (Babylon, modern Iraq), and a mortal who is the sole mortal survivor of the Great Flood. Utnaphishtim is often believed to be the prototype of Noah in the Jewish and Christian religions.

Mithraism

Mithraism was a religion widespread in Persia and India before 1000 BCE, then it spread to the eastern Mediterranean and Rome. Mithraism was the leading religion when Jesus was born. It had a heaven, where the soul of man could go. Rituals included baptism, and a communal meal of bread and wine. A bull was sometimes sacrificed. Mithras was said to have been born of a virgin mother, Isis, and a few shepherds saw the birth. Early Christians were persecuted, so they tried to keep a low profile. They adopted the Christmas, Easter (*Ostara*), and Sun-Day of Mithraism, plus other practices. The Saturnalia Festival of ancient Romans began around December 21. It was celebrated with feasts, drinking, sex, and the unwrapping of the statue of Saturn, the sun god. In the Fourth Century December 25 was officially adopted as Christmas, for the birth of Jesus. Much earlier, around 200 BCE the *Cybelle Cult* in Rome began to celebrate the resurrection of *Attis* after a "death" of three days, much like Easter, later adopted by Christians.

Zoroastrianism

Zoroastrianism follows the beliefs of Zoroaster, who apparently lived in Persia in the Seventh Century BCE. The beliefs were widely known at the time from Greece to India. Jews lived in Babylon when Zoroastrianism was the main religion there. Judaism and Christianity have many beliefs that are similar to Zoroastrianism: The powers of good are led by a Wise Lord; there is an evil Satan, and there are angels, archangels, demons, and fiends. A Messiah will save his people from oppression; there will be a Last Judgment and a Resurrection; a heavenly record is kept of the good or bad actions of individuals; both man and animals have souls, and there is a paradise for the soul in the heavens. Today most of the followers of Zoroaster are in India.

Christianity's Devil or Satan was probably adopted from *Ahriman*, the spirit of evil. Zoroastrianism believed that there was a constant struggle between the powers of light and the powers of darkness.

Lao Tzu

Lao Tzu or "Old Master", the founder of *Taoism* (Daoism), was born around 604 BCE in east-central China. He is said to have been in his mother's womb for 72 years, his father was a shooting star. He advocated *ao* or "the way," it gives birth to all things. He said we must preserve simplicity in all things. Man, animals, insects, and plants all have a particular destiny, which will be fulfilled. Man should be free of conventions. He wrote his beliefs in a sort of Bible, called *Tao Te Ching*. Like Jesus more than 500 years later, he taught people to return good for evil. The main purpose of a Taoist is to become immortal. They also believe in magic.

Confucius

Confucius was a philosopher, sage, and teacher who continues to have a great impact on modern eastern Asia. He lived from about 551 to 479 BCE in northeast China. He advocated the reforming of men and governments, avoiding needless war and taxes. He advocated the love of all men, or *Jen*. He promulgated the golden rule "Do not do to others what one does not wish to be done unto," which has been adopted by some religions, including Christianity. Among his famous sayings were: "Within the four seas, all men are brothers." Confucius taught his followers to respect parents and the family, to help the poor, to seek justice, to be faithful to one's obligations, and to follow the customs of society—to be *proper*. There is little in his teachings about human or individual rights. Some people believe that human and individual rights are not compatible with Chinese society. Many Chinese and others in eastern Asia still follow Confucius. As communism is disappearing Chinese are returning to the worship of ancestors, like many East Asians. Most Chinese are accustomed to hard work. Perhaps that is why they are often more successful than the poor in other countries, such as Africa and Latin America. We should not expect China to have the same respect for individual freedom that we have. However, if China wants to become more influential, its people must have more freedom of speech and the government in power should tolerate peaceful opposition.

Christianity

Christianity, like most religions, has developed with many variations. Let's look at some of the differences. Some early Christians adopted the use of rosary beads from Buddhists. Coptic Christians, common in Africa and the Middle East, follow somewhat the teachings of Nestorian, a Fifth Century scholar. They believe that Jesus the man was son of Mary, but Jesus the god was not. The Roman Catholic Church decided that the Holy Spirit came from the Father as well as the Son. The Orthodox Churches do not agree to adding "the Son." Orthodox Churches use many icons, the Roman Catholic Church does not use icons. Most Orthodox priests are married. Since the Eleventh Century, most Roman Catholic priests are not married, but many have had a great number of sons and daughters, called "nieces" and "nephews." The Orthodox and Roman churches have disagreed on these issues since at least the Eleventh Century. Jesus' disciples Peter and Paul were married. Protestant churches on most of the Pacific Islands will not ordain any man unless he is married. They believe a bachelor priest or minister would have too many temptations. When the Roman Catholic popes moved from Rome to Avignon, France, in 1305, several changes were made. Tithes at the rate of 10 percent were required, something like today's income tax. The marriage of bishops and other Church officers was prohibited, to protect the Church's property. Priests and bishops had many children, with their wife or concubines. The wife and children insisted upon the right to have property that the Church also wanted. However, in many areas, such as Iceland and Scandinavia, Roman Catholic bishops and priests continued to marry. Iceland changed from Roman Catholicism to Lutheranism at the same time as other Scandinavian countries, in the Sixteenth Century, by killing the Catholic bishop and his many children. Before the Fifth Century paintings began to show Jesus, Mary, and saints with a halo over the head. They copied earlier paintings of Roman emperors that showed a halo over the emperor's head. Romans copied earlier Greeks, who painted a halo over the head of some gods. A square halo shows a living person, usually the then-current pope. The St. Prisca Church in Taxco, Mexico, built 1751 to 1758, has a famous painting of Mary, clearly showing her to be pregnant. It was quite controversial for showing Mary to be like all other expectant mothers. In Ireland until recently a woman "could not" leave the home for other reasons on Sunday morning until she had been to church. Women sometimes carried on top of the head a tile from her roof. She could then assure the priest that she had not been anywhere except "under my own roof."

The Roman Catholic Church has often been very intolerant of beliefs and practices that conflict with those of the pope. The Albigenses in southern France said they followed the teachings of Jesus and God, but they did not follow many of the Church's teachings in the Twelfth and Thirteenth centuries. The pope insisted that a crusade be fought against them. The few hundred Albigenses *and* the 20,000 Roman Catholics who tried to protect the free speech rights of the Albigenses were all killed. The Inquisition was very effective at killing thousands who disagreed with the Church's teachings. Men and women who were suspected of having heretical thoughts were also killed. Spain's *El Escorial* has the world's second-largest Christian library after the Vatican. El Escorial was also the center of the Inquisition. My tour showed many of the terrible instruments of torture used by the Church, but guides said other instruments of torture are too gruesome for people to see. The popes encouraged seven or more crusades to regain Jerusalem and to fight Moslems in the Eleventh through Thirteenth Centuries. Crusaders were finally chased out of the Middle East in 1302. The Children's Crusade was perhaps the most cruel. Orphans from all over Europe were sent to fight the heathen. All of the children were killed or became slaves of the Turks. Crusaders killed Jews and Orthodox Christians, as well as Moslems. However, we should not judge the intolerance and cruelty of the Inquisition, Crusaders, and Turks by today's standards. The merchants of Venice became rich during the crusades, trading with both the crusaders and their enemies. The crusades did somewhat unify Europeans and it taught them that there were great civilizations and much learning outside of Europe. We should not criticize any religion because of cruelty by some of its followers in the past, there was much cruelty then.

After Martin Luther's views were publicized in 1519 many people and their kings disagreed with the Roman Catholic Church. The Church had become very rich, with the best farms and many businesses. Kings wanted to get control of that wealth, so they encouraged separation from the Church in Rome. Several million people were killed in religious wars between Catholics and Protestants. In Europe the greatest number were killed between 1521 and 1648. In China a militant group of Christians, the T'ai-pings, tried to overthrow the dynasty that ruled in China. Their leader, Hung, believed that he was a son of God, the brother of Jesus. At least 20 million Chinese were killed in the rebellion in the 1850s and 1860s. Christianity acquired a warlike reputation in Asia. When the Spanish invaded Latin America they wisely merged local religions with Christianity. For example, the San Francisco Cathedral, built in Quito, Ecuador, in 1535, has a statue of Mary stepping on a snake, a symbol of evil. The Company of Jesuits Church, built in 1605 in Quito, has the Inca's symbol of the sun above the entrance. The Saint Thomas Church in Chichicastenango, Guatemala, has always permitted Mayans to swing buckets of incense and chant prayers to Mayan gods on the steps of the church.

Popes often had a large army. They fought kings and acquired much territory, the Papal States. In the mid-19th Century many people in what is now Italy wanted to create their independent country. They had to fight the pope's army but finally won. The people in Rome cheered. Italy was finally united, in 1870. Later that year, in the First Vatican Council, the pope made two announcements. He declared that a pope is "infallible." He also declared that the soul begins when the sperm meets the egg, therefore abortion is a sin. Until 1870 the Church followed the views of St. Thomas Aquinas, the great Thirteenth Century theologian. He believed that a fetus is given a soul only when it looks like a human—after five months or so of pregnancy. Ancient peoples, like Lucretius in the First Century BCE, believed that the "immortal soul" enters the body at the time of birth. Recently the bachelor pope ruled that the decision that a woman cannot be a priest is infallible. A few years ago the pope ruled that a couple cannot use a condom, even though their use would do much to prevent the worldwide epidemic of AIDS. He ruled in 1997 that if a divorced Catholic remarries they cannot have sex with the new wife or husband—it would be a sin. In Italy a railway conductor recently noticed that I was reading *La Repubblica*. After chatting awhile in Italian, he said *"La Repubblica* is a communist newspaper. Communists and the Church have ruined Italy." I heard that view expressed several times in Italy.

Buddhism & Swastikas

Gautama Buddha is often said to have been born in the village of Lumbini, India at the Nepal border in 566 BCE. He died in 486 BCE. Some Chinese claim that he was born nearly 500 years earlier. His clan name was *Shakya*. Buddha or "the Enlightened One" is believed to have had a "virgin birth" from his mother's side. An elephant's trunk is said to have entered his mother's side, and 18 months later he was born from the other side. Each step he took is said to have created a lotus flower, he is often shown sitting on a lotus flower. He married at 16 and left or abandoned his family at age 29. Under a *bo* (bodhi) tree he had an awakening and discovered the *Four Noble Truths*: all existence is suffering, there is a cause for it, which may be brought to an end, and discipline is necessary to end the suffering. The Buddhist calendar began 544 BCE when he had the "awakening." Followers use the *Eightfold Path* of morality, mental discipline, and wisdom to end suffering and reach *nirvana*. Each youth or young man is expected to serve at least a few weeks as a monk. They wear simple clothing, usually an orange robe, and go each morning with a bowl from door to door to beg for food. Buddhist monks are prohibited from lying, stealing, killing people, committing adultery, drinking alcohol, eating solid food after noonday, using comfortable seats, or getting close to a female. In addition, nuns can't use perfume. There are far fewer female nuns than male monks. Female tourists must be careful not to get close to a monk. One sect of monks in China's Yunnan province permits monks to marry and live with the wife.

Eight animals are honored in Buddhism, one for each day of the week; Wednesday is divided into halves. In China and some other countries, each year is dedicated to one of eight animals plus the snake, rooster, rat, and dragon—12 in all. Buddha told followers to take the Middle Path, avoid anger and hatred. To end suffering, stop craving. That may be good advice in today's world, where businesses bombard everyone with messages to buy their product to get happiness. Buddhists do not believe in the presence of God, nor do they believe that destiny is decided by God. They believe that destiny is controlled by men themselves.

There are many sects of Buddhism. The *Theravada*, *Hinayana*, or *Lesser Vehicle* Buddhists believe an individual is responsible for his own progress. It is practiced in Laos, Cambodia, Thailand, Myanmar, Sri Lanka, and India. *Mahayana* or *Greater Vehicle* Buddhism offers salvation to all who have faith and belief in Buddha. Those who have achieved enlightenment should refrain from entering nirvana but help others to achieve nirvana. It is practiced in Japan, Korea, China, Vietnam, Nepal, and Tibet. Nirvana is the ultimate, when one attains wisdom and compassion. The *Zen* sect searches for the Buddha nature within oneself, a search for enlightenment. *Soto Zen* emphasizes the sitting position to meditate. *Rinzai Zen* uses surprises to get sudden enlightenment.

Some people say that Buddha had 550 previous lives, but the last 10 lives are most important. In statues, the right hand of Buddha is important to determine what he is advising, such as "stop doing bad things." Buddhist monks usually have a ceremony for a child when he reaches puberty, when he becomes a monk, even if temporary, and at funerals. The *swastika* has long been a symbol of Buddhism, reincarnation, and total spiritual resignation. I saw several carved on old stone temples in southern China and in Saigaing, Burma, and on Hindu temples in Bali. In the Marquesas Islands the Christian cross has been modified so it looks much like a swastika. Many ancient civilizations, including ancient Romans in Albania, and North American Indians, used swastikas as a symbol of nature or religion. Scandinavian Vikings drew swastikas on rune stones. In Crete men painted swastikas on pottery in 800 BCE. In Bulgaria ancient Roman mosaics show a swastika, symbol of the sun and the four seasons, with Nike, goddess of victory. Many years later German Nazis also adopted the swastika as their symbol, changing it slightly.

Some large Buddhist temples are interesting places to visit, attracting crowds like Disneyland. There are many possibilities or things to do so you will have good luck. Visitors walk left three times around the big pagoda in Dali, China, for good health. Wat Phra That in Chinag Mai, Thailand, has many monks in saffron robes and nuns selling lotus flowers. Other traditional offerings to Buddha, such as incense and candles, are also sold. A worker sells small canoes filled with holy water. When a small amount is bought it is put into a *dagon*, pulled up by cords to the top of the big gold-covered *stupa*. Another cord is pulled, the dagon dumps the holy water onto the stupa, giving "merit" to the donor. The 2600-year-old Shwese Dagon Pagoda in Rangoon, Burma (also called Yangoon, Myanmar), has a gold-covered dome, 328 feet above the octagonal base. A 76 karat diamond is on top. The spire has 6,835 precious stones; 5,452 are diamonds. Four hairs of Buddha are said to be in the temple, it also has a large reclining Buddha. People left offerings to Buddha, including fruit, rice, joss sticks of incense, and flowers. Shops sell candles "to see the truth," tiny umbrellas "to ward off trouble," and flowers. Murals show the eight great victories of Buddha. A man rang a bell three times to attract the attention of Buddha to his daughter's wedding. A woman poured water on an image of Buddha to wash away her own troubles. A father should step over a son born on a Saturday, or when grown the son will step over the father. We watched people at a stone that is claimed to predict the future, if it feels easy to lift their future is good. A bell weighing 24 tons is displayed, it once fell from a barge into a river. The British wondered how to retrieve it, the Burmese re-floated it by attaching many bamboo poles. Students beginning exams visited the "wish-granting spot." They wished for good grades on exams. In 1984, North Korean terrorists with a bomb killed many South Korean leaders visiting the pagoda. Little girls gave us flower petals, expecting us to give them ball-point pens in return. Vendors with a hand-operated sugar cane press sold the juice. We were there on a Sunday. Men and women having a Sunday birthday had the honor of sweeping the temple grounds, in several work brigades. The next day the "Monday birthday" people would sweep. Our guide asked on what day I was born. I said I knew the day of the month but not the day of the week. She was surprised. To every Buddhist and many other Asians the day of the week a person is born affects a person's entire life. There are many "posts" or areas on the temple grounds. People with a Sunday birthday, for example, go to the Sunday post. In China a baby is considered to be a year old when it is born. Age is counted from the Chinese New Year. If New Year is on our February 15, a baby born on February 1, for example, is two years old on February 15. In many Latin America countries age begins with conception. In most other countries age begins at birth.

A typical Buddhist *stupa* has important meanings to followers of Buddhism. The dome represents heaven, and the tall mast symbolizes the world axis. It is often encircled by discs signifying the heaven of the gods, extending into paradise. In some countries the more important Buddhist temples have many serpents or dragons tails on the roof. For example, Wat Sensoukharhan Temple in Vientiane, Laos, has seven serpents tails on the middle of the roof. It is of average importance. Luang Prabang's Xieng Thong Temple has 17 serpents tails on the roof, it is very important. In the Forbidden City or Palace Museum of Beijing important buildings also have the greatest number of roof ornaments. They always have an odd number of ornaments, as pagodas usually have an odd number of roofs.

The "world's largest Buddha" (71 m. or 233 ft. high), in Leshan, Sechuan province, China was carved onto a cliff to stop the sinking of many boats on turbulent water near where three rivers meet. In 713 AD a monk, Heitung, outlined his plans for the statue and asked for government help. The officials agreed to raise funds for the statue but said they would take their personal "commission" out of the cost. The angry monk is said to have torn out his own eyes, given them to the official, saying "Here's your commission!" The monk, now blind, raised the money through friends and other Buddhists. China had a problem with corruption 13 centuries ago, it still has much corruption. Records were not kept to show whether the rivers were calmed down, they are still turbulent.

Some Buddhists believe that everyone goes to hell upon death. They drink a soup, which cuts off all memories of the past life. A kind person will be reincarnated and return to Earth, perhaps as another person. An evil person is reincarnated as a pig, rat, or other creature. Buddhists are taught not to step on the sill of a temple door because some evil people live there. Some Buddhists enter a temple on the left side and leave on the other side. Temples have a big bronze container in front for lighting sticks of incense, then they are thrown into another bronze container. The smoke from incense or candles is said to go to heaven, where it asks for help. Pilgrims in some Chinese temples pay a monk to write their name in characters by calligraphy and leave it at the temple, so their name will be waiting for them at the gate to heaven.

Buddha traveled widely. His collarbone is said to be in the Shwese Dagon in Bagan, Myanmar (Pagan, Burma), part of it is also said to be in a temple in Anuradhapura, Sri Lanka. His left collarbone is also said to be in the Phra That Doi Tung near Chiang Rai, Thailand. A tooth is allegedly inside seven gold caskets in the Temple of the Tooth at Kandy, Sri Lanka. Another is claimed to be in ruins of a pagoda near Mandalay, Burma. A hair is claimed to hold the "Gold Rock," a balancing rock in Burma. Four hairs of Buddha are said to be in the Shwese Dagon of Rangoon (Yangoon), Burma. The Peshawar (Pakistan) Museum claims to have the ashes of Buddha in an urn. The Wat That Long (Temple) in Luang Prabang, Laos is also said to have his ashes. His footprint is said to be on Adams Peak in Sri Lanka. The Odomong Pagoda in Phnom Penh, Cambodia is said to have his eyebrow. His teeth are said to be in a temple on Mt. Emei, one of four sacred mountains in China, some 100 miles (160 km.) southwest of Chengdu.

Shinto

In Japan most people follow both Buddhism and Shinto. Japanese funerals are held at Buddhist temples. Shinto started as nature worship but changed to ancestor worship. Typically, a baby seven days old is baptized at a Shinto shrine, and at age three, boys and girls are taken to a shrine to pray for their health and happiness. Boys aged five and girls aged seven are again taken to the shrine. Most weddings are at a shrine, and students go there to pray for good grades. On New Years Day, up until January 7, Japanese go there to pray for health and happiness. Before entering a shrine building they purify themselves by washing hands and gargling. They leave a money offering, bow two times, clap the hands two times to attract the attention of the deity, bow again, and leave. They often buy a prayer board and hang it at the shrine. *Tori gates* separate the divine world from the outside world. Gate posts often have tree branches and strips of paper, signifying lightning, to purify. At the great Ise Shrine a new building has been built every 20 years for nearly 1300 years, the old building is torn down. Most of the shrines in Nara are also periodically burned and rebuilt. Kyoto has a stone boat to carry believers to Paradise when they die.

Hinduism

Hinduism is the major religion of India, Nepal, and Bali. Hinduism began with the *Vedas* or stories of theology, mythology, and other subjects about 1,500 BCE. Translation or interpretation of the Vedas was reserved to the Brahmins, and they gradually became the highest class. The *Upanishads* are religious essays begun about 700 BCE. The Hindu epic *Ramayana*, with 24,000 verses, has many delightful stories about Prince Raama, his wife Seeta, and brothers Bharata and Lakshama. Many Hindu temples have a small statue of the most popular gods, Raama, Seeta, and Ganesha, the elephant god. Ganesha is believed to bring good fortune. There are some 33,000 gods, which include trees, stones, cattle, and even snakes such as the cobra. Shiva or Vishnu is usually considered to be the most powerful god, but Hinduism varies greatly from one area and one caste to another. The *Holy Trinity* consists of *Brahma the Creator*, *Vishnu the Preserver*, and *Shiva the Destroyer*. There are many Hindu sects.

Islam

Muslims or Moslems believe in the teachings of Mohammed. He was born in Mecca, Saudi Arabia, about 575 AD Mohammed married his employer, a widow, who died in a few years. In 610 while meditating in a cave a voice told Mohammed to lead his people. The angel Gabriel took him to several religious sites in Israel, and at the Dome of the Rock they leapt into Heaven. He met Abraham, then Allah.

Allah gave five "pillars" to follow: (1st) repeat "there is no God but the one God, and Mohammed is his prophet," (2d) daily prayer toward Mecca 5 times daily, (3rd) give at least some of your income to the poor, (4th) during Ramadan eat no food or drink during daytime hours. Ramadan is a 28-day period which rotates, in honor of when Allah sent the first part of the *Koran* to Mohammed, and (5th) go to Mecca and kiss the Kaaba stone once. Men then become *Haji* and women become *Hijah*. The Kaaba is a black meteoric stone. It is covered with a black cloth, which is later cut up into small pieces and sold. Jeddah, the airport near Mecca, has a large terminal building where "pilgrims" to Mecca are greeted.

Moslems believe in most of the prophets of the Bible's Old and New Testaments, but they believe that Mohammed was a greater prophet. By the end of the Eighth Century, Islam had spread across North Africa and east into Pakistan, with its first headquarters in Damascus. Mohammed's secretary, after his death, compiled the sûrahs or his sayings into the Koran. The Koran has 114 *sûrahs*, something like chapters in the Old Testament or New Testament, except that some sûrahs are only two lines. It has the *Six Sunnan Books* that explain the customary ways of doing things, how to live and behave. The *Sharia* is a collection of laws to regulate religious and civil life, including acceptable and unacceptable food, dress, politics, justice, banking, education, and manners. Many Islamic countries apply the law of the Sharia to civil law but use tribal law or enact statutes for criminal law. Saudi Arabia applies the law of the Sharia to criminal law also.

Shiites believe the political leader must also be the religious leader, like Khomeni. They believe that true Islam can't be known without an *imam*, or many imams, chosen by God. A majority of the people in Iran are Shiite. In most other Islamic countries *Sunnis* predominate. In North Africa the poorer people of the inner cities are often Shiites. There are many sects and differences in Islam, especially among Shiites.

Men are permitted to marry up to four wives at a time, and divorce is simple for a man. However, many Islamic countries by statue prohibit more than one wife and permit divorce by a man or woman. Men and women are taught not to look the other in the eye, and to be reluctant to shake hands with the opposite sex. Islamic banks are prohibited from collecting interest on the loan of money. In the past Jews, were welcomed in Islamic countries to perform the needed function of loaning money. When Islamic Turkey controlled much of Eastern Europe it invited the Jews, who fled from Spain during the Inquisition, to Eastern Europe. Islamic banks can invest in businesses that do not conflict with Islamic values and banks can accept a share of the profits from those businesses. Many Arabs are good businessmen, they know that they must hire educated professionals from the U.S. and Europe, and "temporary" laborers from other Arab countries to do labor. Educated Arabs are often well informed about internal political and economic matters in the U.S. and Western Europe. They cannot understand why the U.S. blindly supports Israel, regardless of what atrocities they think Israel does.

Moslem men often wear headdresses without a brim so they can touch the ground or floor during prayers. Muslims do not eat pork but most eat other meat. Never call Muslims "Mohammedans," it is very disrespectful. They respect but do not worship Mohammed. One of the first things a traveler notices in an Islamic country is the call to prayer, five times a day. The wailing sound is usually broadcast on loudspeakers everywhere in villages and towns. Airport terminals always have a corner or a room, with a rug, to kneel for prayers. Some leaders and "believers," frustrated with Arab weaknesses, advocate turning back to the law of the Sharia and keeping out Western influences. Most Muslims abhor the rulings and acts of Islamic fundamentalists—the Taliban of Afghanistan, and extremists in Iran and Algeria. My Islamic friends say their religion is peace-loving and that the Koran advocates that worshippers acquire knowledge. Moslems admire much about modern society but they believe a moral society is more important. Islam is a religion for an entire society, not an individual religion. Islamic people move toward an Islamic State, which must be changed and rebuilt. There is no belief in original sin, and there is no Day of Judgment to be initiated into another kingdom. Reward and punishment is substituted for heaven and hell. Most Islamic people do not steal, because Allah sees everything and will punish them. On the surface, some Islamic countries, such as Oman and the United Arab Republic, seem to be Paradise on Earth for citizens. Much of the money from oil has been used to build modern homes and other buildings, roads, streets, the power and water supply, improve schools and health for everyone, and slums and trash on streets are hard to find.

Conclusions Concerning Religions

World travelers should respect the followers of all religions regardless of our personal beliefs. As a minimum, this means that conservative clothing must be worn when visiting a church, synagogue, temple, or mosque. Men must wear long pants, women should wear a long dress, plus a scarf in mosques. Most Buddhist temples and Muslim mosques with carpets require that shoes be removed or that soft sock-like slippers be placed over shoes. In some Islamic countries on the Arabian Peninsula non-believers are not permitted in a mosque. Moslems wash hands and feet before prayer with water, or with sand if no water is available. Worshippers in some Orthodox churches wash hands before entering the church. Water in the churchyard sink in Plovdiv, Bulgaria is said to cure ailments. Do not deface or treat with disrespect any image. Flash or video cameras are rarely acceptable in a temple or mosque. Sometimes cameras are forbidden altogether in a temple, mosque, or other religious place. Stay away from areas where there is an active prayer or other worship service. Keep quiet or speak in a low voice. Traditional societies in sub-Sahara Africa, and Australia's Aborigines, had a watchman with a bullroarer to warn women, children, and other outsiders to keep away from a men's secret meeting. A bullroarer is usually an oval-shaped piece of wood on a cord. When whirled around it makes a roaring sound, something like a bull.

If a nation establishes a "national religion," it should be tolerant of others. Most of the conflicts among people of various religions are caused by the fundamentalists, the ultra-orthodox. They fight against outsiders. They believe that God, Jehovah, Allah, or Buddha is on their side. The most devout often have the least social compassion—less sympathy for the feelings of others. They try to impose their practices and even their narrow religious beliefs on others. They try to suppress books, science, and teachings that do not wholly support their view. They often seek to limit the education of girls and women, and they want to prohibit them from having control over their own body. Zealots believe they know the right path for all of us, but since we are too dumb to follow, we must be forced to follow their path. They want to prevent, by law or force, our making mistakes—i.e., from taking actions of which they do not approve. But it is all for our benefit. Eric Hoffer, the California longshoreman and philosopher, said in The True Believer "...where a mass movement can either persuade or coerce, it usually chooses the latter. Persuasion is clumsy, and its results uncertain."

Each of the great religions has attractive features and some problems. No one religion has a monopoly on either truth or myths. All religions perform a great service in giving believers a peace of mind and in helping the needy. Many churches, temples, and mosques are beautiful. Some of the most impressive and exhilarating music ever written or composed is played and sung in churches. Let's remember that all men are brothers and all women are sisters.

PART V:

HEALTH CARE

CHAPTER 15:
HEALTH CARE

Health-Care Plans

All of the industrial countries of the world except the U.S. have a government health-care plan that covers most or all medical expenses for legal residents. Health care is expensive in all industrial countries. Costs are rising, some treatments or drugs are no longer covered, and co-payments may be required for some treatments. A common complaint is that a patient must wait for weeks to see a doctor for routine treatment. They may wait for months for a non-emergency operation.

No other country pays even two-thirds as much as the U.S. pays for medical care. Yet, the U.S. has more than 42 million people without health-care coverage. In the U.S., only 75 percent of the cost of health care goes for diagnosis, treatment, and drugs. Many billions of dollars go to lobby legislators, for the cost of processing claims, profits, and expenses. Salaries and bonuses for executives of insurance and health-care plans and hospitals are often more than a million dollars a year! A for-profit health-insurance plan or for-profit hospital must either charge too much, or deny treatment to people who are entitled to it. Health care insurance plans often tell physicians what treatment they may or may not provide, and they sometimes penalize physicians for giving medically-indicated care to patients. While U.S. total labor costs are below costs in most of Western Europe and Japan, the health-care costs paid by employers are far greater. Anyone opposing an efficient government-sponsored health care plan calls it "socialized medicine." How do other countries provide excellent health-care for far less cost than in the U.S.?

Canada's Medical Services Act set up their universal single-payer medical insurance plan in 1968. I spent four summers attending French-speaking universities in Quebec. The other students came from nearly every English-speaking city in Canada. Their plan is very popular. It covers almost everything. Any Canadian politician who closes hospitals and clinics to cut costs is not likely to be re-elected. Administrative costs are only a tiny fraction of the administrative costs in the U.S. The General Accounting Office of the U.S. studied the Canadian plan. It concluded in 1991 that we could save a lot of money and still provide care for everyone under a system like Canada's. Canada has a much lower infant mortality rate, fewer people die from heart disease, and the life expectancy is higher than in the U.S. This is also true for nearly all countries in Western Europe.

In the United Kingdom the National Health Service Plan began in 1948. It covers nearly all costs. Some 11 percent of the people also buy private insurance. Prescription medicines cost around five dollars each. Only about three-fourths of the cost of dental care are covered. Students and the elderly get free dental care. A resident must see a local physician first. There has been a shortage of hospital beds. Health-care costs have increased recently but in 1998 were below seven percent of GDP. The gross domestic product or GDP is the value of all goods and services produced in a country in a year. In Ireland the poor, the unemployed, and pensioners are covered by the government Department of Health plan. Others must pay the actual cost, which is low. Some one-third of the people pay a little more for a P-A-Y-E or Pay As You Earn supplemental plan. Denmark, Norway, and Sweden are known for their complete but expensive medical and social services. In Denmark, we were told in 1996, that their medical care alone costs only about three percent of their GDP, but latest figures show total costs of more than six percent. In Italy, the National Health Care System costs are paid by the employer and by withholding from employees' wages. The patient chooses the doctor but the System pays the fee. The patient pays for part of the cost of a "ticket" for medicine and for care in a private hospital. The Netherlands has a complicated system of government and private insurance, but they provide universal health coverage for all Dutch citizens, at a cost of 8.8 percent of GDP. The Swiss pay slightly more than six percent of GDP for health care. Portugal's constitution guarantees medical services for all, but the unemployed may not be covered for all services. Health care is free for pensioners. In Spain, all but one percent of the people are covered by the Health Care Services, free of charge. In Finland any resident can get free medical care in a government hospital, paid for by taxes. Many Finns pay extra for an insurance plan and better care in a private hospital, we visited a thriving private hospital.

Germany has one of the most expensive health-care systems in Europe, with some 1200 local plans, a type of managed care. Germans pay a fixed percentage of their gross income into the "sickness fund." I lived in East Germany shortly after it merged into West Germany. The East Germans preferred their neighborhood clinics with abortion upon request, to the West German system, but lost. One of the families I lived with in West Germany paid extra for a deluxe plan, to get a private hospital room and earlier treatment of minor problems. But her total costs were less than two-thirds of health-care costs in the U.S. Germans in 1998 paid slightly over 10 percent of GDP for health care. The lady who ran our guest house in Vienna explained why she paid for a supplemental health plan. France's *Sécurité sociale* pays for 100 percent of medical costs. Both employers and employees make contributions, for a total cost of about six percent of GDP.

New Zealand's popular universal health-care plan began in 1938. To reduce costs it has recently begun to charge a small fee for some services. General practitioners charge about 12 U.S. dollars for a visit, and specialists charge more. A prescription costs about 10 dollars. Australia's Medicare plan is administered by each state but it now provides universal coverage. Nearly one-third of the *Aussies* also buy private insurance. Japan has a universal health-care plan for everyone, at a cost of seven percent of GDP. Singapore provides almost-free medical care for anyone in government hospitals. Government workers, the military, and retirees get free first-class medical service in private hospitals, but others must pay for it.

Uruguay began to provide elaborate social services in 1911, patterned after those in Switzerland. It includes free medical care. Argentina's government social services system is also patterned after plans that are common in Western Europe. Care is free only in government clinics and hospitals, but they are common, even in small cities. Chile recently improved its health care system. Most of the countries in South America and Central America have a social security system that provides a pension for workers in industry or the government, and second-class health care for everyone in government hospitals.

My wife and I made a medical tour of the Soviet Union in 1984. Their system provided neighborhood clinics and emphasized regular physical exams and preventive medicine. Equipment in the intensive care units of their better hospitals was adequate but not fancy like ours. When the Soviet Union fell apart, their medical system also fell apart. Alcoholism is worse, life expectancy is less. The same is true for the former socialist countries in Central and Eastern Europe. I've made several recent trips through the Balkans, Hungary, the Czech Republic, Slovakia, Poland, and the three Baltic countries. Everywhere it is the same. Care in State clinics is still free, in theory. Government funding is scarce. Patients must pay for prescription medicine. It may be free for children and pensioners. If anyone needs an operation, he must have a "gift" of 500 dollars or so for the surgeon.

In the U.S., one possibility is to extend Medicare Parts A and B to everyone. It is very popular. Patients go to the physician or other health-care provider of their choice. Administrative costs are only around one percent for Part A and three percent for part B. Medicare now covers only the age group that uses the most health care—the 13 percent of us who are 65 or older. The government has contracted in many states for a private insurance company to efficiently handle claims and payments under Medicare. The elderly pay less than one-fourth of the actual costs of Medicare. Taxpayers pay the balance. Those who can afford it also buy private health-care insurance, so they pay less money out-of-pocket for medical care. An ideal and efficient health plan would emphasize preventive care more than Medicare does, it would have more mental health coverage, and it would pay part of the cost of prescription drugs.

Native Healers

In Itzapa, Guatemala I watched *curanderos* treat patients. They rubbed alcohol on the chest and back of a shirtless man. They spat alcohol onto women patients. Each folk doctor had a small fire, burning sugar and incense powder, with candles of a particular color. A raw hen's egg is rubbed on the patient's ears, then burned in the fire. Evil spirits are believed to leave the body and go into the egg. For good measure, the curanderos also waved a Bible above the patient's head. Priests of the Mosuo tribe of China's Yunnan province used eggs to attract all of the evil spirits—of lightening, thunder, and more. The Mosuo did not eat eggs until recently.

Pilgrims, usually Christian, Islamic, or Buddhist, go to sites where a religious person is said to have made a miraculous cure. I have visited many of these places, in Europe, Latin America, and Asia. Some of the cures are well documented. Physicians say that up to one-half of our physical ailments are caused by a mental belief or condition. If we believe strongly enough in a cure we may be cured. In Buddhist temples in Japan, people rub incense on sore spots to stop the pain. Others throughout East Asia rub a sore spot with healing water at the temple to stop pain, or they buy a wafer-thin, one-inch square of gold leaf for about a dollar and put it on the part of a statue of Buddha where they have pain. In Laos, girls pour water on the face of a statue of Buddha to wash away any ugliness of their face. They then put a gold leaf on Buddha's face so they will be beautiful in their next life. In the Golden Palace Monastery in Mandalay, Burma, believers touch the throat of a sacred lion's statue to cure a sore throat. It didn't cure my sore throat, but perhaps it does for believers. Perhaps I should have asked for help from Saint Blais (Blaize), a Fourth Century AD Bishop in Armenia. He was said to have cured many sore throats and choking because of food lodged in the throat. Parents with a sick child rub the belly button of the "Miller Buddha" in Emei, Yunnan province, China to cure the child. Among the U.S. Navaho Indians, when a member of the tribe is sick, the family may have a *sing* with a shaman or medicine man who claims supernatural powers. The sing may last only 24 hours, or several days for a wealthy family. A trained physician may also be consulted. "Holy water" that has been blessed by a priest, monk, or shaman, or that comes from a sacred stream, is said to cure many ailments.

Bloodletting is still used in parts of Africa and the Pacific. They believe poor health is caused by bad blood, filled with evil spirits. The letting of blood was prescribed by "physicians" using leeches in the U.S. and Europe until only 150 years ago, for all kinds of ailments—for fever, chills, coughs or colds, bloody flux or diarrhea, jaundice (yellow skin), pain in almost any part of the body, distemper, ill humor, and more. Many of the patients became anemic and died.

Herbal Medicines

To be effective, many of the plants must be picked at a particular time, such as early in the morning, or after a shower. It is difficult to control the dosage. Some plants used are poisonous if taken at the wrong time or if an overdose is taken. There is no uniform quality control. However, the cost of herbal medicine is usually less than medicine obtained by a prescription.

Many of our popular medicines began as herbal medicines: Ancient Greeks used willow bark, a source of salicylic acid or aspirin. Digitalis, used for heart failure, came from the leaf of the foxglove plant, which has purple or white bell-shape flowers. The bark of the cinchona tree provides quinine, used to control malaria. In Vanuatu I tasted tea made from the leaf of a local tree, soaked in water. It is said to control malaria. Early settlers in Jamestown, Virginia, learned quickly which plants would help or harm them. Their *Jamestown Weed* or *Jimson weed* ointment was used to stop pain. Local Indians taught other pioneers how to use local remedies. Ginseng was used to "revive the spirits," to "warm the blood," and to "strengthen the stomach and comfort the bowels." It is still popular in East Asia. In Central America, juice of the cockspur, a stinging plant if touched, is drunk to delay the effect of snakebite until the victim can get to a doctor. The chewed fiber is put onto the place of the bite as a poultice. The plant can be boiled to make a tea, to drink to help asthma or to put onto skin acne. In the U.S. rattlesnake root was used for rattlesnake bite, as a tincture for gout, for purging, and much more. For asthma, ancient Mayans used a mixture of hot chocolate, hot pepper, and the peeling of oranges or lemons. Miners in the U.S. learned that eating a wild plant, miner's lettuce, would prevent scurvy. British ships in the Nineteenth Century carried barrels of limes or lemons to prevent scurvy. British sailors were still called "limeys" during World War I, today they are called "fish heads."

On a recent visit to Cuba we were told that even common drugs such as aspirin are scarce, because of the archaic blockade by the U.S. The government has encouraged people to use traditional herbal medicines. The public market in Belize City, Central America, had several tables selling herbal medicines. Each buyer got a short handwritten description as to how it was to be used. In La Paz, Bolivia, my wife and I heard about the "Magic Market" where Quechua Indian women sold traditional medicines. We looked for it for several days, and finally found it in an alley. Many herbs, bones, dried fetuses of llamas, skunks, sulfur, and other things were sold. We tipped one of the vendors to explain how some of the things are used. She said it is *muy complicado*. The wisdom and folklore of many generations were used to assemble her goods. How could a *yanqui* expect to learn it all in a few minutes?

People for centuries have looked for a drink, food, or anything else to preserve or regain youth. In Vanuatu the leaf of a particular plant is chewed for long life. A man who died on Malakula Island in 1997 was said to be 149 years old. In Papua New Guinea a medicine man washed his hands with a particular leaf. He put several leaves into a joint of bamboo, with water, and recited "magic words." When a customer who wants to live longer drinks the water he must look to the east, then look west. The medicine man said he is over 50 but he looked much younger, and had a full head of black hair. Guides from another tribe led our small group on hikes in their big rain forest, explaining what food or herbal medicine each tree provides, and how they use the wood. Big logging companies from Malaysia, Japan, and Taiwan search the Pacific and Southeast Asia for forests to cut. Much of the money is paid to politicians, who persuade the tribes to sell the trees. Typically, in a few months the money and the forest are gone. The tribe is gone, the members must leave to try to find work. Our guides said a logging company offered them an insufficient sum for the forest. It was rejected. Two months later the offer was tripled. Rejected. The minister of forestry then came with the loggers, making promises and subtle threats. The offer was rejected. The last offer was 10 times the first offer. It was rejected. The guides said "The forest is our father and mother. We could never sell it." Loggers have apparently given up trying to log on Vanuatu's big Erromango Island. The few remaining villages made conflicting claims to own the land. Local people were unwilling to work on the island because missionaries are said to have put a curse on it, since cannibals there ate missionaries from Samoa some 150 years ago. Logging creates a muddy runoff that is killing coral around many Pacific islands.

Korea's Folk Village has a herbal pharmacy. Hundreds of plants and animal parts are in drawers, labeled by the source. A chart of the human body shows acupuncture points. Exhibits show equipment used for acupuncture. Warriors and other people in Ghana's Ashanti tribe chew a particular local plant to stop bleeding by making it clot. In the

Marquesas Islands, juice of the *mio* or oceanic redwood tree is put onto centipede stings as an astringent and to help stop the pain. Minor skin cuts are treated with leaves or flowers of particular plants, usually the *ati* or *burau*. Bruises are treated with other leaves, the *taa* or the *vainau*, mixed with *monoi* oil and rubbed gently over the bruise. In Central America a red pepper is rubbed on the skin at a painful place. For a sore throat American Indians in Arkansas tied a smelly dirty sock around the patient's neck until the throat was cured—probably soon. In Yemen onion is eaten to prevent a sore throat and to adjust to unusually hot days. In China's Guanzi province tea is made from eucalyptus trees and is drunk for a sore throat or a cold.

Papua New Guinea's rain forest has many plants that local people have used as medicine for hundreds of years. The sap of the breadfruit tree is drunk for diarrhea. Tea made from the leaf of a particular plant is drunk to prevent infection. Another leaf is used for an antiseptic. A wild ginger's leaf is sucked to stop a sore throat. Another plant is used as a contraceptive, and to abort a fetus. Young men drink the sap of a particular vine "to make big muscles." Drivers chew the seed of a pepper plant to avoid becoming drowsy. One village has young men of the Huli tribe who stay isolated for 18 months or more while they grow an elaborate wig to sell to richer men. The head man explained that his ancestors have developed a medicine to put on hair so it grows faster. He said "clean living," away from smoke or women, and a good diet and plenty of rest is required for those who want to grow hair there. Ancient Egyptians use a concoction made of mustard seeds to stop the loss of hair.

Wherever coconuts grow, the "milk" made by grating the copra is drunk in quantity, used as a laxative. Three or more raw candlenuts are also eaten, for a laxative. Another common laxative used in Polynesia is made by cooking a mixture of grated coconut, starch, and *tiare* (gardenia) leaves. In Vanuatu the sap of the breadfruit tree is put onto a bruise to reduce swelling. In New Caledonia sap from leaves of the niaouli tree, related to the eucalyptus, is used to rub on sore muscles. Tea made from the leaves is drunk "for poor respiration." In Vanuatu, a woman expecting a baby squeezed the leaf of a particular tree to get the sap, rich in iron; the umbilical cord of a newborn baby was cut with a sharp piece of bamboo. A Vanuatu mother who is nursing a baby and needs a lot of energy mashes the bark of a particular kind of hibiscus plant and drinks the tea made from it. In West Africa both animals and local pregnant women eat the "dirt" from salt licks and big termite mounds. They know that it has minerals they need. The dirt is sold in markets. Chinese have for centuries drunk a mixture made of powdered ants, rich in protein. They claim that it can also cure various ailments, such as rheumatoid arthritus.

In Vanuatu the sap of a tree is applied to stop bleeding. Most large villages in the Solomon Islands have a medicine man who grows medicinal herbs. The people boil wava leaves and drink the tea for diarrhea and hepatitis. For mouth sores, they boil the seed, like licorice, of a fern-like plant that grows on coconuts. For stomach problems they boil the leaves of *loku loku*. They drink tea made from *leru baru* for early-stage cancer. For back pain they drink tea made from leaves or bark of the *totuno*—it tastes bitter. If someone falls from a tree they rub tea made from leaves of one of the two types of *burongo* on the sore places. The inside of the *nute* fruit is said to be good for diabetes or high blood pressure. For high blood pressure they also drink tea made from bark of the big *bosi* tree. For sexually transmitted disease they drink the sap or tea made from leaves of the *chomo*. If a child has asthma Solomon islanders split a plant that looks like pitpit grass, but is different, and scrape and eat the sap in its center. For stomach problems pioneers in Newfoundland ground juniper and boiled it, or they boiled alder buds, for the patient to drink. For ingrown toenails they dropped hot tallow from a lighted candle onto the sore part—the burn probably hurt more than the ingrown toenail. To stop a cough they mixed wild cherry juice and turpentine, or kerosene oil and molasses, and drank a little. For a toothache Newfoundlanders put vinegar into the mouth and tried to keep it there. In the Marquesas Islands, *morinda* juice made from the fruit of the *noni* tree is sold to lower blood pressure and to prevent or stop all types of cancer. It smells awful, and tastes bad, even after any of several flavors are added. Also, in the Marquesas, hibiscus flowers are crushed and the raw juice helps digestion and acts as a tranquilizer and sedative. Bark of the North American Pacific yew tree contains taxol, said to control cancer of the ovaries. North American Indians made tea from the bark of cascara trees, to drink for a laxative. In Europe leaves of the feverfew plant are chewed to help migraine headaches. Saint Johns-wort, a popular low-growing shrub, taken in large doses, is used in many countries to reduce depression. Tea made from its yellow flowers is used to help digestion, and its oil is rubbed onto skin for gout and rheumatism.

The manager of a large aquarium in New Caledonia recommended putting hot water (about 50 degrees C or 122 F—like hot coffee) onto the painful sting of many sea creatures—stone fish, jellyfish, or rays. She warned to carefully pull off the stingers of jellyfish, then put on meat tenderizer. Never rub the skin back and forth. When I swim on Australia's beaches I carry part of a lemon or orange to put on the sting of "blue bottle" jellyfish.

Along the upper Amazon several tribes grind the bark of a particular tree to make *nunu*. They take it at bedtime and have visions during their sleep. Hunters told us they can then see places where they will find prey the next day. The blowgun, made by hollowing out part of a plant seven or eight feet long, with a dart tipped with a poison that paralyses, is their favorite weapon. Some tribes carefully collect secretions from a particular kind of frog by gently scraping its back and legs. They burn their own skin and rub it with the frog's secretions to produce hallucinations, like those produced by LSD.

Man learned long ago that smoke drives away mosquitoes and other insects. In Guangzi province, China, eucalyptus leaves are burned to make smoke to keep away mosquitoes. Many homes in the tropics keep a smoldering fire of coconut husks burning underneath a home built on stilts. In Papua New Guinea the bark of the breadfruit tree is burned to kill mosquitoes. Unfortunately, the smoke is also bad for humans. Many plants are used to repel insects. Lemongrass or citronella grass is rubbed on the skin to keep away mosquitoes in many places. Oil squeezed from the copra of coconuts is often rubbed on skin for some protection against insects and sunburn. In the Marquesas Islands monoi oil is put on the skin to drown the little *no-see-ums*, both the white kind found on beaches and the black ones found higher. Oil is used on the skin in much of Africa to protect against insects and the sun. Some trees or bushes are planted near a home to keep away insects. Along the Amazon one kind of palm has a network of roots with spines that keep away insects. Local people carefully split the wood from it to make house walls and floors. They claim that the wood keeps away insects. A kind of cedar keeps away moths. Young women in America and Europe liked to have a cedar chest to store linens and clothes. Until the late 1930s it became part of their "hope chest" or wedding dowry. In Vanuatu the *croton*, a decorative plant with a pleasant smell, somehow drives away insects.

In the foothills of northern Argentina, my wife and I participated in a herbal medicine study with Earthwatch. Local people rub a wound with the *aloe verde* leaf. Tea made from the *inca juju* plant, found only in that area, is drunk for liver problems. Bark of the *chañar* plant is ground and taken for bronchial problems and as an expectorant. *Marcella* is used to help digest foods. The *contrayerba* plant is rubbed on insect bites to stop pain and itching. It is also drunk, with *brea*, as an antidote for bites of a poisonous snake. In the pleasant town of Capilla del Monte, two shops were busy selling herbal medicine.

A *curandera* or folk doctor in Argentina had a large herbal garden. She used a quartz crystal to examine a patient. She said it emits "good energy." She was very observant, and prescribed local *romero* and *ajinco* plants to treat my upset stomach. Another curandera said she became aware as a girl that she had a special gift to see things that other people could not see, to diagnose ailments, and to heal. She "listens to plants and nature." She said she could see auras with her "third eye." She saw a rose-colored light above my wife, and asked whether it was her birthday. My wife's birthday was the next day, a few hours later. The curandera demonstrated how she treats patients, moving her arms faster and faster to build up the aura. She said that the vibrations can cure even cancer or AIDS. In private, she attacked the tumor of one woman in our group, the patient later said the area near the tumor felt warm, even hot. The curandera said she seems to float away from her body, that we must get out of our bodies, to "see ourselves." Local Argentine physicians, trained in Western medicine, said they send patients with some ailments to the curanderas. The curanderas have had good luck in treating patients with *patas de cabra*, a skin affliction that looks like a goat's footprint.

In China my wife and I studied Western and traditional medicine with a small group. Beijing's Institute of Acupuncture and Moxybustion had many patients. Traditional medicine is not concerned with functions of the body, how or why a treatment cures, but only with does it help? We smelled something like incense and other strange smells. Acupuncture charts show the many points on the body, each is numbered. My wife volunteered to have a needle inserted. She said there was no pain. A man had many needles in his face, to stop problems in the intestines. A patient who had lost her hearing was given needles in the ears. A boy suffering from asthma had needles in the left ear, and in his chest and left leg. A girl who was too nervous was hooked up to an electric stimulator, with weak current. As a needle was inserted quickly between another patient's toes, he reported that he felt something moving in his ear. For a patient suffering from myopia or nearsightedness, a doctor washed around the eyes, and tapped him gently with a hammer all around the eyes, then straight up the forehead, on the top of the head, and down the rear of the head. Another man had several wooden boxes on his back, with a plant burning inside. The heat is said to stimulate the body's natural protectors in the area. I bought pills for laryngitis. They included rhinoceros horn, bear gall, cow bexear, and toad cake. It didn't cure my laryngitis. China's Friendship Stores sell "Ass Glue" for diarrhea but did not list the ingredients.

In Chengdu's College of Traditional Medicine we saw other treatments. For a nearsighted patient bits of a herbal medicine were fastened to a patient's ear with adhesive tape. Herbal "seeds" are placed at particular acupuncture points. The patient rubs the seeds regularly, helping the herbs to spread. Many patients had wooden boxes with smoking herbs inside. However, one doctor applied a smoking herb, a *moxa stick*, like a cigar, to a patient's skin, through several layers of cloth. The college has a collection of more than 3,000 raw specimens, in glass jars or drawers. They are classified by the source, such as rhinoceros, deer, other horns, snakes, fish, rocks, seeds, insects, tree bark, nuts, and various sea creatures and plants. They are also classified by their function, such as laxatives or drugs for headaches. Some herbs are for growing hair. We ate a banquet in the pharmacy's retail store and restaurant. We had at least 19 foods, each was served separately in a dish. It included liver, chicken, rabbit, soup with a seahorse, wolf berries, rat fish, turtle, mushroom soup with a pigeon's egg, and fresh pear for dessert. It was designed to make us feel good. Our drink was made from a yellow flower. For three days our stomachs were unsure how to react to the "uppers" and "downers." There is little distinction between food and medicinal herbs. Some foods or herbs are believed to be *yin*, to be used for particular ailments; others are *yang*, to be used for other ailments. Things that are yin are the Earth, feminine, and responsive. Those that are yang are Heaven, bright, and masculine.

On other trips in China we visited the hospital and pharmacy in each of two communes. They used both traditional medicine and Western medicine. The herbal pharmacy had 2,000 specimens in drawers. To fill the prescription of a traditional doctor, the pharmacist took a few things from each of 11 drawers, divided it into four piles, and wrapped each in a newspaper. The patient is told to boil a little of each in the morning and drink the tea. We visited two clinics staffed by "country doctors." They were at first called "barefoot doctors" and received only a few days of training. As China progressed they were given six months of training, and return each year for another month. They had a wooden box of medicines, which they carry on a bicycle. They gave injections. In Dali, Yunnan, Doctor Ho Shi Xiu, well-known as Doctor Ho, said he has 2,000 kinds of herbal medicines. The fenced-in yard behind his clinic has many plants, grown to be used for treating his patients. He gave several in our group herbal teas, with directions on how to use it for curing various ailments. Several said it helped to cure or improve their ailment. My wife, a trained physician, said his tea cured her chronic cough. China is known for its herbal medicines, and the hundreds of vendors of herbs on or near Mt. Emei, Sechuan province, have perhaps the greatest variety, picked or gathered nearby.

Nicaragua under the socialist Sandinistas of 1987 followed China's plan to train many people to give health care. Health *brigidistas*, usually young women, were also taught about protein, vitamin deficiencies, milk, the advantages of breast feeding, and oral rehydration. Diarrhea is a major health problem. They used things that are readily available to a peasant woman: boiled water, a little sugar, salt, and bicarbonate of soda, plus lemon and a pinch of the leaf of the local *juabo* plant. It is eaten with mashed bananas. We also visited several hospitals, clinics, nursing schools, and two medical schools. The volunteer European doctors and nurses complained that the blockade then in effect by the U.S. caused a shortage of all medical supplies. Across the Pacific, the Philippine government trained more than 400,000 village health workers in basic medicine, how to dispense medicine, and on family planning. Some of the rich landowners opposed their giving treatments, and the Catholic Church opposed their giving information on family planning. The Philippine islands are crowded with many people living in extreme poverty, and the rate of population increase is high.

Health Care & Disease

In Latin America and in Islamic countries nurses and others who work closely with the human body and its wastes have a low status. In most of the world, outside of Europe, the U.S., and Canada, little nursing care is given by the paid staff in hospitals. Relatives or friends of the patient give the care. Dormitories sometimes provide sleeping cots for the caregivers. Sometimes they pitch a tent on the hospital grounds. They buy food for the patient and themselves from vendors on the edge of the hospital grounds. In Syria, when my wife fell in an ancient Roman funerary tower, fractured several bones, and had to spend a few days in a hospital, I gave her most of the nursing care. However, we were served trays of tasty food and the physicians were well trained. Half of the nurses were Christian, half were Islamic, wearing a shawl. All were well-trained and younger than 30, except the older evening-shift head nurse. My wife and I talked with her in German, and with a day-shift nurse in French. We speak little Arabic and the other nurses spoke only Arabic. In many countries the relatives must provide food for the patient. My wife worked as a physician in a hospital in India, and in clinics in Pakistan and Guatemala. Basic medical care is adequate in the cities, and cheap.

The plague hit Europe hard several times. The period from 1348 to 1350 was perhaps the worst. Since it was usually carried by fleas on rats and mice, seaports were hit first. Marseilles suffered in 1348, 1720 to 1723, 1780, and 1825. Museums in France, such as the Fine Arts Museum in Marseilles and the Gadagne History of Lyon Museum in Lyon have many exhibits, written only in French, describing what it was like. Treatment included a quarantine of the area, and the burning of infected objects or holding them over a fire—all good methods. Bad air was believed to cause the plague, so physicians wore a cape and a mask with a long nose that filtered the air. Physicians were therefore called "long noses." Other treatments may not have been effective at all in stopping the plague. It included building a new church, burning perfume, and drinking medicine made from snakes or from opium. Malaria once plagued the U.S. South, as it still does much of the world. In the U.S., John Gorrie, a physician in Florida, discovered, a little more than 150 years ago, that a person kept in an enclosed cool room did not get malaria. He designed the first compressed-air refrigeration machine, to make ice to cool a room. That was the forerunner of air conditioning and refrigeration, both of which revolutionized the world.

      Cholera has hit many areas hard. The cholera demons were believed to cause it. Until recently, in Burma, the treatment was to make a lot of noise to drive away the cholera demons. They pounded roofs and walls, and beat metal pans and drums, to drive the demons away. In West Africa, the people armed themselves with clubs and torches, yelled and made noise to drive the demons out of the village. The demons were chased some distance outside of the village. Roosters in the village were then killed, their crowing might lead the demons back into the village. In China's Yunnan province, priests of the Mosuo minority group have an elaborate procedure to drive out the demons of illness from a sick person. They include loud drums and gongs, dancing, a ritual sacrifice of a rooster to the spirits of the ancestors, and a priest wading through a bonfire and licking red-hot metal with his tongue. The priest then carries a burning pot of oil and a sword all around the building to chase out demons. One Western observer, Joseph Rock, anthropologist, said a very sick man was cured. Rock built a nice home on a peninsula of Lugu Lake and lived there many years. In the November 1924 issue of the National Geographic magazine, he describes the ceremony to drive out the demons of sickness. Ecuador's Achuar Indians believe that if a person suddenly becomes sick a shaman has been hired to send a supernatural psychic dart at the sick person. A second shaman must be hired by the sick person's friends or family to suck out the harmful dart, according to an article by Mary Roach in *Discover Magazine*, December 1998.

Index of Countries

Europe

Asia

Africa

West Africa

Other Books by Wesley M. Wilson

Countries & Cultures of the World, Then & Now
(3 Volumes);1997

Five Languages Made Simpler; French, Italian, English,
Spanish & German, 1997

Know Your Job Rights; 1976

The Labor Relations Primer; 1973

Labor Law Handbook; 1963
cumulative pocket supplements (1968-1985)